A Guide for Implementing a Patent Strategy

Scrivener Publishing
100 Cummings Center, Suite 541J
Beverly, MA 01915-6106

Publishers at Scrivener
Martin Scrivener (martin@scrivenerpublishing.com)
Phillip Carmical (pcarmical@scrivenerpublishing.com)

A Guide for Implementing a Patent Strategy

How Inventors, Engineers, Scientists, Entrepreneurs, and Independent Innovators Can Protect Their Intellectual Property

Donald S. Rimai

Scrivener
Publishing

WILEY

This edition first published 2018 by John Wiley & Sons, Inc., 111 River Street, Hoboken, NJ 07030, USA
and Scrivener Publishing LLC, 100 Cummings Center, Suite 541J, Beverly, MA 01915, USA
© 2019 Scrivener Publishing LLC
For more information about Scrivener publications please visit www.scrivenerpublishing.com.

Wiley Global Headquarters
111 River Street, Hoboken, NJ 07030, USA

For details of our global editorial offices, customer services, and more information about Wiley products visit us at www.wiley.com.

Library of Congress Cataloging-in-Publication Data

Names: Rimai, Don, author.
Title: Guide for executing a patent strategy / Donald S. Rimai.
Description: New Jersey : Wiley-Scrivener, 2019. | Includes index. |
    Identifiers: LCCN 2018041062 (print) | LCCN 2018041347 (ebook) | ISBN
    9781119407102 (ePub) | ISBN 9781119407102 (ePDF) | ISBN 9781119407058
    (hardback)
Subjects: LCSH: Patent laws and legislation--United States. |
    Patents--Economic aspects--United States. | BISAC: LAW / Intellectual
    Property / General.
Classification: LCC KF3116 (ebook) | LCC KF3116 .R565 2019 (print) | DDC
    346.7304/86--dc23
LC record available at https://lccn.loc.gov/2018041062

Cover image: Russell Richardson
Cover design by Donald S., Benjamin E., and Nancy I. Rimai. The figure is from U. S. Patent 7,823,996,
issued to Benjamin E. Rimai *et al.* (2010).

Set in size of 11pt and Minion Pro by Exeter Premedia Services Private Ltd., Chennai, India

10   9   8   7   6   5   4   3   2   1

Dedicated to the memory of my uncle, Emanuel Rimai (1912–1984). From one generation to the next. The lessons you taught me when I was growing up have now been passed on to my son.

Contents

Preface

Several years before retiring from my 33-year career at Eastman Kodak as a researcher in the area of electrophotography, I was asked to assume the responsibilities of an intellectual property manager for digital printing. My responsibilities included devising patent strategies that would protect Kodak's technology, participating in asserting Kodak's patents, improving the quality of our patent portfolio, and producing and prosecuting patent applications.

In this role, I was fortunate to work with a world-class group of scientists, engineers, and technicians, coming from a wide variety of disciplines. The disciplines included physics, chemistry, mechanical, electrical, and computer engineering, mathematical modeling, and imaging science. Educational levels typically ranged from technical staff with associate degrees, to professionals with BS, MS, and PhDs. Most had many years of experience and routinely advanced electrophotographic and ink jet technology by solving almost intractable problems on a routine basis.

The technology advanced by Kodak's technical team members was highly innovative and allowed electrophotography to go from being limited to office copiers to its rivaling both silver halide photography and offset printing in quality, reliability, and speed, while being able to integrate the capabilities of the digital era with hard-copy printing.

Yet, despite the high level of skills of these individuals that routinely led to great innovations, these inventors often failed to recognize that they had inventions. Yes, invention disclosures were submitted by the members of the technical staff and patent applications were filed and prosecuted by the attorneys. Kodak was highly successful in both the quantity of applications filed each year and the number of patents received. Nonetheless, many of the inventors failed to precisely define their inventions and, in fact, very often did not recognize that they even had inventions. This was because the legal concepts of an invention often differ from the perception held by many members of the technical community of what constitutes inventions. Obviously, prioritizing inventions and patent applications into a coherent patent strategy was unlikely to occur. Adding to these complications was the fact that electrophotographic technology was a very mature field with much ongoing R&D, resulting in much prior art that had to be circumnavigated.

Despite these challenges, I found that the problem of formulating and implementing a coherent patent strategy is not beyond the capability or desire of most members of a technical team. Rather, it occurs because technical people are rarely educated in patents.

This book is the result of the experiences that I had working with these world-class technologists, as well as many patent attorneys. It addresses the questions that have been routinely asked of me by engineers and scientists. It is, in effect, a compilation of my experiences working with a variety of teams and is written as one technical person talking to another, explaining each step of what has to be done and why it is important in order to successfully design and implement a patent strategy that protects your technology and is of value to your company.

Don Rimai
Rochester, NY
August 2018

Acknowledgements

I would like to thank my wife Nancy I. and son Dr. Benjamin E. Rimai for their support throughout the writing of this book. I am especially gratified for their discussions, comments, and reading of the drafts. Their questions contributed to my being able to address the needs of members of the technical communities as they formulate and implement their patent strategies.

1

Background for Developing and Implementing a Patent Strategy

Why Should You be Seeking Patents?

You are a scientist or an engineer working for a corporation. The technology that you are developing is very exciting and quite novel and the resulting products should allow your company to outcompete its competitors. It does not matter whether your company is a so-called "high tech" firm, whether you are involved in biomechanical technology, life sciences or pharmaceuticals, or the development of more mundane products such as the gears or tools. The issues are the same. Your technological advances need to be protected.

You are an entrepreneur who has invested your life savings, after also obtaining financial backing from principal investors, into your company and are hoping to see the value of your company grow exponentially. You are, of course, worried about foreign companies pirating your products and, because of their lower labor costs and the fact that they have not invested heavily in R&D or in developing the markets, they may be able to produce comparable products at substantially lower cost. You need to prevent that, while increasing the value of your company.

You are an innovator who develops neat and novel products in your garage or basement. You are hoping to make millions of dollars from your innovations by producing and selling the products directly or by convincing an established company to produce these products and pay you royalties. However, your proposed products are so unique that you are worried that another company can simply steal them. After all, they can be easily reverse engineered. Concerns over how to protect your innovations keep you awake at night.

While the three specific scenarios presented here differ in many aspects, there are still underlying similarities. Let us address both the similarities and the differences by first focusing on the scientists, engineers, and other technologists who are employed by companies, as these individuals have certain benefits in obtaining patents.

Why Should an Employed Scientist or Engineer Seek to Obtain Patents?

The obvious issue faced by most scientists and engineers is that they are assigned complicated tasks as part of a project team by their managers. These projects have tight schedules and market windows open and close rapidly and a delay in introducing a product can be very expensive. In addition, scientists and engineers are generally much more proficient at solving technical problems than they are at writing detailed descriptions of the problems they have solved and how they have solved them. This becomes even more pertinent as the resulting documents will be intended for a legal, rather than a technical audience.

Despite the pressures placed on these individuals, there are very good personal reasons for them to pursue the obtaining of patents. The benefits to the employer are similar to those of the entrepreneur and, accordingly, will be addressed in the next section of this chapter. Suffice-it to say is that innovative companies should have good patent portfolios, as discussed in *Patent Engineering* [1].

In years past, an engineer or scientist might have served one employer throughout a long career. Those days are gone. The average tenure at a company today is approximately five years and scientists and engineers need to constantly think about their next employer. Most of us who have worked in industry have signed nondisclosure agreements whereby, typically, we have agreed not to disclose company information for a specified period of time, typically about two years after leaving the company. This serves the company quite well, but how about the employee who has either been laid off or is seeking better opportunities? What accomplishments can one present to a prospective employer? You simply cannot talk about what you are working on.

However, patent applications 18 months after filing and all patents are public record. They are, in fact, your publication record – a publication record that highlights your skills and accomplishments for everyone to see. Your patents clearly distinguish you from all others against whom you are competing for those coveted career opportunities.

In addition to serving as your publication record, many companies have financial incentives to encourage inventors to file patent applications and obtain patents. If your company has such incentives, this is a way to increase your paycheck.

Having to explain what you have accomplished also makes you take a step back and look at the thoroughness of your work. Have you really solved the problem on which you were working? Are there opportunities to enhance your products? Do you know how your advancements and products compare to those of your competitors? The process of filing quality patent applications and building a patent portfolio that protects your technology forces you to address these issues in a more critical manner than how you may address them otherwise. We have all learned about the "scientific method" whereby, when commencing research in an area, one first does a literature search to learn about what was previously done. This certainly is valuable in today's competitive world where time pressures require that we work as efficiently as possible. This means that we need to know how others previously tried to solve similar problems and what they learned. It does not do either you or your employer any good to reinvent the square wheel. Moreover, as discussed in Chapter 10 of *Patent Engineering* [1], it is very important to know whether or not the products that you plan to introduce infringe upon the patents held by others.

Why Should Entrepreneurs and Companies Seek to Build Patent Portfolios?

There is no question that building and maintaining a solid patent portfolio that protects your intellectual property can be both expensive and labor intensive. However, not having a strong patent portfolio can be even more costly and time consuming as competitors try to force you out of business, sue you for infringing their patents, seek injunctions against your company to block the sale of your products, and wring expensive licensing fees out of your revenues.

It should be noted that the term "patent portfolio" has been used extensively. As was discussed in *Patent Engineering* [1], a single patent, or even a few patents, does not provide the level of protection needed in today's market. There are often alternative ways of achieving an objective and, in case you choose to enforce your patents against a competitor (often referred to asserting your patents or an assertion), there is great strength in numbers as your competitor's attorneys will seek to have your patents ruled invalid or irrelevant, claiming that their clients are not, in fact, practicing the technology that you have patented This is far more difficult if your competitor's attorney has to challenge numerous patents.

In addition, there is marketing value to patents. Although a patent is not a measure of how great a technological advancement is, the fact that a device or process is patented is often used as a marketing tool to entice potential customers to buy your products. And, as will be discussed more fully later in this chapter, a solid patent portfolio can allow your company to have access to the intellectual property owned by others, as well as being able to profit from collecting licensing fees.

Why Should the Independent Innovator Build a Patent Portfolio?

Obviously, the reasons that patent portfolios are valuable to entrepreneurs are also valid for the independent innovator. However, there are reasons that are even more pressing for the individual than for the entrepreneur, assuming that the entrepreneur has already launched a company. The reasons include being able to exclude other, more established companies from simply copying your innovations. Without a proper patent portfolio protecting your advancements, any company which you believe might be interested in producing and marketing your products can simply copy them, perhaps even incorporating some further improvements that may make them more desirable to potential customers. Absent proper patent protection, there is no reason why a company should pay you anything to practice the technology that you so painstakingly advanced.

Moreover, you may be seeking to produce and market your own products. If you are an independent inventor, you probably will have to seek funding from investors. Today, there is a popular television show called *Shark Tank*, comprising several successful businesspeople who are seeking investment opportunities. Individuals with novel products present their ideas to these businesspeople (known as *Sharks*), seeking to exchange a percentage of the start-up company in exchange for funding. A common question asked by the businesspeople is "What prevents someone else from simply copying the product?". On more than one occasion, the individual(s) seeking support were able to show that they had either obtained patent protection or had, at least filed, patent applications. This was one factor considered by the sharks when deciding whether or not to invest.

Certainly, an innovator does not have to be prepared to appear on a TV show. However, potential investors are looking to make money and they want some assurances that the novel products will not simply be copied.

What is a Patent?

Thus far, we have argued that it is important for those advancing technology to obtain patents. We have not yet told the reader what a patent is.

A patent is a legal document that allows the owner of the patent to exclude others from practicing the described invention. It should be noted that a patent does not give the owner the right to practice that invention if that practice infringes on patents held by others or if that patent describes an invention that is illegal. For example, suppose you invent a platform attached to a chair that allows someone sitting in the chair to rest one's arms on the platform. However, if someone had previously patented the chair without the arms, you cannot produce arm chairs because you will be infringing on the prior patent. However, your patent is still valuable because it would allow you to enter into an agreement with the holder of the chair patent that would allow both of you to produce arm chairs while excluding all others from doing so. This type of agreement is frequently referred to as a cross-licensing agreement and can allow you to gain access to technology that you need in order to commercialize your innovations.

Two things that a patent is not. First, a patent is not the equivalent of an academic award, such as a Nobel Prize, that signifies the importance of an invention. Second, although a technical disclosure describing the background of the problem and the invention, itself, must be included in a patent, a patent is not a technical paper such as might be published in a scientific journal or presented at a technical conference.

Popeil was awarded a patent for a fishing rig [2]. I doubt that many would equate either the significance or technological innovation of this invention with that of the transistor [3]. However, Popeil was a successful businessman who marketed the "Pocket Fisherman", and it is likely that his patent kept potential competitors out of this area.

Indeed, there are many patents that describe technology of dubious importance, either because the item was ill-conceived to begin with or because the world moved away from needing that technology.

It is interesting to note that neither John Bardeen nor William Shockley, who shared the 1956 Nobel Prize in physics for the development of the transistor with Brattain, legally qualified as inventors on these transistor patents. Alternatively, neither Gerald Pearson [4] nor Robert Gibney [5], both of whom made inventionable contributions to the development of the transistor and worked closely with Brattain, Bardeen, and Shockley, shared the Nobel Prize. Scientific advances and patentability are totally different concepts. What constitutes an invention and who are inventors will be discussed more fully in this book. For now, it should be remembered that, rather than being a scientific document aimed solely at educating readers, a patent is a legal document whose principal role is to establish the rights of the owner of the patent to preclude others from practicing the invention without the permission of the owner. It is important to keep these concepts in mind when developing a patent strategy aimed at generating valuable patent applications.

What is an Invention?

If a patent conveys the right to exclude others from practicing your invention, it is then appropriate to ask what an invention is.

Webster's New Collegiate Dictionary [6] offers several definitions of the word "invention". Perhaps their most apropos definition is "a device, contrivance, or process originated after study and experiment". Indeed, this definition probably captures what most technical people envision as an invention. Unfortunately, it is, in large measure, incorrect as far as patentability. Just as the term "patent" has a specific legal meaning, so does the term "invention" and it is this legal definition of invention that must be used when filing patent applications.

Legally, an invention is a solution to a technical problem that is novel and nonobvious to one of ordinary skill in the art. This definition introduces three terms that now must be defined: 1) novel; 2) nonobvious; and 3) ordinary skill in the art.

Let us first address what is and is not meant by "novel". The term novel does not simply connote a new product, no matter how useful or innovative, that was put together using known components so that the components function exactly as expected. As an example, let us consider a window screen, invented by John. The patent states that the invention comprises an interwoven mesh of wires or fibers with the spacing between the wires or fibers being between 0.1 and 1.5 mm affixed to an opening. The stated purpose of this invention is to prevent insects from entering John's house by affixing the mesh to a window, thereby preventing the insects from passing through the open window while allowing John's house to be ventilated.

Subsequently, Sam discovers that the stream that he has been using to obtain his water has been carrying too many stones and pebbles that he wishes to filter out. He devises a filter comprising an interwoven mesh of wires or fibers with the spacing between the wires or fibers being between 0.1 and 1.5 mm affixed to an opening through which the water flows. Sam files a patent application on his filter, only to have the patent examiner* reject it as not novel in light of John's patent. Sam responded to the examiner's office action by claiming that John did not disclose attaching the mesh to a frame, but, rather, required that the mesh be directly affixed to the window by nails. However, the examiner rejected that argument, stating that it is known to stretch a painter's canvas to a frame prior to painting in order to rigidly attach the canvas. It would have been obvious to affix the mesh to a frame so, therefore, novelty was absent. Sam's arguments and his patent application were again rejected.

Joan had the same problem as did Sam regarding filtering the water. However, she also realized that the filtered sediment would rapidly clog the mesh. She realized, however, that if the mesh were mounted at an oblique angle to the flow of the water, some of the water would pass through the mesh while the rest would wash the sediment from the mesh. She applied for a patent for a self-cleaning mesh to filter sediment from water comprising an interwoven mesh of wires or fibers with the spacing between the wires or fibers being between 0.1 and 1.5 mm affixed to a frame that is mounted obliquely to the flow of the water. As the prior art does not teach the oblique mounting of the mesh, she has a novel concept and is awarded a patent for her invention. What is the invention? She solved the technical problem of filtering the water while preventing the filter from clogging.

Let us now address what is meant by the term "one of ordinary skill in the art". Most of us tend to view ourselves, despite our education, experience, and knowledge, as having ordinary skills in the art in which we are employed. That is not the correct measure. If you have been working in a

---

* The individual who ultimately receives a patent application at a patent office is called the "patent examiner" or "examiner". This individual, in conjunction with his supervisor, or "primary examiner" will review the application and determine whether or not it meets the criteria for issuing a patent and produce an "office action" that will communicate the findings to the applicant.

field of endeavor, perhaps with other team members, you would probably be considered as one of extraordinary skill in the art. I doubt if anyone would have considered Bardeen, Brattain, and Shockley as having ordinary skill in the art of semiconductors when they invented the transistor. What would be considered ordinary skill in the art at that time? Radios existed and television sets were becoming commercially available. Certainly, a consumer who had the ability to plug in a radio or TV, hook it up to an antenna if necessary, turn it on, and tune in a station of choice would be a person of ordinary skill in the electronics art. Perhaps a service technician who could replace vacuum tubes and solder connections might be considered one of ordinary skill in the art of electronic component fabrication. It would certainly not be the members of the team of highly educated condensed matter physicists who recognized that, by appropriately doping semiconducting crystals and biasing sections of the crystals appropriately that amplification and rectification could be accomplished. It is very important that you not underrate your skills and, a priori assume that you merely possess ordinary skill in the art in which you are professionally engaged.

Let us now discuss what is meant by the term "nonobvious". Let me illustrate this concept by an actual example in which the author was involved in the field of electrophotography.[†]

In an electrophotographic printer such as a laser printer or office copier, a toner image is transferred from a photoreceptor to a receiver such as paper. This is most often accomplished by applying an electrostatic field that urges the toner from the photoreceptor to the paper. If it is desired to print on both sides of the receiver (e.g. making a duplex print), it is generally necessary to first fix the transferred toner to the first side of the receiver by fusing it. The receiver must then be flipped and sent back through the printer so that a second toner image can be transferred to the second side. The toner is then fixed to the receiver by fusing for a second time.

This is obviously a complicated process that reduces the reliability of the printer by making it more subject to experiencing paper jams and making the entire process more time consuming and expensive.

To improve the process of duplex printing, the author was part of a team tasked with designing a printer that can produce duplex prints with one pass of the receiver through the machine. To do this, the team designed and built a printer that contained a transfer intermediate. For one side of

---

† Throughout this book appropriate examples from the area of electrophotography will be utilized. To make these examples more comprehendible to the reader, I am including a brief description of electrophotography in Appendix 1.

the printed page, the toner image would be electrostatically transferred directly from the photoreceptor to the receiver. For the other side, the toner image would first be electrostatically transferred to a transfer intermediate member and then, by reversing the direction of the applied electrostatic field between the intermediate and the receiver after the first toner image had been transferred to the receiver, the second toner image would be transferred from the intermediate to the second side of the receiver. The resulting invention was awarded a US patent [7].

Producing and transferring a toner image electrostatically in an electrophotographic printer was well known, as was the use of a transfer intermediate. What was not known in the literature was the fact that the polarity of the applied transfer field could be reversed without significantly disrupting either the image on the first side of the receiver or that on the intermediate, thereby allowing both images to be transferred. To a team comprising two Ph.D. physicists and a professional electrical engineer (all of whom had years of experience in this field and would be considered highly skilled), the concept of reversing the field seemed pretty obvious. However, reversing the direction of the applied electrostatic field was not discussed in the prior art and it was not known that this would work. Therefore, this was not obvious to one of ordinary skill in the art and the resulting technology was a novel solution to a technical problem.

With this discussion in mind, let us reexamine the Pocket Fisherman patent [2]. What was the invention for which Popeil was awarded a patent? It was not simply for the idea of producing a small fishing rod. Ideas are not patentable. Only solutions to technical problems are patentable. Popeil solved several technical problems‡ including how to store tackle, how to reversibly pivot the rod to reduce its size for transport and storage while allowing it to be expanded into a functioning fishing rod, and how to integrate a casting reel and fishing line into the design.

Whereas none of the patented features of Popeil's rod would exhibit the same technical complexity as the transistor, Popeil designed and marketed a product that fit the definition of novel (as a child, I had a drop line for fishing in which the line was wrapped around a wooden frame. It was small and easily stored, but there was no way of to cast the line.) In contrast, a conventional fishing rod is long and often difficult to store. Neither the

‡ Since the time of Popeil's patent, the US Patent Office has become stricter on limiting a patent to a single invention. It is likely that, if Popeil's application were to be filed today, it would have to be filed as several distinct applications. Alternatively, were it to be filed as one application, it is likely that the examiner, in his office action, would insist that it be broken up into several applications. These are known as divisionals.

drop line nor the conventional fishing rod has a means of storing tackle, thereby also requiring that the fisherman have an auxiliary tackle box. Popeil's invention was deemed to be nonobvious to one of ordinary skill in the art (a fisherman).

Why Do I Need a Patent Strategy?

To paraphrase the above question, if I have what I see as an invention, why can I not simply file a patent application on that invention?

The answer to the above question is that you obviously can file an application on that invention, but it may not be wise to do so. Rather, it is far better to think in terms of all patentable aspects of a project so as to fully protect the technology being developed. By doing so, you can develop a patent strategy that can be of much greater benefit and value to you than just having a collection of individual patents relating to specific innovations within your project.

The importance of a patent strategy is discussed in *Patent Engineering* [1]. The economic value of a patent portfolio has been discussed in *Rembrandts in the Attic* [8]. The message from both these references is that patent portfolios are very important. Specifically, patent portfolios can have great commercial value. They can generate revenues through the sales of licenses to use the patented technology. They can give you access to technology that you need that is owned by others through cross-licensing agreements. Perhaps most importantly, they can provide protection for your intended market by preventing competitors from introducing competitive products. Even when the patents within a portfolio fail to totally block a competitor, they can cause your competitor to face delays in introducing products. They can also result in an increase of the cost of those products. Moreover, properly designed and implemented patent portfolios can limit their effectiveness by having to implement work-arounds to avoid infringing your patents, block piracy of your technology by allowing you to obtain court-mandated injunctions against those products, and allow you to establish a legal monopolistic position in the marketplace. However, the aforementioned benefits can rarely be achieved by a single patent that protects a single solution to a problem. Please remember that, today, a patent is limited to a single invention. You cannot claim multiple inventions in a single patent.

Moreover, there is strength in numbers. You are more likely to obtain beneficial cross-licensing agreements and higher royalty payments if you can present a stack of patents to your competitor instead of a single patent. In addition, when asserting a patent against a competitor, the competitor will first try to argue that 1) your patent is not valid and 2) that it is not being infringed. In the famous instant photography patent infringement lawsuit filed against Kodak by Polaroid, Polaroid argued that Kodak was infringing eleven of Polaroid's patents. Kodak argued that the patents were obvious and, therefore, invalid. Indeed, two of the eleven were found to be invalid, leaving nine. Kodak lost that lawsuit, had to pay Polaroid over $900,000,000, and was forced by court order to exit the instant photography business.

There is yet another reason why you need a patent strategy. Despite your best efforts, you will not be awarded a patent for every application you file. Your goal is to protect your technology as best you can and, if you have a holistic strategy, you will be able to build a wall around your intellectual property and your markets. You simply cannot rely on one or two patents providing the degree of protection you need. However, when filing applications, if you do not design an effective strategy, you may undermine your own efforts by prematurely or erroneously disclosing information. It is important to assess the entire technology program and implement a strategy that will benefit you.

As a Technical Innovator, What Do You Need to Do?

As the focus of this book is on how to obtain patents and devise and implement a strategy that will protect your intellectual property and allow you to establish a solid position in the marketplace, the discussion presented herein will focus on this topic. It is clear that you know how to solve problems and innovate. You have a vision of where your technology will lead and how you will get there. This book is aimed at providing the tools so that once you reach your destination, you do not find it crowded with competitors who are taking advantage of your discoveries.

What you need to do and how you go about developing and implementing a good patent strategy will be discussed in detail in this book. At this point, however, it is beneficial to provide a general road map so you see where you will need to go.

First, identify what is the goal of the technology that you and the others working with you are developing. Obviously, you have some innovative product or products in mind. The products may introduce revolutionary technology that changes the way your customers will conduct their lives or businesses. This is often referred to as disruptive technology because it changes the world. Cell phones have disrupted conventional land lines. Modern computers have transformed all aspects of our lives from the way we communicate and process documents to the way our cars run to the way medical records are kept and shared. Other changes may not be as revolutionary. For example new tools are being introduced each day that facilitate tasks. Hiking clothing that keeps us warm but sheds perspiration is now commonplace, displacing the old woolen garments of years ago. Manila climbing ropes have given way to modern kern mantle ropes made of synthetic fibers that better resist moisture and abrasion. And the list goes on. How well you can maintain your position in the marketplace and how much value you can extract from your intellectual property depends on how well you design and implement your patent strategy. Alternatively, failing to implement a proper patent strategy will result in your simply educating your competitors through their ability to see and reverse-engineer your products, perusing the information you present either on-line or in trade journals and instruction manuals, and from patents and patent applications that either are not allowed or that do not provide enough protection.

Now that you have identified the goals of your technological developments, it is necessary to identify the key problems on which you have been working. The key problems are those that will drive customers to buy your product or which are mandated by law. The solutions to these problems will likely form the basis, but not the totality, of your patent strategy. However, because of prior art search results, this might not be the case. This contingency will also be discussed more fully later in this book.

If you have difficulty identifying what you have that might be considered inventions, ask yourself what prevented you from introducing this product a year or two ago. The issues that prevented you from introducing your product at an earlier time are often are the solutions to the technical problems that you have had to solve and may constitute patentable inventions.

It is very important that you identify the potentially patentable items with your other team members. Please remember that the disjointed filing of applications by individuals who are not working cooperatively with the rest of the team may prematurely disclose information that prevents obtaining a more holistic patent portfolio and may actually contradict statements in the other applications. The latter can set the stage for subsequently having patents declared invalid. It is always important to keep in mind the goal of protecting the technology in the product that you are introducing, rather than just obtaining one or more individual patents.

Above all else, you and the team members should write a detailed draft of the patent application. It is recognized that this is time consuming. In addition, the writing process is often disliked by members of the technical community. However, if you are going to get valuable and accurate patents that protect your technology, you will generally have to do this. What this entails will be discussed in detail in Chapter 2.

Why Do Technical Team Members Need to Do This? Is this not for Legal Counsel to Do?

Legal counsel is absolutely necessary to compose and file patent applications. After all, patents are legal documents and it is vital that all legalities be properly handled if you are to get the protection and value from your patents that you expect. However, obtaining those patents has to be a cooperative effort between the technical and legal experts. Very often inventors write a short description of how they solved a problem, or even communicate orally with their legal counsel and expect their attorney or patent agent[§] to transform the rather cursory communication into a patent application.

Unfortunately, this approach is neither efficient for anyone involved nor does it allow you to obtain the quality patent portfolio that is so important. First, attorneys are legal, rather than technical, experts. Yes, patent attorneys generally have some sort of technical background. Moreover, those of us who have been fortunate to work with in-house attorneys (attorneys who are employed by the same company as you) have had the pleasure of working with attorneys who also have some knowledge of the technology. However, they still do not have the intimate knowledge, nor should they expect to have that knowledge, of the project on which you are working. Smaller companies, entrepreneurs, and independent inventors more often than not have to rely on outside legal counsel – lawyers who hire their services to any appropriate clients. It would be rare that those attorneys would have the specific technical expertise related to your project. Moreover, outside counsel tends to be very sensitive to not running up excessive billing hours for their clients. This often results in all-too-cursory efforts if they have to put together entire applications based on minimal technical input.

---

§ A patent agent is not an attorney. Rather, a patent agent is an individual who has taken an intensive course in patent law and is licensed by the United States Patent and Trademark Office to practice patent law up to, but not including, arguing in the Patent Court.

Not only do you, as a technical expert, have a much better understanding of the background and the problems on which you are working, but you and your team members have a complete picture of the integrated technology. A legal expert will generally not have this. As previously stated, integrating all aspects of the technology is crucial when implementing a patent strategy. Moreover, the engineering team can define the problems being solved. Properly defining the problem is the first step in the successful prosecution of a patent application. In addition, there will be times, especially when dealing with mature technologies, that the proposed inventions may not constitute novel or nonobvious solutions that are patentable. However, those solutions may solve a different problem in a patentable manner. As the owner of a patent is entitled to the full protection of the technology in that patent, defining multiple or alternative problems can be very important.

Often members of the technical community state that patents sound too legalistic and are hard to understand. There are even times when an inventor will say that he invented one thing, but the final patent application is totally different. Comments like these are very troubling. First, each inventor must sign a declaration, under penalty of law, that he has read and understood the patent application. Although rare, it is conceivable that, if you fail to read and understand the application, you can be prosecuted. Moreover, picture yourself in court. You have been called as an expert witness by attorneys working for your company during an assertion. You need to be able to explain your invention to a jury that probably is not technically oriented. If you do not understand your own patent, or if the issued patent does not accurately reflect your invention, do you think your employer will win the lawsuit? What will happen to your career if your company loses because of your testimony?

Patents are written in legalese because they are legal documents. That being said, there is a reason for this. As a technical person, you are able to bridge implicit statements. Remember all the textbooks in which a derivation is left as an exercise for the reader or a problem in the back of the chapter? When writing a patent application, every aspect of the invention must be explicitly stated so that someone without imagination can follow the teachings laid forth and practice that invention. There can be nothing that is not explicitly stated. This brings forth the use of a language that is somewhat foreign to the way technical books, papers, and presentations are written and takes some getting used to. The good news is that, when putting together a patent application, the inventor must carefully state exactly what the problems and inventions are. If you, as a technical team member, actively participate in the writing of the application, you will develop a much better understanding of what you have done and what the patent actually says.

There is yet another reason why you should be directly involved in writing the applications. Remember that the focus of this exercise is to formulate and implement a patent strategy that protects your product in the marketplace. This generally involves filing multiple applications, as only one invention is allowed per patent.

In past years, in the United States a patent would be issued to the first person to invent. However, with the United States signing onto GATT⁵, the US began the process of transitioning to the standard used by the rest of the world whereby the patent would be issued to the first person to file the application. In other words, the timeliness of the filing became a more significant issue in obtaining patents. However, when developing technology, not all inventions occur at the same time. Rather, some problems take longer to solve. Moreover, sometimes the existence of important problems is not even realized until after certain advances are made. Premature disclosure can adversely impact your ability to obtain important patents. Sometimes patent applications need to be filed on the same day. Other times, it is important not to discuss a topic as it can constitute a prior disclosure (*i.e.* prior art) that precludes the ability to obtain future patents. There is often a delicate balance between filing in a timely manner and delaying for sound legal reasons. This balance can only be determined by a comprehensive examination of all the advancements made on a project and what has yet to be accomplished. It is really up to the technical team, working with legal counsel, to decide on the proper time to file applications.

It is the goal of this book to provide technical innovators, including engineers, scientists, entrepreneurs, and individual inventors with the tools necessary to design and implement strategies that will result in their being able to obtain valuable patents that allow them to control the marketplace in which they are competing.

References

1. D. S. Rimai, *Patent Engineering: A Guide to Building a Valuable Patent Portfolio and Controlling the Marketplace*, Scrivener Publishing, Beverly MA (2016).
2. S. J. Popeil, U.S. Patent #4,027,419 (1977).
3. W. H. Brattain U. S. Patents Nos. 2,537,255, 2,537,256, and 2,537,257 (1951).

---

⁵ General Agreement on Tariffs and Trade

4. G. Pearson and W. Shockley, U. S. Patent #2,502,479 (1950)
5. W. H. Brattain and R. Gibney, U.S. Patent #2,524,034 (1950).
6. *Webster's New Collegiate Dictionary*, G. & C. Merriam Company, Springfield, MA (1981).
7. D. K. Ahern, W. Y. Fowlkes, and D. S. Rimai, U.S. Patent #4,714,939 (1987).
8. K. G. Rivette and D. Kline, *Rembrandts in the Attic*, Harvard Business School Press, Boston, MA (2000).

2

The Structure of a Patent

Information Contained in a Patent Application

Certain precise information is required by a patent office when submitting patent applications. While the specific format of that information may vary with each country, the information required is generally fairly similar. In this book we will focus on the format of US patent applications. The reader is referred to the United States Patent and Trademark Office (USPTO) [1] for more detailed information. It is important to remember that legal formats and grammar, as required by patent offices, must be adhered to or the application will be rejected. It is also important to remember that the patent application, if successfully prosecuted, will result in an issued patent with exactly the information contained in the application. In other words, the writing of a patent application must be done precisely and correctly. Throughout all of this, it should be remembered that a patent application is not a technical paper. However, the underlying premise as to why patents exist is that countries such as the United States recognize that it is vital to advance technology and offer inventors the ability to exclusively practice their inventions for a defined period of time (presently 20 years from the date of filing for new applications) in exchange for teaching others how to practice the invention. It is also important to remember that 18 months after an application is submitted to the United States Patent Office, it will be published, thereby teaching everyone in the world all about the invention, irrespective of whether or not a patent is eventually issued. It is very important to get the application process correct and not forget that the goal is to protect your technology rather than just the present invention.

With this preface, let us list the sections that comprise a patent. These include:

a. Title. The title is generally quite brief (typically not more than 7 words) and rarely very descriptive.

b. List of Inventors. There are specific legal requirements as to who is an inventor. Failure to get this correct can result in a patent being declared invalid if challenged in court. This will be discussed more fully in this chapter.

c. Field of the Invention. This section is short and simply relates to the technological area of the invention and is used by the patent office to direct the application to the correct division.

d. Abstract. This is generally a restatement of the field of the invention and a brief description of the problem solved.

e. Summary of the Invention. This is also often referred to as a Brief Description of the Invention and is generally just a restatement of the first claim.

f. Background of the Invention. This is a very important section. It is in this section that the problem that the present invention solves is presented to the patent examiner. This section also discusses the prior art and why that art has not solved the problem. This topic will be discussed in more detail later in this chapter.

g. Detailed Description of the Invention. This is the section in which how the invention solved the problem or problems discussed in the Background section has actually solved the problem(s). What should and should not be included in this section will be discussed in more detail later in this chapter.

h. Figures. These are part of the Detailed Description of the Invention. All aspects of the invention should be diagramed in the figures. Figures can include the apparatus or variations of the apparatus, flow charts, graphs, chemical structures, and whatever else helps to illustrate the invention. It is also appropriate, if necessary, to use figures to illustrate the prior art. All components in each figure should be numbered and each number should be referred to in the List of Parts and in the text of the Detailed Description of the Invention sections.

i. List of Parts. This section reads like a shopping list for a hardware store. It enumerates each component listed in each figure in order to facilitate the reading of a patent. It is, in essence, a lookup table of the components.

j. Claims. These are the heart of the patent. It is in this section that the invention is described in full detail.

Writing Claims

It should be noted that, once a patent application has been submitted to the patent office, very few revisions are allowed to any of the sections with the exception of the claims section. The proposed claims can be modified or omitted and, if desired, additional claims can be added. It should be noted that the Patent Office assesses a fee for each claim in excess of 20.

The claims are the heart of a patent application. These define the invention and, if allowed by the Patent Office, convey the exclusive right to practice the invention to the owner of the patent. All other material in a patent application is present in order to support the claims. If it appears that material is present that is irrelevant to the claims, that material should probably be omitted.

Recognizing an invention or, perhaps even more importantly, a set of inventions seems often to be difficult for members of the technical community. They know that they are solving problems and they comprehend both the difficulties they have encountered achieving project goals and how they have gone about overcoming those hurdles. However, all too often, the same individuals will insist that they have invented nothing and, in fact, have nothing new. It is extremely important to overcome this mindset if, first, you are to obtain patents and second, if you will be able to assert those patents against infringing companies. Inventors who do not believe they have invented anything can be absolutely devastating to a case should they be called to the witness stand in an infringement trial. Let us examine why this difficulty arises and how to overcome it before we discuss the actual details of what must be included and not included in a set of claims.

First, as a word of caution, members of a technical team should never put forth any documentation stating that what they have are not inventions or are not patentable. Those are legal rather than technical decisions and should be left for an attorney. Additionally, any such documentation is subject to the discovery process prior to the commencement of a trial. It would be most inopportune for your opposition to find that your own team members have documented why any allowed patents that you are trying to assert should be found to be invalid.

Engineers, scientists, and other individuals striving to advance technology and introduce novel products have generally given their concepts a lot of thought. Add to that their in-depth background, experience, and education. These are people who have extraordinary skill in the art, rather than ordinary skill in the art. Differentiating between those of ordinary and extraordinary skill in the art is the first stumbling block that must be overcome.

Moreover, these individuals have been working on their projects, in general, for an extended period of time. If they have not actually been involved in that specific project, they have generally worked on closely related projects. This tends to distort the terms "obvious" and "novel". Again, it is important to remember that these terms have specific legal meanings in the world of patents. Let us see how they interplay.

You have been struggling with a problem for some time. Think of Archimedes in the bath tub allegedly shouting "eureka" when he discovered that he could distinguish a gold-lead alloy from pure gold, an assignment given to him by his king who was concerned about counterfeiters passing fake coins, by measuring the specific gravity of the material in question. The solution to this problem was not obvious prior to his legendary bath, but was certainly obvious to him once he realized the solution to his assigned problem. However, Archimedes was assigned that problem, not because he had the ordinary skill in the art, as possessed by the Grecian merchants who routinely handled the money, but because of his extraordinary skill in the art. I am confident that he had to explain his discovery to the king.

What was the prior art from which Archimedes had to distinguish his discovery? Surely Archimedes recognized that rocks sink, ships float unless their hulls have been breached, and people could swim. However, the concept that the mass and volume of the displaced water are related to an intrinsic property* that is specific to a material appears to be a novel discovery. Had a patent office existed at that time, Archimedes could have

---

* An intrinsic property of a material is one that does not depend on the amount of the material that is present. For example, the temperature or the specific gravity or the density of a material is independent of whether one has one kilogram or ten kilograms of that material. Properties such as the mass or volume of a material that depend on the quantity of that material are known as extrinsic properties.

applied for a patent on his process for distinguishing pure gold from gold-lead alloys.

It should be recognized that Archimedes had to explain his techno-logical advancement to a knowledgeable colleague (the king). If you have to explain the solution to the problem on which you are working to a knowledgeable colleague even one time, it probably is not obvious. It is also important to recognize that the king could not have obtained a patent on his perceived need for a method to distinguish pure gold from gold-lead alloys. That is an idea. It is not a solution to a technical problem.

With that, let us now recognize that discoveries and technological advancements do not occur in a vacuum. There is always prior art. In his book *Connections* [2], Burke argued that modern technology stems from advances that were made centuries ago and that it is only the realization of how various unrelated products can be combined that has allowed the world to advance.

Example 1. Let us delve into the questions of what constitutes obvious-ness and novelty with a hypothetical example. Assume that your team has been assigned a project to improve fuel mileage by decreasing the weight of the gears used in truck transmissions that use continually varying conical gears. In this application, the transmission speed varies by having a drive gear traverse across a conically-shaped gear as the speed varies so that the gear ratio continually changes. Your first thought is to change the heavy steel gears for plastic ones. Indeed, you are aware that manufacturers have produced transmissions with plastic gears. However, there are reports that the gears tend to break, with plastic shards fouling the transmissions. Your team will try to address the reported shortcomings of using plastic gears for this application.

With this idea in mind, you write a proposed claim for a transmission for use in a truck comprising:

1. A conical gear composed of plastic;
2. A second gear that is composed of plastic;
3. Whereby the second gear engages the conical gear in a man-ner so that the gear ratio varies continuously with vehicle speed.

Would this claim be allowed by a patent examiner? The answer is prob-ably not. The examiner, in his office action, would argue that plastic conical gears are known, as is using plastic gears in transmissions. It would be obvi-ous to use a plastic conical gear in a continuously varying transmission.

There are other problems with the proposed claim in that it does not specify any attributes of either of the gears. Are the gears composite materials such as graphite or fiberglass embedded substances? If so, what are the characteristics and concentrations of the fibers that would allow this to work? If there is too much filler, would the gears become brittle? If there is too little, would the gears be too weak? Are there specifications of the size and number of the teeth on each gear, as well as their diameters and neutral axes? Finally, what are the characteristics of the plastic used? Is it a thermoplastic (a polymer that softens above a certain temperature known as a glass transition temperature or T_g) or is it a cross-linked polymer that does not soften and is known as a thermoset material? It is important that every factor that allows the invention to solve the reported problem be explicitly stated.

Is it possible to get a patent on using plastic gears for this purpose? Quite possibly, but you would have to show that a specific type of plastic, with well-defined properties, exhibited a substantial improvement over other plastics commonly used for gears for similar applications. This would require that you have test results that illustrate the performance improvement of the plastic in which you have an interest compared to other types of plastics used in similar applications. However, if the plastic that you are proposing to use has already been disclosed, then it is known and you cannot obtain such a patent, even if that plastic had not been previously claimed in a prior patent.

Now, let us continue with this example. Let us assume that the problem encountered with plastic gears for comparable applications is that the teeth would break off after a short time. The problem is exacerbated by the use of known transmission fluids, which plasticize the gears. You find two things: 1) if small holes with diameters within certain limits are present between all the teeth, the gear is strengthened sufficiently to avoid breaking; and 2) if DOT 5 brake fluid† is used within the transmission instead of normal transmission fluid, the gears do not get plasticized and last longer. Can patents be obtained on these discoveries?

The use of holes to reduce the propagation of cracks by eliminating stress amplification sites, thereby increasing the fracture toughness of a material, is known. However, the use of holes within a specific range of diameters being able to impart sufficient strength for this particular product is not known according to the premises set forth in this example. Also,

---

† DOT 5 is designated by the Department of Transportation as a brake fluid comprising silicone oil rather than mineral oil.

although DOT 5 brake fluid is known for use in hydraulic brakes, it is not known for use in transmissions. Accordingly, there would be no logical reason to combine the use of DOT 5 brake fluid with plastic gears for use in a transmission. That would probably be patentable. However, unless there is some demonstrable benefit for combining the use of the holes and the DOT 5 brake fluid so that the combination gives some benefit beyond those obtained by using each separately, two separate patent applications would have to be filed. Please remember that a patent is limited to a single invention. If the use of the holes and the DOT 5 brake fluid each has a beneficial effect and the two can be used separately to obtain such an effect, even if it is not as great as the combined effect, there would be two separate and distinct inventions.

Example 2. Let us now examine a second hypothetical example. You are part of a team that has been assigned the task of designing an apparatus that would allow tree surgeons to more efficiently and safely climb and prune trees. In this example, let us assume that the only related art is the fall-arresting harness and rope used by rock climbers [3–5]. The rock climber's harness is designed so that the rope can be clipped to it by a pair of carabiners, placed in opposition to each other so that, at most, only one carabiner will be opened should a force be exerted onto the latch of one or both carabiners. The two main features of the apparatus are that 1) a so-called dynamic rope [6]is used so that it stretches to dissipate the force felt by a climber should the climber fall‡; and 2) the apparatus has to be light, as the climber has to be able to comfortably carry both it and the rope, as well as any hardware used to affix the rope to the harness or to the rock wall.

Typically, the belt and leg loops on a rock climber's harness are relatively thin and the rope has a typical diameter of less than 10 mm. Comfort is not a major issue, as, unlike the tree surgeon who may spend hours suspended by a harness, the rock climber would only be suspended by it for brief and occasional periods upon falling. Also, the rope used by the rock climber is not used as a climbing aid, but rather as a fall-arresting safety feature. Moreover, as the rope would not be expected to routinely and repeatedly be subjected to intense frictional rubbing, abrasion resistance, while somewhat important, is not as critical a factor as is weight and the rope's ability to stretch under an applied load. In addition, the rock climber can attach the rope to multiple camming devices that are wedged into multiple openings in the rock wall, thereby affording multiple points of contact. The

---

‡ A dynamic rope will stretch between 5% and 10% under a static load and between 30% and 40% under a dynamic load. See reference 6.

camming devices can be readily removed and inserted into other openings as the climber ascends or descends the wall.

In contrast to the rock climber's apparatus, a tree surgeon does not usually have to hike to the tree. As a result, the weight of the apparatus is less critical. However, as the rope will repeatedly, and under load, be dragged through the crotches between the trunk of a tree and its branches, abrasion resistance is critical. Moreover, as friction causes heating to occur, the rope should not weaken at elevated temperatures. Also, the rope is used as a climbing aid. A dynamic rope that stretches would make using it as such an aid more difficult (two steps up and one step back). Rather, a static rope[§] would be more appropriate.

Another problem addressed by your team is the lack of ability of the tree surgeon to affix his rope to more than a single attachment point (e.g. a single crotch or branch). Should the branch break, the tree surgeon would fall with no means of arresting that fall. This differs from the rock climber who can affix multiple cams onto which to attach the rope.

Your team addresses the need to have multiple points of attachment by designing a detachable lanyard whose length is adjustable, to compensate for the varying thicknesses of tree trunks and different sizes of tree surgeons. The proposed lanyard comprises two lengths of rope, shown in Figure 2.1. Attached to each rope is a hook, preferably a snap hook[¶] that can attach the lanyard to the harness. The lanyard is at least partially wrapped around the tree to be scaled and each end is then attached to the harness using the hooks so that the lanyard could be easily detached, if necessary, as when a branch needs to be traversed. To allow the length of the lanyard to be adjusted, the second rope is attached to the first using what is known as a Prusik knot or hitch, as shown in Figure 2.2.

Your team comes up with multiple innovations that comprise the harness and the rope, in addition to the aforementioned lanyard. Let us first discuss the innovations to the rope.

[§] A static rope stretches less than 5% under a static load. See reference 6.

[¶] In order to practice the invention, it is necessary that the lanyard be able to attach to the lanyard rings. This requires the use of a hook. However, it should be apparent that it is preferable that the hooks not unintentionally slip out of the lanyard rings, but still be readily detachable when desired. To achieve this, it is preferable to use snap hooks. Accordingly, the independent claim would be written to include the hooks. The snap hooks would be included in a subsequent dependent claim. This would also establish a fallback position should the patent examiner cite prior art disclosing the use of a hook. In that case, the dependent claim could be rewritten as an independent claim. While this would limit the scope of the patent, it would still encompass the preferred mode of use.

Figure 2.1 Lanyard comprising two lengths of rope and a hook attached to each rope. It should be noted that even if two or more hooks were attached to a rope, this would still meet the criteria of the invention because it has at least one hook attached to each rope.*

Figure 2.2 A Prusik knot.

*This is an example of where the terms "comprises" and "consists of" have distinct meanings. If the claim comprises a featured item, it may contain more of the same or other items and still be within the coverage of the claim. Alternatively, were the claim to read "consists of a hook attached to each rope", the presence of additional hooks would place the item outside of the claim.

As differentiated from the rock climber's rope, your team specifies a static rope with a diameter between 11 mm and 14 mm. The larger diameter enhances the abrasion resistance and strength of the rope while the use of a static rope facilitates its use for climbing.

The features of the rope are probably not patentable. The use of a thicker rope to increase strength and abrasion resistance is known, even if not for this specific application. Moreover, the use of static ropes for climbing is also known, as sailors in tall ships used such ropes to climb masts. Had the team done anything to alter the properties of the rope, such as applying a coating that reduces the friction between the rope and the branch but still allowed enough friction to allow the Prusik hitch to function as required, there may have been an invention.

Your team made a number of modifications to the climbing harness to make it better suited for the tree surgeon. The belt and leg loops that support the weight of the tree surgeon were made much thicker than those used in a rock climbing harness. This was done to spread the pressure felt by the tree surgeon when suspended by the harness. However, this change is probably not patentable as the examiner would probably say that it would be obvious to make this change.

Your team has also made two other changes. First, instead of a harness consisting of a single belt, they designed a harness comprising a double belt system comprising an inner belt and an outer belt. The outer belt goes from being between 1 ½ and 2 ½ inches wide near the front to between 3 and 5 inches where the belt would contact the waist of the wearer from each hip across the back of the wearer. The outer belt is comprised of a material that is of sufficient strength so as to allow the belt to support the wearer both statically and in case of having to arrest a fall. In addition, there is an inner belt that is attached to the outer belt by a suitable means including, but not limited to, being sewn to the outer belt or adhered to the outer belt using a compliant adhesive or mechanical fasteners. The inner belt is at least as wide, but not more than 1 inch wider, than the outer belt and comprises a padded material that is between 3/16 and 3/8 inches thick. The original purpose of the inner belt was to enhance comfort, but it was also found that it helped to reduce injuries when arresting a fall when the wearer was using a static rope.

The thickness of the inner belt is important as a thinner material would not provide enough comfort or injury mitigation, whereas a thicker material would tend to shift and not provide a secure fit to the wearer.

The harness also comprises two leg loops that would support the wearer's legs so as to decrease the force applied to the wearer's back by the dual-belt. Each leg loop would also comprise an outer strap having a width of between 1 ½ and 3 inches and an inner strap comprising a padded material that would increase comfort and also mitigate injury when using a static rope in the event of having to arrest a fall. The inner strap is at least as wide as the outer strap, but at no point exceeds the width of the outer strap by more than 1 inch.

Your team has also incorporated a climbing rope attachment ring at the center of the harness to which the climbing rope could be affixed by either a mechanical fastener such as a snap hook or carabiner or by directly tying the rope to the ring. Two additional rings, called "lanyard rings" are located on the harness so that, upon properly wearing the harness, the rings would be no further back than the front of the hip bone of the wearer. The two lanyard rings allow the lanyard to be attached to the harness. In addition, the lanyard rings are located in positions that are no further forward than 3 inches from the front of each hip bone of the wearer. The lanyard rings are attached to the harness so that the attachment is between the outer belt and the inner belt. This is done because simply sewing or adhering the lanyard rings to the belt would not provide sufficient strength for the attachment of the lanyard rings to the harness.

The rope attachment and lanyard rings are made of a strong metal, preferably steel that can support at least 1,000 pounds and have inside diameters of between 1½ and 3 inches and are between ¼ and 3/8 inches thick.

Are there inventions in the design of the lanyard and the harness? The answer, within the context of the assumptions made herein, is "probably yes". I say "probably" as one can never fully anticipate what the examiner will find in the prior art. Let us examine the possible inventions, starting with the lanyard.

Making the length of the lanyard adjustable using a Prusik hitch would probably be patentable. However, it is likely that the examiner would find safety belts that allow window washers to attach themselves to window frames, thereby safely affixing themselves to the window frames while establishing a sufficient distance to allow them to clean the windows. The examiner would probably argue that it would be obvious to use the lanyard for that purpose. However, as the prior art does not reveal a lanyard that is continuously adjustable in length, nor one that is adjustable while still attaching the wearer to the object, the use of the Prusik hitch would be patentable.

The harness also contains several inventions. The dual-belt structure would probably be patentable as each belt serves a distinct function that has not been previously taught. Whether or not the use of the padded layer to increase the comfort of the harness is an invention is questionable, as cushions are known to exist. However, the use of the padded layer to decrease injury when arresting a fall when climbing with a static rope is novel. It does not matter that the use of the invention may have additional benefits. The invention (the padded layer) was a novel, nonobvious solution to a technical problem (injury upon arresting a fall when using a static rope). If you can get that claim, no one else can use your invention for any other purpose. The owner of a patent has the full rights to exclude others from practicing the invention, regardless of the specific application or embodiment that someone else envisions.

While the use of the rings, per se, would probably not be considered an invention, as rock climbing harnesses employ a ring to which a climbing rope is attached, the position of the lanyard rings and the fact that they are between the compliant layer of the inner belt and the outer support belt, is patentable. This is because 1) the position of the lanyard rings is important when using the lanyard. If the lanyard rings were too far forward, they would not allow the tree surgeon to effectively climb a tree. If they were too far backward, the tree surgeon would not be able to readily detach the lanyard from the harness when necessary to traverse a branch or rapidly rappel down the tree. And, 2) if the lanyard rings were simply mechanically attached to the exterior belt of the harness by stitches, rivets, etc., instead of secured between the inner and outer belts, the connections would not be sufficiently strong to allow them to safely support the tree surgeon.

Why are the various aspects of the inventions being explained in such painstaking detail? This is necessary as the claims must explicitly define the invention. Let us consider, for example, what might result if one did not accurately specify the properties of the lanyard rings and how and where they are attached to the harness, but merely stated that lanyard rings are attached to the harness. Someone could have used plastic rings. Someone else could have made very small rings from 18 gauge wire. Someone could have even poked the wire through the harness and simply twisted the ends together. None of these options would have worked. It does not matter whether or not you and your teammates knew better. The claims must explicitly describe the invention.

With the warning about including explicit detail in the claims, if something is not required to practice the invention, do not include it. For example, it does not matter how the tree surgeon snugs up the belt as long as it is sufficiently tight. There is no sense requiring a specific type of buckle to be used, as, in order for a claim to be infringed, every aspect of the claim must be practiced by the infringer.

To summarize, it appears that your team designed a device that contains at least four distinct inventions: 1) the adjustable lanyard; 2) the double layer harness (that includes both the belt and leg loops); 3) the location of lanyard rings; and 4) the attachment of the lanyard rings between the outer and inner belts so that the strong outer belt would hold them on the harness. How many patent applications would have to be filed?

It would appear that three patent applications would be required, as attaching the rings between the two belts and the specific location of the rings would probably constitute a single invention. Specifically, sandwiching the rings between the two belts is required to ensure sufficient strength. The location of the rings could then be incorporated into a separate claim within that patent application as it would not be feasible to practice the invention of the location of the rings without first securing them adequately to the harness. However, the other inventions could each be practiced separately from one another. Please remember that a patent is restricted to a single invention.

Background of the Invention

The writing of claims is explored in further depth in Chapters 11 and 12. At this time, let us turn our attention to the section entitled "Background of the Invention".

As previously discussed, the claims completely describe the invention. As an invention is a novel and nonobvious solution to a technical problem, it is now time to discuss what the solved problem actually is. That information is contained in this section of a patent application.

It is important to clearly define the problem solved and why the prior art, either as individual pieces or as any combination thereof, does not solve the problem. If you do not clearly define the problem and explain why a solution is not obvious in light of the prior art, the patent will probably not be allowed by the patent office.

As an actual example, I was part of a team devising a new method of transferring toner from a photoreceptor to a thermoplastic coated receiver in an electrophotographic printer.** In this transfer process, the thermoplastic-bearing receiver is heated prior to entering a transfer nip formed by two rollers that press the heated receiver against the toner-bearing photoreceptor. As the receiver is heated to a temperature above the glass transition

----

** See Appendix 1 for a description of the electrophotographic process.

temperature (T_g) of the thermoplastic, the toner is able to embed into the softened thermoplastic [7–9]. Upon exiting the transfer nip formed by the two rollers, the receiver is separated from the photoreceptor. The thermoplastic, acting as a hot-melt adhesive, causes the toner to transfer from the photoreceptor and adhere to the receiver.

The problem encountered was that the thermoplastic would not only adhere to the toner, but also to the photoreceptor, making separation of the two elements difficult and often resulting in one or both members being damaged.

The problem of the receiver adhering to the photoreceptor could be mitigated by incorporating a release agent into the photoreceptor. Indeed, it may appear obvious to do so because the release agent could also enhance the transfer of the toner to the receiver. However, there are several difficulties with this approach. The first is that release agents rapidly wear down and become depleted to the point of not functioning within a few prints. As discussed in Appendix 1, the photoreceptor, after transfer of the toner, is cleaned and reimaged thousands of times, if not more, before being replaced. In order to use a photoreceptor-bearing release agent, a mechanism to constantly recoat the photoreceptor would have to be implemented. This is costly and complicated and, in addition to requiring the coating technology, would also require devising a reservoir for the release agent.

Another difficulty encountered with incorporating the release agent into the photoreceptor is that it can affect the development of the electrostatic latent image by the toner. This can occur because of either or both triboelectric or adhesive interactions. It is clear that, although a release agent is desirable to improve the thermal transfer process, it is simply not practical to incorporate the release agent into the photoreceptor.

This is the entire problem, as was spelled out in the background of the invention section. It is very important that it be clearly stated. The problem is not simply the photoreceptor and receiver bonding to each other. Simply introducing a release agent would address that. The problem that had to be solved included the fact that the release agent could not be practically introduced by incorporating it into the logical component, namely the photoreceptor, because of the reasons stated above. As will be seen forthwith, the precise statement of the problem was instrumental in our receiving the patent, U.S. Patent #4,968,578 (1990) [6].

Detailed Description of the Invention

Now that the claims, which totally describe the invention, and the background section, which describes the problem and how others attempted to solve the problem, as well as the limitations of the previously proposed solutions, have been described, it is now time to discuss how you solved the problem. In this case, a method of continuously introducing a release agent into the transfer nip in a manner that does not degrade or impede the transfer of the toner to the receiver was devised.

In order to continuously introduce new release agent into the transfer nip, the release layer was incorporated into the thermoplastic layer of the receiver. Ordinarily, it would be expected that putting a release layer onto the surface to which something should stick would be detrimental. However, in this particular circumstance, since the toner embeds into the thermoplastic, it was able to penetrate through the release layer and we were able to transfer the toner.

It should be noted that the first claim[††] explicitly describes the method of transferring the toner to the receiver. Reading the claim clearly shows that every aspect of the invention is described in the claim. Moreover, everything in the claim must be supported explicitly within the detailed description of the invention. There should be nothing left to the imagination of a potential reader.

The detailed description of the invention section should also include figures that illustrate every aspect of the invention. These can include structures, chemical reactions or compounds, flow charts illustrating methods, graphs, etc. Each component in a figure should be enumerated and the number and item explicitly discussed in this section.

The purpose of this section is to describe the invention. In other words, every aspect of every claim must be precisely described in this section. A discussion covering the preferred manner of practicing the invention should also be included. It is also worthwhile to include enough material

---

[††] Claim 1 of U.S. Patent #4,968,578 reads: "A method of non-electrostatically transferring dry toner particles which comprise a toner binder and which have a particle size of less than 8 micrometers from an element to a receiver comprising

(A) contacting said toner particles with a receiver which comprises
  (1) a substrate;
  (2) a coating of a thermoplastic polymer on the surface of said substrate, where said thermoplastic polymer has a $T.sub.g$ less than 10.degree. C. above the $T.sub.g$ of toner binder; and
  (3) a layer of a release agent on the surface of said coating in an amount sufficient to prevent said thermoplastic polymer from adhering to said element during said transferring;
(B) heating said receiver to a temperature such that its temperature during said transferring is above the $T.sub.g$ of said thermoplastic polymer; and
(C) separating said receiver from said element at a temperature above the $T.sub.g$ of said thermoplastic polymer."

so that more limited claims can be submitted should the original claims be rejected.

In the example of the release agent applied to the receiver sheet, the inclusion of the release agent on the receiver sheet was included in the discussion section, as were methods of incorporating the release agent into the thermoplastic. The inclusion of this information was crucial in our successfully being able to prosecute this patent application and ultimately obtain a patent. Had we merely stated that we were incorporating a release agent to improve the separation of the receiver from the photoreceptor, we would never have received the patent. Specifically, the examiner originally rejected the application stating that using a release agent to improve separation was known so that this invention was obvious. However, our attorney argued that the release agent was applied to the member to which the toner had to adhere and that "no one in his right mind would do this in order to improve transfer". As the improvement was unanticipated, it was considered novel. Moreover, its inclusion solved a technical problem, thereby fitting the criteria for allowing the patent. Had the problem not been clearly stated in the background section and the solution discussed in the details section, the patent would not have been allowed.

Although not required, it is often helpful to include a discussion of how the invention works, as this can help convince the examiner that the invention is not obvious. However, this is not necessary and understanding how an invention works is not required in order to obtain a patent. It is only required that the patent application describes the problem and how to practice the invention so that a reader could follow the description and practice the invention.

A patent is awarded to an inventor or group of inventors as a means to advance technology by teaching others about the invention. In exchange for teaching how to practice the invention, the owner of the patent obtains the right to exclude others from practicing that invention without permission for a legally defined period of time. However, it should be recognized that being required to teach about the specific invention does not mean that you have to teach everything you know about the technology that is not directly related to that invention. In other words, be careful not to disclose more than is required to support the claims, which, please remember, are the exact descriptions of the invention. If a topic is not directly related to the claims, it probably should not be included.

That being said, as you make progress on a problem, you may come up with multiple inventions. Again, please remember that a patent is restricted to a single invention, so multiple applications may be required. Consider, once again, the hypothetical example of the tree climbing harness, lanyard, and rope.

As previously discussed, during the course of that hypothetical project, several inventions ensued. Each would require a separate patent application. However, that does not mean that separate background and detailed description statements would have to be written. In a situation like this, where the inventions are all strongly interacting, a common disclosure could be written, differing principally in the claims, which must be distinct from one another and unique. You cannot claim the same item more than once. However, if the team is working on further developments such as ascenders, descenders, and rappelling devices to facilitate vertical or horizontal movement within a tree, any mention or discussion of such devices and how they would interact with the present inventions should be omitted totally.

It should also be noted that using a common disclosure, or even different disclosures that discuss the inventions filed in other patent applications, even if necessary to demonstrate how the invention is practiced, generally would require that all related applications be filed on the same day so that one disclosure does not become prior art against the others. Extreme care must be exercised when implementing a patent strategy to protect one's technology to avoid premature disclosures while recognizing that patents will be issued to the first to file and that we live in a highly competitive world.

Who Are the Inventors?

Teams normally consist of highly motivated and competent individuals who are working closely with one another. Under such circumstances, it is normal for you to want to share credit with your other teammates. However, this is an urge that you should resist as there are legal requirements for what constitutes inventorship.

When publishing a scientific paper, someone is listed as an author if that person made an intellectual contribution to that paper. This is not the case when deciding inventorship. To be an inventor an individual must make an inventionable contribution to at least one claim. It does not matter which claim that is, but there must be at least one where the proposed inventor can state "I came up with that". A person who conducts experiments or builds equipment under the direction of another individual is not an inventor. Moreover, as understanding how an invention works is not required in order to be awarded a patent, someone who explains an invention would not be considered an inventor, no matter how complex that explanation is. Each inventor must have his or her name associated with at least one claim.

As claims can be modified, added, or deleted during the prosecution of a patent application, the list of inventors may change. Someone originally listed as an inventor may be removed or another individual might be added. It is important to have the correct individuals listed because improper inventorship can lead to a patent being declared invalid if challenged in court.

As inventorship is a legal issue, it is suggested that, in case of a question, you and your teammates talk with your legal counsel. Each team member can discuss what he or she contributed to the invention and your attorney can then decide who should be listed as an inventor. It should be apparent that, when implementing a patent strategy for a proposed product, different team members may be listed as inventors on the varying resultant patent applications.

Concluding Remarks

Writing a patent application differs greatly from writing a technical paper, even though the application does discuss the technical features of the invention. The invention is described totally in the claims and this section should be written first. All other sections of the patent application should be supporting material used to establish that the proposed invention does, in fact, meet the legal requirements to be considered an invention. This includes defining the problem clearly and addressing why the prior art, either by itself or in combination, does not solve the problem being addressed. The description of the invention should include all aspects that make the invention work. While multiple patent applications can be written using a common disclosure, i.e. writing encompassing background and description sections, the claims have to be distinct and can represent only a single invention. If a common disclosure is written, it would probably be necessary to file all the applications on the same day to avoid prior disclosure of an invention.

References

1. www.USPTO.gov
2. James Burke, *Connections*, Little, Brown and Company, Boston, MA (1978).

3. D. Mellor, *Rock Climbing*, W.W. Norton and Company, New York (1997).

4. J. Long, *How to Rock Climb*, Falcon, Helena, MT (1998).

5. J. Long and C. Luebben, *Advanced Rock Climbing*, Chockstone Press, Conifer, CO (1997).

6. https://www.ems.com/ea-how-to-choose-climbing-ropes.html

7. W. A. Light, D. S. Rimai, and L. J. Sorriero, "Method of Non-Electrostatically Transferring Toner", U. S. Patent #4,968,578 (1990).

8. W. A. Light, D. S. Rimai, and L. J. Sorriero, "Thermally Assisted Method of Transferring Small Electrostatic Toner Particle to a Thermoplastic Bearing Receiver", U. S. Patent # 5,037,718 (1991).

9. W. A. Light, D. S. Rimai, and L. J. Sorriero, "Thermally Assisted Transfer of Electrostatographic Toner Particles to a Thermoplastic Bearing Receiver", U. S. Patent #5,043,242 (1991).

3

The Path to Obtaining Patents

Introduction

You and your teammates have drafted documents that you hope will lead to patent protection for your innovative technology. In doing so you have followed the steps discussed in Chapter 2. In subsequent chapters, we will discuss how to formulate a patent strategy (including how to prioritize your applications), how to conduct a prior art search, and delve into more detail about drafting suitable claims. In this chapter, we will address what transpires between your having drafted the text that discloses your invention(s) until the time when, hopefully, one or more patents are ultimately issued.

During the course of drafting your proposed patent applications, you have taken an overview of your project and decided what patent applications should be filed now and what would be more beneficial to postpone. You have conducted the prior art searches, drafted proposed claims, and written the sections on the background and description of the invention or inventions. You have taken care not to disclose more than you need to in order to support the claims you are proposing, while leaving enough supportive material to write more restrictive claims if ultimately necessary. You are now asking where you go from here. You are about to enter the stage of what is termed "prosecution" or "prosecuting a patent application".*

Initial Meeting with Legal Counsel

You are now ready to meet with your legal counsel. You might ask, why do you now need to undergo the expense of hiring legal counsel after having gone through so much effort writing your patent application(s)? The straight forward answer is that a patent is a legal document that, upon successful prosecution, conveys to the owner of the patent certain legal rights. In order to obtain the best patents, one needs to employ someone with legal expertise.

When filing patent applications, those individuals with the appropriate legal expertise will typically have one of two sets of credentials. The first is a patent attorney. A patent attorney is someone who has attended law school, has been admitted to the bar, and has been certified in the specialty field of patent law. In general, a patent attorney will have some technical background, often a bachelor's degree in either science or engineering.

The second group of individuals with expertise in patent law is the patent agents. A patent agent is not an attorney and cannot represent you in patent court. However, a patent agent can conduct all other business involved in patenting inventions. Typically, patent agents are individuals who have worked as engineers and have then decided to take a course in patent law and pass a bar exam that certifies them to practice patent law as an agent. Alternatively, a patent agent can be someone who worked as an examiner at the patent office for a specified period of time and is now allowed to work as a patent agent.

Hiring a patent agent can save you money, as their hourly billing rate is often substantially less than that of an attorney. My own experience working with both patent agents and patent attorneys in writing and prosecuting patent applications is that both do excellent work. A cautionary note is that a patent agent is not an attorney so client-attorney privilege may not

* The term "prosecution" is generally used to denote the process of attempting to have a patent allowed and ultimately issued by the patent office. When enforcing a patent against an alleged infringer, the term used is "assertion" or "asserting a patent".

always occur, and may depend on whether the agent is independent or works for a law firm that was hired by either you or your employer.[†]

Upon reviewing your draft with legal counsel, your attorney [‡] or patent agent will probably want to revise your proposed claims. Counsel may also seek further information about the invention to more fully define it in the claims, as well as additional background information and details in the disclosure. Your attorney will have had prior experience with the patent office and will want to ensure that your invention is legally distinguishable from the prior art. Please remember that it is not sufficient that you are doing something different from that discussed in the prior art or that you are solving a totally different problem. Your attorney will be focused on whether the invention is novel, as defined by patent law, and nonobvious to one of ordinary skill in the art.

Manuscripts are written with specific audiences in mind. Scientific papers are generally written for members of the technical community who are conducting research in areas comparable to the author's. Service manuals are written for technicians who repair or maintain pieces of equipment. Owner's manuals are aimed at individuals who will actually use the described device. Whereas scientific publications may include high-level mathematics or other details leading to a depth of understanding, service manuals will not include such information unless directly pertinent to the needs of a technician. Similarly, owner's manuals will provide information on how to use a device, but not discuss the underlying theory or information on the servicing or repairs that are assumed to be performed by a trained technician. In all instances, the documents are written with the intended audiences in mind.

Patent applications, too, must be written with the intended audience in mind. In this instance the intended audience comprises the patent examiner and primary examiner.[§] Although both individuals have tech-

---

[†] It should be noted that, if your employer hired the patent attorney, it is your employer's interests that are protected by attorney-client privilege. Under these circumstances, the attorney is not representing you personally and, if discussions go beyond those stipulated by your employer, they may not be subject to that privilege.

[‡] Unless otherwise explicitly stated, the terms "attorney" and "legal counsel" will be used interchangeably and are meant to include patent agents. However, it should be noted that when asserting patents (i.e., suing an alleged infringer), your legal representation must be an attorney rather than a patent agent. When discussing assertions, legal counsel will refer to attorneys and not agents.

[§] The individual working in the patent office who is directly responsible for determining the patentability of your application is the patent examiner. The primary examiner is the patent examiner's supervisor and will review the patent examiner's decisions and communications, known as office actions, before they are issued.

nical experience in the field of the invention, they are not considering the application in terms of scientific information contained therein. They are strictly considering whether or not the application describes a legally patentable invention.

A secondary audience to be considered is the potential jury members who will be deciding whether or not someone is infringing upon your patent during an assertion. However, one must first obtain a patent before asserting it. Writing claims with the intention of being able to assert those patents is discussed in Chapters 7 and 8.

As an example, let us consider US Patent #5,772,779 [1]. The invention described in this patent involves a cleaning roller used in an electrophotographic printer to remove residual toner from the photoreceptor after transferring the toned image to a paper receiver. The rotating roller brushes residual toner from the photoreceptor and is itself cleaned by vacuuming.

The roller comprises acrylic fibers that are manufactured by one company. A second company weaves the fibers into a rug that is then sold to others for a variety of applications ranging from linings for coats to paint rollers. In fact, a company whose major product was paint rollers then bought the rugs and made the cleaning rollers that were used in the printers.

The problem we faced was that, if a new, previously unused cleaning roller was used to clean a previously unused photoreceptor, a scum would quickly form on the surface of the photoreceptor. This would prevent light from properly discharging the photoreceptor, thereby degrading the electrostatic latent image and resulting in observable defects in the printed image. The problem we faced was how to prevent the formation of the scum. This was quite challenging, as we had no idea why it was forming, especially as the problem did not occur if either, or both, the cleaning roller or photoreceptor had been previously used.

Upon extensive scientific analysis, we found that the new cleaning rollers were depositing an unknown material onto the photoreceptor. This material would serve as an adhesive that would glue the calcium carbonate filler particles from the paper to the photoreceptor during the transfer process, thereby producing poor quality images. The presence of toner on the used cleaning rollers and photoreceptors separated the fibers from the photoreceptor, thereby preventing the transfer of the adhesive material to the photoreceptor.

Now that we understood what the scum was, we needed to answer the next questions: What was the adhesive material, and what was its source?

It was apparent that the material came from the fibers, but the fiber manufacturer would not supply us with any information. Apparently, that material was part of a proprietary manufacturing process that they did not wish to share with us. Moreover, as the manufacturer made thousands of tons of these fibers each year, mainly for the carpet industry, they were not about to alter their process to supply the relatively miniscule quantity of fiber that we would need each year to produce our cleaning rollers.

We ultimately learned that the material that was plaguing us was a finishing agent coated onto the fibers in order to facilitate manufacturing. Moreover, we were able to identify the physical properties of that material that resulted in our observed problem with scum formation. We also found that we could remove that material from the cleaning rollers by washing the rollers in hot water with suitable surfactants or organic solvents. We now had a solution to a technical problem that we figured was not obvious. We ultimately obtained patent coverage, but not before receiving an initial rejection from the examiner. Let us examine what information we had to discuss with legal counsel and what constituted the inventions.¶

It should be emphasized that the present example is relatively simple because it involves a single patent aimed at solving a specific problem instead of a family of patents designed to protect a technological area. However, as the focus of this chapter is to describe the steps in obtaining patents, this example suffices.

With this discussion in mind, what information should you present to your legal counsel? The answer is to provide everything related to the problem solved, even if much of the information does not find itself into the patent application. Again, a patent is a legal document and your legal counsel will have the skills and knowledge to maximize your chances of actually obtaining the necessary patent protection. However, there is some information that would be vital and other information that may or may not be of significance. In the above discussion of remedying the scum formation problem, the research into the cause of the problem, while potentially the subject of an interesting scientific study and possibly of some value in explaining the invention, would not be critical to obtaining the patent. One does not have to explain, or even understand, how or why an invention works. One needs to clearly state what the invention is and how it can be practiced. Accordingly, the

---

¶ At the time this patent was issued (1998), it was possible to obtain coverage for what today would be considered separate inventions. Thus, we ultimately were able to get coverage for using cleaning rollers that did not have the materials used as finishing agents and a method of removing the finishing agents from the finished roller. Today, this would probably be considered two separate inventions as either could be practiced separately.

inventor-drafted version of the claims is important, not because they will be the final version of the claims submitted in the patent application, but because they define in total detail what the invention is. Equally important is a statement of the problem that the invention solved, along with a discussion of why the prior art did not solve or address the problem. Also important are actual examples showing the benefits obtained by practicing the invention and contrasting those benefits with examples showing the occurrence and severity of the problem when the invention is not practiced. Drafts of figures, even if not in total conformity to the legal requirements for patents, are very helpful when illustrating the invention and will assist draftsmen in formalizing the figures. In other words, include all the information that will help your patent attorney or agent understand your invention.

What You Should Expect from Your Legal Counsel

While your attorney may or may not be knowledgeable in your area of endeavor, do not assume that he or she possesses your expertise. Your legal representative is an expert in patent law. And, while your attorney may help you to define your invention(s), it is really up to you to do so. Legal counsel can review your material, suggest issues that an examiner may raise, and solidify your patent protection if the patent office ultimately allows your application. Your attorney may also suggest possible fallback positions that should be included within your disclosure should your initially proposed claims be rejected due to prior art found by the examiner, but which could be traversed (a legal way of saying "get around") if there is sufficient material within the initially filed disclosure to support an alternative, presumably more limited, set of claims.

Your legal counsel may also question what contributions each of the proposed inventors actually made. Alternatively, if there is a question of who should be listed as an inventor on a patent application, your attorney can help sort that out.

It is very important that you indicate to your legal representative all applications that you are considering filing at this time. Also, discuss ongoing R&D so that your attorney will understand the larger picture. Remember that you are trying to generate a patent portfolio that will protect your valuable technology and not, in general, just a single patent. By properly working with your legal counsel, you will ensure the highest probability of success in prosecuting your patent applications and devising and building a valuable patent portfolio.

After Your Patent Attorney or Agent Has Reviewed Your Application(s)

It is extremely important that all inventors carefully read the proposed application. Do you understand it? If not, now is the time to question your attorney. It may be that your attorney has misstated something. Alternatively, it may be that you are not cognizant of the legal reasons why certain statements are made. In either event, any issues or concerns should be addressed before the application is submitted to the patent office (the term "filed" is often used). Again, please remember that only the claims can be modified once the application has been submitted and that all modifications to the claims must be supported within the application by an appropriate and complete disclosure that is present in the original application.

Once you and your counselor have finished revising the application and you are preparing to submit it to the patent office, you will be asked to sign several forms. These include an affidavit that you have read and understood the application and that you attest that everything in it is true and correct. You will also be asked to affirm that you are the inventor. Finally, you may be asked to sign an assignment granting ownership and all rights to another person or entity such as your employer. With work done for hire, that assignment may be the contractual company. If funding were obtained from a government agency for you to work in conjunction with a nonprofit entity such as a university, you may have to assign all rights to the nonprofit institute. Whomever obtains the assignment will own the patent and can do with it whatever he, she, or it desires.

Filing the Application

Your attorney will now file the application or applications with the patent office. This is preferably done electronically, both for convenience and timeliness of the filings, but also because there are additional fees should you elect to file using a paper application. Once the filing has been done, you begin the waiting process. In some instances a patent may be issued within a year. More often than not, it will take two to three years before a patent is ultimately issued. If there are complicating factors, as will be discussed in Chapter 13, the application process may take longer.

After 18 months, the application will be published. From this time forward, you can track its progress at the website of the United States Patent

Office (assuming that you filed in the United States). This can be done by accessing the website of the Patent Office at www.uspto.gov. Once there, click on "Patents". You will want to obtain the publication number by clicking on AppFT under Patent Tools and Links. Copy that number. You can then find the application by searching on the name of the inventor – last name, semicolon, space, first name.

Once you have the application number, click on the tab designated PAIR (Patent Application Information Retrieval). Then click on the Public PAIR tab.** Once in the Public PAIR section, click on the publication number bubble and enter the number that you retrieved from the application link. You will be able to access the history of the application and all correspondence, including the application and all office actions.

It is important to recognize that this information is published and accessible to anyone, whether or not you actually receive a patent. It is a tradeoff. You are educating the public in the hope of being able to exclude others from practicing the claimed invention for a legally determined period of time. Your goal is to exercise due diligence in conducting and analyzing your prior art searches, carefully define the problem solved, and write your claims so that your invention is meticulously but thoroughly defined, while not narrowing the claims to the point that they would not exclude competitors from commercializing similar products. If done properly, you should be able to successfully prosecute between about 70% and 80% of your patent applications. This is one more reason why you should view your portfolio holistically to protect your technology rather than just filing patent applications on individual inventions.

Laying the groundwork by conducting a thorough prior art search, the results of which are incorporated into the background of the invention, defining the problem, and carefully describing the invention in a manner that renders it nonobvious in light of the prior art is the first step in successfully obtaining a patent. The steps involved in actually prosecuting your patent applications are described in detail in Chapter 13. However, as the need to carefully examine prior art and define your invention accordingly has been mentioned, it is worthwhile to further discuss the cleaning roller patent and examine one of the office actions – in this case an initial rejection of the application.

** The Private PAIR tab has limited access only to licensed patent professionals and has information that is not accessible to the general public.

Some months after submitting the aforementioned patent application, we received an office action rejecting the patent on grounds of obviousness. The examiner cited a patent describing a paint roller. In her office action, the examiner acknowledged that the patent does not describe cleaning the roller, but argued that the painter must have cleaned it.

Had our disclosure merely described the problem as the formation of a scum on the surface against which the roller articulated due to contaminants in the roller, the examiner would have been correct in her arguments that cleaning the roller would prevent the contamination of the contacting surface. It did not matter that a paint roller and a cleaning roller and their applications are different. If the problem solved – the transference of material from the roller to a mating surface, could simply be solved by suitable cleaning, the solution would have been obvious. However, we presented two arguments against the examiner's position. The first was that the patent did not state that the paint roller was ever cleaned. We responded that perhaps the painter merely threw the roller away after using it, as paint rollers are inexpensive but would require solvents and be time consuming to clean. Second, if the painter were to clean the roller, he would have done so after rather than before using it. It would not make sense to clean a clean paint roller.

In the present application, as clearly stated in the claims and in the supporting detailed description of the invention, the roller had to be cleaned prior to its initial use to avoid scum formation. The examiner allowed the patent in her next office action.

There are several lessons from this that the reader should bear in mind. The first is that the problem and its solution must be explicitly described. Had we just disclosed cleaning the roller to remove the finishing agents to avoid contaminating the contacting surface, without clearly stating that this must be done prior to its being used, the examiner would have been correct in her assertion that a paint roller could be cleaned to avoid such contamination. Second, the prior art cited by an examiner does not have to be within the field in which one is working. A corollary to this is that it simply will not be possible to preclude everything that the examiner can find that may relate to your invention. This can be especially problematic because the examiner can string together an arbitrary number of prior disclosures. What you can and must do is focus on a representative selection of the closest prior art and define the problem so that that art does not teach, either by itself or in any combination with other art, your invention. If this information is contained in your patent application, you stand a good chance to traverse any objections raised by an examiner or even preclude your receiving a rejection.

The Path Forward

An examiner may find nothing relating to your patent and issue, what is termed, a first office action allowance. This is desirable because it creates minimal documentation within the file folder of your application in the patent office – a file folder that is searchable by your competitor's attorneys in the event of an assertion. However, it does raise the question that perhaps the claims in your application are too narrow. This issue can be addressed by filing what is termed a "continuation" (if there is no new material introduced) or a "continuation in part" in the event of having to include new information. In either case, this requires the filing of new patent applications, and will be discussed more fully in Chapter 13.

The examiner can reject your claims. Claims can be rejected for a variety of reasons, most of which are legal. However, most common rejections are for a lack of novelty or because of obviousness. You can argue with the examiner, as we did in the cleaning roller application. Alternatively, you can revise your claims to circumvent the art cited by the examiner. Discussions between your legal counsel and you should lead to a proper course of action.

If you have been thorough, and perhaps also have a bit of luck, you will eventually receive a notice for an office action that allows your patent and also states the reasons why the patent is allowable. Congratulations! Now, it is merely a matter of paying the issuance fees and waiting. The patent will eventually arrive.

References

1. D. S. Rimai, T. H. Morse, J. R. Locke, R. C. Bowen, and J. C. Maher, U. S. Patent #5,772,779 (1998).

4

Identifying Patentable Inventions

Introduction

Over the years, I have often met with teams of scientists, engineers, and technicians who have been building the technological basis for an innovative product. They are creative, hard-working, and incredibly intelligent and capable. Their solutions to the problems that have prevented the previous commercialization of the perceived product are innovative and imaginative and are the result of long hours spent on R&D. Yet, more times than not, they have not submitted any invention disclosures. When asked about this, they respond that they have not invented anything. Why do they have this disconnect between their making technological advances and recognizing inventions? On other occasions they submit invention disclosures prematurely or even when they do not have inventions. Why are such highly skilled and creative people disconnected from patentability? In order to understand the origins of this disconnect, let us consider several situations.

The first situation that results in the failure to recognize patentable inventions occurs when a solution to a problem appears obvious to the team members who have expended considerable time and efforts in seeking out a solution to a problem. Their error in this analysis is that, after diligently working on a problem with dedicated and skillful team mates and coming up with a solution, the solution, in hindsight, seems obvious to members of the team. However, 20–20 hindsight does not make a nonobvious solution obvious.

A second situation, which is often related to the first that results in the failure of the team members to recognize patentable inventions, arises from a confusion between the extraordinary skill in the art typically possessed by the technical team members and the legal requirement that an invention must be nonobvious to one of ordinary skill in the art. What may seem obvious to one of extraordinary skill in the art does not preclude it from being inventive as long as it is nonobvious to one of ordinary skill in the art.

A third situation can occur when inventors believe that they have an invention and submit an invention disclosure* without first considering the project as a whole, including the technical challenges that have to be overcome in order to make the project a success. They may or may not have an invention. Sometimes they do have a patentable invention, but not necessarily for the problem that they solved. Rather, patent coverage could be obtained, but the problem solved has to be redefined so as to render its solution nonobvious. And, even though they may have patentable solutions to technical problems, they are focusing on a specific solution to a problem, rather than taking a holistic view to protect the technology.

Filing patent applications without considering the project as a whole may result in other team members erroneously believing that all inventions associated with the project have now been patented. Alternatively, filing such patent applications can, and often do, result in prematurely disclosing information that pose difficulties or even precludes obtaining more complete patent coverage subsequently.

How should inventors recognize material that can be used to generate a valuable portfolio that protects the entire advancement and does not jeopardize future filings with premature disclosures in patent applications? This issue will be discussed throughout this book.

---

* The term "invention disclosure", as used in this text, generally refers to a brief description of the problem and its solution. The entire disclosure is often less than one page in length.

A fourth situation often arises when members of a technical team realize that they have a new innovative product. However, they do not recognize that the product is rendered possible simply by combining known technologies. Simply combining known technologies in a manner wherein each component functions in a known manner is generally not patentable but can give rise to patentable solutions to the problems encountered when combining the technologies As is almost always the case, new technology is not developed in a vacuum. Rather, as discussed by Burke [1], advances occur because someone recognizes that the previously known components can be combined to yield something new. The team members then try to obtain patent protection on their new product by filing what is often referred to as "combination patents," whereby known technology is combined with each component acting as it is known to do, to produce a novel product. This approach is a waste of time and money, as the patent examiner would deny such patents, arguing that using a combination of known technology in a known manner and obtaining the expected result is obvious. What Burke and the inventors miss is that the inventions are not simply the combination of known technology. Rather, the inventions are overcoming the problems encountered while integrating the known technological components into a functioning product. Again, the problem solved must be properly and clearly defined in the background section of the patent application. What gives rise to patentability of an innovative product is solving the problems that have previously prevented the integrating of otherwise known technologies.

Let us examine the third and fourth scenarios in more depth using an actual example. A team of engineers was developing a high speed black and white electrophotographic printer. This printer increased productivity by coupling two printers serially, so that the first printer would print one surface of a page and the second, sequential, printer would print the reverse side. A conventional printer would print duplex prints by first printing one side of the page, flipping the page, and then printing the second side. I was asked, in my role as a patent engineer,[†] to develop a patent portfolio around this perceived product [2].

I met with the engineers on this team. All of them were highly motivated, educated, and skilled individuals who were dedicated to delivering

---

† A patent engineer is an individual with in-depth technical knowledge of the subject material, along with a solid working knowledge of patents. Part of the patent engineer's responsibility is to help develop appropriate patent portfolios to protect a company's intellectual property and help establish a proprietary position in the marketplace.

a successful product in a timely manner. Several already were named inventors on numerous patents associated with previous projects. All were loyal employees who wanted to do everything they could to benefit their employer.

Upon asking the team members what inventions they had, they responded that they had none, as they had not invented anything. In fact, they asserted that all they did was to couple two printers together serially. Then asked, if all they had to do was to couple two printers, why were they not able to complete the project a year earlier? That question immediately evoked a litany of technical problems they had to solve, including being able to properly time two machines perfectly, as millisecond timing differences between the coupled printers could lead to gross misregistration and poor justification,‡ the ability to couple two printers together while maintaining cross-track registration, the requirement to selectively flip pages that were to be duplexed and not flip sheets that were to be printed in simplex mode, the ability to control the timing of the printing in the coupled printers when varying the paper size, etc.

In other words, the team members did not recognize the problems they were solving. They assumed that the problem was to improve printer speed and productivity by coupling two printers together in serial fashion so that each printer would print on one side of a sheet of paper. To them, combining the known technologies was obvious, as indeed it would be to one of ordinary skill in the art, such as one in the graphic arts business who prints pages for a living. However, the patentable solutions they were finding were to the technical problems encountered when attempting to couple the printers. Once they understood this difference, they were able to succinctly enunciate how they solved each problem, which immediately gave rise to claims. Numerous patent applications were filed and successfully prosecuted [3–9]. The patents that were obtained formed a solid portfolio that would present barriers to the technical problems that a competitor would have to overcome in order to introduce a similar product. Inherent in filing these applications were two realizations: 1) it would simply not be possible to anticipate all alternatives that a competitor may use to circumvent a given patent and it would be costly and difficult to circumvent all the patents; and 2) it would be unlikely that patents would be allowed for all the applications filed and that both successful and unsuccessful applications teach how to solve technical problems. However, with the problems

---

‡ The registration of the printing between the front and back sides of a printed paper is referred to as justification.

properly stated and a prior art search conducted and discussed in the background section so that the examiner understands both the problem solved and why that solution was not found in the prior art, a sufficiently high success ratio of the patents awarded to the applications filed could be obtained so that serious obstacles would be presented to potential competitors.

It should be apparent from the preceding discussion that identifying what is patentable and building an encompassing patent portfolio that protects your intellectual property can be challenging upon occasion. There are times that a certain product is sufficiently novel that it, by itself, can be issued a patent, if it solves a technical problem in a manner that is novel and nonobvious. Even then, there will probably be opportunities to enhance your patent coverage within the concept of the product to make a stronger and more valuable portfolio.

The example cited from electrophotography was chosen because there is substantial prior art in this field that has to be circumscribed. Even though electrophotographic printers are well known and the idea to use two coupled printers rather than slowing down the process by requiring it to invert the paper would be fairly obvious, the solutions to the problems encountered while implementing the coupling met the legal requirements for patentability. It is necessary to think, not just in terms of what the novel product is, but what problems you had to overcome in order to develop that product. We will now turn our attention on how to identify such solutions.

Owning the Problem

Most patent strategies revolve around filing distinct and independent patent applications that disclose solutions to distinct problems. More often than not, there is little connection or coordination between those filings. This tends to promote weak patent portfolios that teach much about a technology, are expensive to both build and maintain, and which provide relatively less protection than would be optimal. In fact, such a strategy leaves many opportunities to work around the patents, having taught the competitors who have read the patents and who also tend to possess extraordinary skill in the art, about the problem and how it was solved.

A better patent strategy was introduced in *Patent Engineering* [2]. This strategy, called "owning the problem", focuses on obtaining patents that protect the entire technological basis for your product, rather than just solutions to specific problems.

The goal of owning the problem is that you have enough patent protection surrounding your technology to prevent others from marketing similar products. In other words, you have protected your place in the market. This approach also allows you to obtain licensing fees, should you desire, from companies that want to sell competitive products and to control where and to what extent those products could be sold. If your patents are too narrowly focused on what your company is doing and are of little interest to others, the patents are not worth much financially. As a result, owning such patents would not enable your company to enter into patent exchange agreements and thereby avoid having to pay licensing fees.

There is yet another advantage to your owning the problem rather than just owning specific solutions. The broader your patent protection is, the more likely that other companies will need access to your intellectual property. By owning the problem, you can obtain access to intellectual property that you need, but that is owned by others, through cross-licensing agreements.

There is one other issue that should be of concern for companies, both large and small, as well as individual inventors and entrepreneurs. This concerns the effect of non-practicing entities (NPEs), also known as patent trolls.

A patent troll is an individual or company that just obtains patents, but does not produce anything. They make money by suing other companies, claiming that those companies are infringing their patents.

Traditionally, the targets of patent trolls were mainly large corporations with deep pockets. However, as discussed in a recent Wall Street Journal (WSJ) Article [10], this is no longer the case. As litigation costs have increased, with discovery costs in the hundreds of thousands of dollars and court trials costing millions, some patent trolls are now targeting smaller companies that simply cannot afford to defend themselves in an assertion lawsuit. Instead, these companies often opt for paying tens of thousands of dollars in licensing fees, whether legitimate or not, to the NPE just to settle the case and be able to move on. Many of these companies can ill afford such extortions, but, faced with a costly legal defense, have little choice.

In one example alleged in the WSJ, the company that filed the most lawsuits in 2016 has never gone to trial. Accordingly, the issue of whether or not their patents are actually valid has not been adjudicated. Suffice-it to say, it merely holds issued patents.

Can a patent strategy that enables your company to own the problem reduce your exposure to the demands of patent trolls? The answer is perhaps.

As stated, a patent troll does not produce anything. Trolls do not need your intellectual property, so cross-licensing agreements are unlikely. Similarly, the threat of a countersuit in the advent of an assertion, which is a tactic that is often employed against product producing companies, is not an effective threat against trolls. Granted, there have been changes in the patent laws that make trolling more difficult, but these are mainly effective for larger companies that choose to defend themselves in an assertion.

There are two ways that you can reduce the probability of being sued for an alleged patent infringement. The first is to conduct a clearance search, as discussed in *Patent Engineering* [2]. A clearance search compares the technology used in your products with the claims in active patents. While conducting a clearance search will reduce the chances of being sued, especially by reputable companies, it does not eliminate the possibility as there may be legal gray areas. In addition, trolls that are intent on extracting licensing fees, as opposed to prosecuting assertion suits, may not care whether or not you are actively infringing their patents. They are simply trying to use the threat of your having to undertake an expensive legal defense in order to extract licensing fees from you.

A second, complementary, course of action is to develop and execute a patent strategy that will allow your company to own the problem. Doing so would greatly impede the ability of someone else to obtain patents that read[§] on your products. Granted, in order to be patentable, the invention must be novel. Any sort of prior disclosure, including using the technology in a commercialized product, disclosing the information in a scientific or trade journal, or demonstrating the technology in a trade show, etc., all constitute prior disclosures and can be used by an examiner to deny allowing a patent. That being said, it is far more probable that an examiner will find prior art in the patent literature, including, but not limited to, both issued patents and patent applications, rather than in other sources. If you can deny a troll, or for that matter any other company, the ability to obtain patents that read on your products, you will be better off.

Identifying Inventions

Let us now turn our attention to how to identify patentable inventions. Specifically, let us look at recognizing inventions that will, when considered in their entirety, form a patent portfolio that focuses on owning the problem instead of just a series of individual, disjointed patents, each of which discloses a solution to a particular problem. The reader is reminded that by owning the problem you will have formed a bulwark around your

---

§ If a product practices a claimed invention, that product is said to "read on the claim".

technology that establishes and protects your products in the marketplace. In addition it will allow you to gain access to the intellectual property owned by others through cross-licensing agreements. Finally, such a patent portfolio would allow you to enhance your company's revenues by obtaining licensing fees from others who require access to your intellectual property.

Having previously discussed the common pitfalls that prevent inventors and other team members from recognizing their inventions, it is now time to discuss how you actually start identifying inventions and constructing a patent portfolio that will allow you to own the problem, instead of building a collection of disjointed, independent patents that just provide limited protection to specific solutions. As previously discussed, the latter provides very limited protection that is expensive to both obtain and maintain.

To start formulating a patent strategy, you need a seed. A seed is a problem and a technical solution to that problem and has the potential to become a patentable invention or to "grow" into a patent portfolio. More importantly, a seed serves as a focus for the evolving problems and their solutions as a project advances. Seeds need not have complete solutions at the time they are identified. Rather, they are opportunities that you recognize. These opportunities can include obtaining fundamental patents on a new product or process. They may include doing something a bit differently than others, thereby reducing complexity or costs of the product or making it easier to use. A seed, in and of itself, may not be patentable. An example of an unpatentable seed is the previously discussed serial coupling of two black and white printers to improve duplex printing.

Seeds can arise from the analysis of competitive products that leads you to an understanding of the limitations and shortcomings of those products. Most likely the project on which you and your team are now working came from just such an analysis. Seeds that come from this type of study can be especially important as they identify the problems encountered with products offered by your competitors. As such, they will need your solutions. Please remember that patents are valuable only if someone else needs that invention. It should be noted that seeds can also come from your competitors' patents. After all, did they not define a problem and their proposed solution to that problem in their patent? There may be better solutions or important augmentations to the problems they discussed.

Seeds can also originate from an introspective analysis that extends beyond your present products into the future. After all, a patent typically takes several years from the date of filing to the date of issuance and has a lifetime of up to twenty years. In this era of rapidly evolving technology, twenty years could represent multiple product lifetimes. Think long range.

Do not neglect the ideas that found themselves on the cutting room floor when your team was discussing alternative approaches towards developing your anticipated product. These, too, have the potential to generate patents and may serve as seeds for further inventions. After all, you decided on your perceived best alternative based on assumptions that you made. What would happen if the assumptions changed? Consider, for example, that for many years, automotive ignition systems relied upon a rotating mechanical device known as a distributor to send a spark at the appropriate time to each cylinder in an internal combustion engine. Varying the timing of the spark was done using a vacuum mechanism or centrifugal weights that would vary the timing of the spark with engine speed. At that same time, massive computers such as the IBM 360/370 existed. It was assumed, for many years, that computers would be too big and/or too slow for use in an automobile. But what if those assumptions were challenged? What if someone assumed that, within the next generation, fast, small, and inexpensive computers could be built. Can you imagine the value today of patents that proposed using a computer to generate and time the sparks in an internal combustion engine, thereby eliminating the distributor, while improving fuel economy and reducing emissions? Always question your assumptions! In effect, seeds comprise any idea that may generate novel and nonobvious solutions to technical problems – the fodder of patents.

The project on which you are working is an obvious source for seeds. In this case a seed often comes from identifying the critical challenges related to the particular field of the invention. Critical challenges are problems, limitations, or shortcomings in existing products or services. In particular critical challenges are those problems that:

- Determine the cost, functionality, or profitability; or
- Are the result of regulatory requirements; or
- Drive customer buying decisions or habits.

Presumably, the project on which you are working presents at least one, and perhaps several, of these critical challenges. Such challenges can range from there being nothing in the market that addresses them to improvements that enhance customer buying decisions or address the ever changing regulatory requirements. All present significant market opportunities for you.

Once you have listed all critical challenges, ask yourself what problems have you encountered when attempting to address those challenges. In other words, what prevented you from producing a product at a previous time (perhaps a year or two ago) with the desired features that overcame the critical challenges? Moreover, are you presently able to implement all those features that address the critical challenges in a satisfactory manner or are you still facing problems? If all problems have been addressed, it makes it rather simple to put together a patent strategy. Alternatively, if you are still facing problems, you will have to carefully balance what you can presently disclose in order to file in a timely fashion. However, this must be done while still including enough additional information to revise your claims, if necessary, without compromising your ability to file additional patent applications on forthcoming developments.

The project on which you are working may or may not constitute a critical challenge and, accordingly, may or may not be patentable by itself. If a product combines known features in a manner that results in the combination of those features giving rise to an unanticipated (i.e. novel and non-obvious) result, the device would be patentable. An example of this is the compact fishing rig patented by Popeil [11]. Specifically, making a fishing rod more readily portable and storable by decreasing its length would be obvious. However, solving the problems including safely and readily storing the associated tackle was considered novel. It should be noted that it is likely that, under today's patent law, this device would be considered to comprise multiple inventions and, therefore, require multiple patents to claim all the then patented features.

Even when the device itself is patentable, do not omit filing applications on the solutions to the problems encountered when combining the individual components into the product.

In contrast, many would consider the transistor to be a single invention. However, legally, the device comprised numerous distinct inventions [12–19]. The references cited do not constitute an exhaustive list, but are, instead, used to illustrate that the transistor actually consists of multiple, inventions and not just a single one.

Also, do not neglect critical challenges that one is faced with when using or interfacing your product. For example, if your product can interface with any computer, printer, or other electronic device despite the specific protocols of those devices, and that ability distinguishes your product from those of your competitors, that ability can drive customer buying decisions and is, therefore, a critical challenge.

There are, of course, problems that do not rise to critical challenges. For example, while using an adhesive to bond auto body components instead of using welds or mechanical fasteners may facilitate manufacturing and reduce vehicle weight, it is unlikely that anyone would decide to purchase a vehicle based upon a manufacturing adhesive, even if it is a high tech or specialized adhesive. Although you may want to consider filing patent applications on challenges that are not critical, as such patents may be valuable, they are not the focus at the present time.[5]

Once you have identified all the critical challenges, it is time to list the problems encountered when addressing those challenges. The solutions to these problems will form the core of your patent strategy. It is important to differentiate between the terms "fundamental advancement" and "critical challenge". Fundamental advancements may or may not address critical challenges. Consider some years back, the VHS and Beta-Max recording systems. Both represented fundamental technologies, but those offered by Beta-Max did not represent critical challenges, as they did not drive customer buying decisions, and sales rapidly declined.

Similarly, consider Kodak's foray into instant photography – a field pioneered by Edwin Land and his Polaroid Corporation. In order to circumvent Land's patents on the fundamental chemistry of instant photography, Kodak developed its own chemical packets. While Kodak's chemistry was quite distinct from that of Polaroid, no one purchased an instant photographic system because of a certain chemistry. Land's chemistry offered, at the time it was introduced, the ability of a customer to obtain color photographs within minutes and without having to have a roll of film processed. This drove buying decisions and, therefore, represented a critical challenge. By the time Kodak introduced its competitive instant photographic product, the ability of the consumer to produce and view a photograph without having to bring a roll of film to a processor was no longer a critical challenge. The Polaroid product already allowed the consumer to view a photograph within minutes of having taken the picture. Customers wanted instant photographs and were not concerned with, nor did they understand, the chemistry. The timing of the Polaroid technology enabled customers to do something that they could not have done previously. The different Kodak chemistry did not. Yes, there were other critical challenges that could have been met. The image quality of an instant photograph is poor compared to a conventional photograph. Improved image quality could have represented a critical challenge. In addition the consumer had to coat Polaroid photographs with a rather odious material. Elimination of this step may have also constituted a critical challenge, but was not addressed by the Kodak technology. In summary, critical challenges are

---

[5] One exception to this can arise if such noncritical challenge patents are sufficiently valuable as to warrant filing. If filing patent applications on the critical challenges will result in disclosing the noncritical technology, then it would behoove you to include such applications in your proposed portfolio.

temporal and, what constitutes such a challenge at one time may not constitute one at a later date.

In addition to the fundamental advancements/technology described above, Polaroid developed enabling technology for which a number of patents were granted. For example, Polaroid had a patent on pairs of rollers that form a nip through which the film packet is pulled by the consumer. This set of rollers squeezed the developer into the film packet, allowing the exposed film to produce an instant photograph. It was easy to use and addressed the problem of how to get the chemicals into contact with the exposed film to allow development to occur at the time chosen by the consumer, as opposed to the consumer having to transfer the exposed film to a photofinisher in order to produce visible prints. The ability of the customer to snap a photograph and develop it, either on the spot or at a later time of the customer's choosing drove buying decisions. In fact it was this and six other relatively simple enabling patents that cost Kodak over $900 million and forced it out of the instant photography business. In summary, simple enabling technologies may address critical challenges and recognizing and patenting such inventions can be extremely valuable.

Fundamental technologies can also drive buying decisions. For example Kodak used dyes in its color photography business that closely matched natural colors, believing that that was what the consumer wanted. In fact, the professional market preferred those colors. However, Fuji Film developed dyes that were brighter, even if unrealistic. Consumers preferred these resultant colors, which allowed Fuji to increase its share of the marketplace. Here, a fundamental technology also represented a critical challenge because it drove customer buying decisions.

Once you have identified the critical challenges, you need to identify how you solved them. This will form the basis of your patent strategy. Also, as previously discussed, reexamine the alternatives that were not among the solutions chosen to these problems and identify why you chose the solutions that you did. If the alternatives had fundamental flaws, move on. However, if they were not chosen because of assumptions or because your chosen path was easier to integrate into your prospective product, you may also want to include the alternative solutions in your strategy. Again, the life of a patent is relatively long and controlling alternatives can allow you to control the future markets.

Determine What Your Competitors Are Doing

You have, by now, identified both the problems encountered and their solutions in developing your own technology. Now is the time to take another look at how your competitors are addressing similar problems.

Closely and repeatedly examining competitive products is important. First, such examination forces you to compare your offering to that which is already in the marketplace or soon to be introduced. Does your product address the critical challenges in a manner such that customers will choose to pay for your product instead of that of your competitor? In a worst case scenario, you may learn that the product about to be introduced by your competitor may totally undermine your market and you may have to decide to cancel your program altogether.

Another advantage that you will gain by examining your competitors' products at this time is that you now recognize their limitations and opportunities for improvement that will distinguish your products from those of your competition to potential customers. After developing your product, you may know how to fix their problems. These solutions to their problems can be very valuable additions to your patent portfolio because your competitors will probably need those solutions, especially after your product, which does not have those problems, is introduced.

Now that you have identified the critical challenges and the seeds, it is vital to clearly explain how your inventions address those challenges. In particular, when discussing the background of your inventions, it is important to explain why the prior art, either as a single piece or in combination with an unlimited number of other pieces, does not fix the problem. Remember that, in order to be patentable, your solution must be novel and nonobvious. Being able to cite actual limitations of your competitors' technology will go far in establishing the patentability of your invention(s). After all, why would a competitor introduce a product with problems if the solutions to those problems were obvious and easily fixed?

However, there is one cautionary caveat in discussing the limitations of the technology disclosed in the prior art. Be very circumspect about discussing any limitations to the technology especially in your own existing patents when seeking new patents. Such discussions will be found by a defendant and will likely be used against you in the event that you choose to assert the patents. Moreover, such information can be used by competitors to establish patentability for their patent applications.

File on the Patentable Enabling Technology

As discussed above, the enabling technology that actually is required to make your fundamental advancements work can represent critical challenges and may be more valuable than the fundamental patents. This was discovered by Kodak when it attempted to defend itself against Polaroid's assertions. Simply stated, one does not know, a priori, which patents will be valuable. You simply have to cover all bases to the best of your ability.

Concluding Comments

It is important to remember that, these days, each patent is limited to a single, distinct invention. In general, inventions that focus on materials will be considered distinct from inventions that disclose the advantages gained by a piece of apparatus that uses those materials. Methods for using either the apparatus or the materials are, in general, distinct inventions. This is because the advantages gained by using a material can be obtained with a different piece of equipment. Similarly, a method to accomplish something can be used with either a different piece of equipment or a different material.

As will be discussed in more detail in Chapter 8, it is important to always keep in mind one's ability to assert a patent when identifying the inventions. You should preferably patent inventions that would only require a single entity, be it a person or a company, to infringe. Thus, an invention that first requires someone to construct a piece of equipment or formulate a new compound and then use that equipment or compound may be difficult to assert because more than one entity may be infringing upon it. Accordingly, such advances are likely to constitute more than a single invention and should be filed as separate applications.

Finally, it is important to remember that you are constructing an encompassing patent portfolio that owns the problem and will protect your place in the market, rather than just a collection of disjointed patents that present specific solutions to problems. As such, there will be much overlap in the applications. Carefully identify what is ripe for filing and what is not. Keep in mind that the patent will be issued to the first to file, not the first to invent, so that the filing, or priority, date is crucial. However, you need to avoid prematurely disclosing any information on which you plan to file in the future. This is a delicate balancing act and is made even more complicated by the fact that your disclosures will have to include enough information that can be used to support revised claims in the likely event that the examiner rejects your initial claims. It is vital to focus, at all times, on implementing a successful patent strategy and not just on being able to prosecute an individual patent. However, building a solid patent portfolio requires that most of your individual patent applications be successfully prosecuted thereby resulting in issued patents.

References

1. J. Burke, *Connections*, Little, Brown, and Company, Boston, MA (1978).
2. D. S. Rimai, *Patent Engineering*, Scrivener Publishing, Beverly, MA (2016).
3. M. T. Dobbertin and A. E. Rapkin, U.S. Patent #8,019,255 (2011).
4. M. T. Dobberton and T. J. Young, U.S. Patent #8,000,645 (2011).
5. M. T. Dobberton and T. J. Young, U.S. Patent #8,224,226 (2012).
6. T. J. Young, D. J. Fuest, M. T. Dobberton, and C. B. Liston, U.S. Patent 8,180,242 (2012).
7. T. J. Young, D. J. Fuest, M. T. Dobberton, and C. J. Liston, U.S. Patent #8,099,009 (2012).
8. J. A. Pitas, A. E. Rapkin, and M. T. Dobbertin, U.S. Patent #8,301,061 (2012).
9. M. T. Dobberton and T. K. Sciurba, U.S. Patent #8,355,159 (2013).
10. http://www.wsj.com/articles/americas-biggest-filer-of-patent-suits-wants-you-to-know-it-invented-shipping-notification-1477582521.
11. S.J. Popeil, U.S. Patent #4,027,419 (1977).
12. W. Brattain, U.S. Patent #2,663,829 (1953).
13. W. Brattain and J. Bardeen, U.S. Patent #2,589,658 (1952).
14. J. Bardeen and W. Brattain, U.S. Patent #2,524,035 (1950).
15. W. Brattain and R. Gibney, U.S. Patent #2,524,034 (1950).
16. G. Pearson and W. Shockley, U.S. Patent #2,502,479 (1950).
17. W. Shockley, U.S. Patent #2,502,488 (1950).
18. W. Shockley, U.S. Patent #2,654,059 (1953).
19. W. Shockley and M. Sparks, U.S. Patent 2,623,105 (1952).

5

Identifying What Has Yet to Be Invented

Introduction

Identifying patentable inventions with solutions to problems in hand is sufficiently challenging under most circumstances. This becomes even more challenging, as discussed in Chapter 4, when you have to integrate multiple solutions to a plethora of problems so that you can develop a coherent patent strategy. You are now being asked to identify inventions that you do not yet have, possibly solving problems that you do not yet know that you have. Why is this necessary and how do you go about achieving this?

Looking forward is beneficial for several reasons. First, it keeps you focused on the problems that face you. The list of problems will change. Some problems will be solved. Others that may have been anticipated will not be the subject of R & D. Still others will seem to appear from nowhere.

More often than not, the problems transition from fundamental technology building to solving the problems that enable the implementation of that technology. The reader is, again, reminded not to confuse the terms "fundamental technology" and "critical challenge". While fundamental problems are usually associated with critical challenges, this may not always be the case. For example, U.S. Patent #5,678,617 [1] describes a method and apparatus for making a drink hop along a bar from the location where a bartender prepares the drink to a patron's location.*

It is very clear that the inventors had to solve some fundamental problems in order to make this device function. The reader, however, is reminded that, in order to be a critical challenge, the invention must

    a. Determine cost, functionality, or profitability; or
    b. Address regulatory requirements; or
    c. Drive customer buying decisions.

It is unlikely that the technology described in this patent would drive any customer buying decisions. It certainly does not address any regulatory issues. Moreover, it does not determine costs or profitability. Functionality could be debated, but so far it would appear that the technology can better be described as sleight-of-hand† rather than an actual mechanism that allows the transport of an actual drink.

Expanding Electrophotographic Printing into New Applications

With that, let us turn our attention to an example of an innovative technological development, wherein the problems encountered were often unanticipated and had to be addressed sequentially over a period of several years. This activity occurred in an area of electrophotography in which I had the privilege of working.

Up until around 1990, the role of electrophotography was limited to copiers. The image quality was fine for the reproduction of alpha-numeric text. The advent of the "plain paper copier", brought about by the ability to electrostatically transfer a toner image from a photoreceptor to paper,‡

---

* At the time this patent was issued, the USPTO allowed patents that contained both apparatus and method claims. It is likely that, today, this would be considered to be two separate inventions, as either could be practiced without the other.
† The wording in the abstract of the patent states "The drink then seems to hop from some remote spot on the bar and take one or more leaps, ultimately landing in the patron's glass".
‡ Prior to the advent of the electrostatic transfer process, electrophotographic copies were generally produced on paper coated with zinc oxide, which is a photoreceptive material. This paper had an unappealing look and feel and the images made on it were poor compared to those produced lithographically.

expanded the use of this technology into the areas that had been dominated by lithography [2].

However, the world changed due to advancements in digital electronics. The invention of the digital camera eliminated the need for conventional photography using silver halide-based film image capture. And computer electronics and associated software such as Adobe Photoshop gave individuals the ability to download digital images from an image capture device, enhance the features of those images, and, if appropriate printing technology were available, print those images. Other opportunities such as replacing silver halide-based medical imaging with digital imaging also existed if high quality printing could be implemented.

One possible printing technology was based on electrophotography. However, the image quality at that time was too poor to allow it to be used for high-quality applications such as photofinishing. One such limitation was the electrostatic transfer process. Surface forces holding the toner particles to the photoreceptor were stronger than the maximum electrostatic transfer forces that could be exerted as the toner diameter decreased [3, 4]. This limited the ability to transfer toner images to those having toner diameters greater than about 12 μm [5]. (The advent of silica-coated toner particles decreased the maximum diameter of transferable toner particles to about 7 μm [6].) Transfer efficiency was also limited to about 90%, with approximately 10% of the toner remaining on the photoreceptor.

Transfer presented two very significant challenges in order to meet the demands of photographic quality printing. First, the grain introduced into the prints with 12 μm, or even 7 μm, toner would far exceed that of a silver halide photographic print and would not be acceptable to most customers. To match the grain of a silver halide print would require the use of toner particles having diameters no greater than 3 μm. Second, a failure to transfer virtually all the toner in the image would give rise to a mottle and would also be unacceptable. In other words, producing photographic quality prints would require a higher transfer efficiency than is normally achieved to be obtained using toner particles that are so small so as to be considered essentially nontransferable.

There is yet another significant problem. After transfer, the image is permanently fixed to the paper by fusing, whereby the toned image is subjected to heat and pressure. This softens the toner particles, thereby spreading them in order to bond them to the receiver. However, by spreading them, their diameters are increased, thereby increasing the grain of the print to unacceptable limits. In addition, electrophotographically produced documents tend to have relatively low gloss levels, whereas photographs are much glossier.§ This challenge will be discussed in more depth later in this chapter. Let us, for the present time, continue with the discussion of toner transfer, its critical challenges, and recognizing and handling problems as they evolved.

The first challenge that we faced was the need to transfer toner images made with previously nontransferable small toner particles with an efficiency not generally obtained with conventional-size transferable toner. This, obviously, called for a fundamental advancement. Moreover, as the ability to produce such images would drive customer buying decisions governing the use of electrophotography for novel, high quality applications, it was a critical challenge.

The challenge was met by designing a novel transfer process that did not rely on electrostatics at all. Rather, the process called for enhancing the adhesion of the toner to the receiver by heating it to a temperature so that it would soften, but not fuse to the receiver. It should be noted that thermal transfer processes that combined the transfer and fusing steps were known at the time. However, those processes tend to be rather slow and subject the photoreceptors to sufficient heat as to degrade them.

The transfer process discovered, denoted as a "thermally assisted transfer", to distinguish it from conventional combination of thermal transfer and fusing (often referred to simply as "thermal transfer") was issued U.S. Patent 4,927,727 [7]. Let us examine the first claim of this patent and discuss what it contains.

Claim 1 states:

In (sic) method of making a hard copy wherein a latent electrostatic image on an image-bearing substrate is developed by applying to said image dry thermoplastic charged toner particles comprising a toner binder, and said developed image is transferred to the surface of a receiver by contacting said developed image on said substrate with said surface, then removing said surface from said substrate, the improvement which comprises

The above part of the claim essentially states the field of the invention. It should be noted that the examiner will probably ignore this section, although it would be important when asserting the patent. The claim continues:

---

§ A typical document, even one containing graphic content, would have a gloss level, as measured with either a G-20 or G-60 gloss meter of less than 10. In contrast, the gloss of a photograph typically exceeds 90.

(A) *developing said latent electrostatic image with a toner having a particle size of less than 8 micrometers;*

Section (A) establishes that an electrostatic latent image is converted into a visible image using toner with particle sizes less than 8 μm. This is included, as the toner image has to first be formed on the photoreceptor. In other words, a toner image must exist. Moreover, the process is designed to transfer small toner particles (at the time, less than approximately 8 μm). This limitation was put in to avoid any prior art, including conventional thermal transfer processes, that used larger toner.¶

(B) *heating said surface before it contacts said developed image, to a temperature such that said surface heats said toner particles when it contacts said developed image to a temperature between 10.degree. C. above the T.sub.g of said toner binder and 20.degree. C. below the T.sub.g of said toner binder, where said temperature is sufficient to fuse discrete toner particles that form said image to each other at points of contact between said particles, but insufficient to cause said contacting particles to flow into a single mass;*

Section (B) states that a critical factor in the claimed method is that the receiver was heated to a specified temperature prior to its contacting the toner. This helps distinguish it from conventional thermal transfer whereby the toner image on the photoreceptor is heated. Moreover, the restriction that the contacting toner particles do not flow into a single mass further differentiates this invention from conventional thermal transfer. This restriction is important to the present invention because it was desired that this be a relatively high-speed process, compared to conventional thermal transfer and that the heating of the photoreceptor be minimized.

¶ It should be noted that the claim specifies toner particles less than 8 μm even though the envisioned usage requires 3 μm toner particles. The claimed process does work with toner particles up to 8 μm. Claiming this size in the independent claim broadens the protection afforded by the patent. Dependent claim 8 specifies the preferred size range of less than 5 μm. If the proposed first claim were rejected, the patent application could still have been salvaged by rewriting the claims so that claim 1 would have been omitted and claim 8 could become the independent claim. Claims are discussed more fully in Chapter 8.

> (C) *non-electrostatically transferring said developed image to said surface, where said surface has a roughness average less than the radius of said toner particles; and*

Section (C) states that the transfer process does not rely on the application of an electrostatic field. This is at the core of the invention. The technique requires that the toner contact the receiver in order to allow the surface forces to effect transfer and further requires that the receiver roughness be small compared to the toner particles. By comparison, paper often has a surface roughness that is greater than twice the toner radius. Again, the requirement that the surface be smooth is vital for this invention to work and, is, therefore, included in this claim.

> (D) *heating said developed image after it has been removed from said substrate to a temperature sufficient to fuse it to said surface.*

Section (D) establishes that the transferred image has not been permanently fixed to the receiver. This is a distinguishing feature between this claimed transfer process and conventional thermal transfer, also known as transfusing.

What is included in Claim 1 is every component that makes this invention work. What is also included are aspects that are not practiced in this invention, but help to distinguish it from the prior art. It should be noted that the information within the claim is also stated exactly within the detailed description of the invention.

What is absent from the claim and from all discussion within the application is any speculation of how to address future problems, be they known (e.g., the issue of fixing the toner without increasing the cross sectional area of the particle, which would increase grain; or the issue of obtaining a very high and uniform gloss) or unanticipated problems that we encountered as we developed this technology. In other words, you have to anticipate that you will discover further problems in need of innovative solutions when you write your applications. You should avoid speculation because that can constitute a premature disclosure. Write your applications with the intent of filing additional applications in the future.

At this time we turned our attention to developing the enabling technology that would improve the performance of the thermally assisted transfer process. We quickly recognized that, in contrast to most electrophotographic uses at the time, the presently envisioned usage would require printing on very smooth, high quality, reflective receivers that appeared similar to those used in photofinishing. In other words, paper was not going be treated as a commodity item, as is normally the situation for electrophotographic printers. Rather, for any envisioned applications of this technology, the consumer would anticipate a certain look and feel to the receiver. In other words, a specialized paper would be required for the envisioned applications of this technology. This recognition allowed the thermally assisted transfer process to be facilitated by using as the receiver, a paper that had been overcoated with a thermoplastic layer designed to enhance toner adhesion to the receiver during the transfer process. This is described in U.S. Patent 4,968,578 [8].

One problem that we encountered was that the method described in U.S. Patent 4,968,578 often required that some sort of release aid be coated onto the photoreceptor prior to the deposition of the toner (e.g., development). This had to be frequently replenished *in-situ*, which is complicated and adds expense. In addition the release aid on the photoreceptor tended to degrade the development process.

It was clear that we had to develop enabling technology that would be able to address these issues in order to produce photographic quality prints. As these solutions would be required to drive customer buying decisions, it was clear that these constituted critical challenges, despite the fact that they would be classified as enabling, rather than fundamental, technologies.

As the receiver did not have to be treated as a commodity item (i.e. the customer would not expect to simply put any type of paper into the printer and make it work), we decided to increase the adhesion of the toner to the receiver by coating the surface of the receiver with a thermoplastic that would soften during the preheating phase of the transfer process. Upon application of pressure, the toner particles would partially embed into the thermoplastic, thereby effecting transfer of the toner image to the receiver upon separation of the receiver from the photoreceptor.

This was an effective, enabling advancement and definitely a solution to the problem of transferring the toner image. More specifically, it was a solution to a technical problem, but was it an invention that is, was it patentable? The answer, according to our attorney, was "no". The reader is reminded that the patent examiner** is going to ignore all verbiage up to the word "comprising" in the claim. In other words, the use for the invention is not relevant when applying for a patent, although it would be very

---

** A patent examiner, first defined in Chapter 3, is an individual employed by the Patent Office and is responsible for determining whether an application describes a patentable invention.

pertinent during an assertion. The examiner is going to look to see what is novel. In this case, a piece of paper bearing a thermoplastic on its surface is known, as numerous items that comprise paper with a thermoplastic coating, such as playing cards, laminated signs, and cafeteria trays , exist. Thus, novelty would be considered to be lacking. It does not matter whether the item in the prior art is being used in a different manner or is even totally different. The fact that the ability to be used in this fashion is inherent to known items is sufficient to negate novelty.

However, one problem often leads to another, giving rise to more opportunities to invent, as was with this technology. Specifically, the thermoplastic effectively allowed the toner to transfer to the receiver because, under heat and pressure, it acted as a hot melt adhesive. As a result, the thermoplastic not only adhered to the toner, but it also adhered to the photoreceptor.

Four solutions to the problem of the receiver adhering to the photoreceptor were found. Three of these consisted of using, as the thermoplastic coating on the receiver, various types of polymers with surface energies restricted to a narrow range [9–11]. This range of surface energies is not inherent to these classes of polymers, but are, rather, subsets of the range of surface energies that such materials typically possess. Since their use in this application was not taught anywhere, they were considered patentable inventions. The fourth comprised incorporating a release aid into the thermoplastic [8] - that is the layer to which the toner particles are expected to transfer. By including the release agent in the receiver, it becomes automatically self-replenishing so that coating the photoreceptor was not necessary. It also addressed the problem of having a release aid on the photoreceptor degrading development, as the release agent was not coated onto the photoreceptor.

The list of enabling technologies that were developed, including being able to transfer to plain paper, textured graphic arts papers, and stiff papers that could not be wrapped around a roller to allow sequential transfers of multiple primary colors, is extensive. Patents were granted for many of these enabling technologies and, therefore, allowed the assignee to own the problem. Moreover, as they impacted customers' buying decisions, they were critical challenges even though they were not fundamental technologies.

Now that many of the transfer problems were addressed, it was time to look for solutions to the fundamental critical challenge of permanently fixing the toner image to the receiver without increasing grain and obtaining the high gloss that one expects with a photograph.

Typically, a glossy print is made by casting the print, under pressure, against a smooth roller. This approach, however, did not work, as the thermoplastic- coated receiver would adhere to the roller. In other words, the solutions to the problem of adherence to the photoreceptor were not sufficient to prevent adherence to a shiny fusing roller. A solution to this problem was found by allowing the fusing member to cool prior to separating the image-bearing receiver from it. However, that could not be done in a continuously running printer, as the time to cool the roller would have been prohibitive and would have adversely affected productivity. Instead, a shiny web was made whereby the image could be cast against the web in a heated fusing nip formed between a heated roller behind the web and a pressure roller located on the opposite side of the printed receiver. The web was then transported away from the heated region, thereby allowing cooling to occur. Separation of the printed receiver from the web was effected after cooling [12]. The use of this technique drove the toner particles into the thermoplastic without spreading them, while imparting a glossy sheen onto the exposed toner and the thermoplastic. These results would not have been obtained without the use of the thermoplastic that was uniformly coated over the entire surface of the receiver.

By this time, the reader probably realizes that a solution to one problem often leads to other problems that must be addressed in order to enable the use of the invented technology. In this instance, heating the receiver to a temperature that was sufficiently high to fix the toner image and impart a gloss (and significantly higher than that needed to accomplish transferring) the image caused the receiver to curl. A curl preventing layer on the obverse side of the receiver was necessary [13, 14]. By this time, the construction of the receiver was sufficiently novel that we were also able to have claims allowed that incorporated the fact that the receiver contained a toner image.

Lessons Imparted

The above history of what innovations were necessary to transfer, fix, and gloss prints made with 3 μm toner was included to illustrate a number of factors that go into developing a patent strategy and portfolio.

The first and foremost lesson is that you should not just patent a specific solution to a problem. A patent portfolio is much more powerful and valuable if it is harder for a competitor to traverse the claims in the patents. You should to try to patent as many aspects of both the fundamental and the enabling inventionable technology as is possible.

The second lesson is that a nonobvious solution to a problem does not necessarily imply novelty. As discussed earlier, the use of the thermoplastic- coated receiver itself was not an invention because similar items already existed; just because a device is used in a novel fashion does not make it a novel device. That thermoplastic-coated papers such as playing cards were already known precluded obtaining patent coverage on the receiver. It should be noted that the term "known" does not mean "well-known" or common knowledge. If a technological solution that, by itself or in combination with other technologies, has been disclosed at all and can be used to obtain your solution to your problem, it is known. Whether or not it has been used specifically in solving your particular problem is irrelevant.

Let us now focus on the main subject of this chapter, namely addressing how you handle problems for which you do not presently have solutions or even problems that you do not know you have while implementing a patent strategy. It is certainly clear, from the above examples, that, in some instances such as the need to fuse and gloss an image, we knew that we faced critical challenges at the start. We did not, initially, have any idea of what the solutions would be. In other instances, such as those encountered during the post-transfer separation process, we did not even anticipate the problems that were uncovered. How do you develop and implement a patent strategy that includes problems for which you do not have solutions and which you may not know even exist?

There are several factors that, added together, do much to address the handling of future developments. The first is to realize that time is a critical factor. You have come up with a solution to a critical challenge. As such, you want your team to evaluate this solution as quickly as possible. You need to be working closely with your team mates so that any issues that arise during the evaluation process are made known to you quickly. Considering the time involved between putting together the initial draft of an invention disclosure and actually filing the application with the patent office, you generally will have time to make sure that your presently proposed application does not prematurely disclose any information that may endanger obtaining further coverage.

Another cautionary note is to avoid disclosing any information that is not directly correlated with describing the problem being solved and how the present invention solves the problem. Yes, you can use a common disclosure when appropriate for filing multiple applications, but anything not directly related to the proposed claims should not be disclosed. That being said, there does need to be sufficient information to support revised claims, if necessary. However, in all cases, it is necessary to narrowly focus on the goals of the specific patent application or applications under consideration, without disclosing more than is necessary. In short, do not speculate on solutions to problems that are not being claimed. Also, be cognizant of how the application(s) being filed can be combined with prior art to impede the successful prosecution of future patent applications. Please remember that, even though generalizations may not be considered to support claims, they may be considered to disclose enough technical information that that can result in future applications being rejected.

Stay in close communication with the other technical team members to make sure that the applications that you are envisioning are complementary to those being advanced by the others, as well as being aware of the problems being addressed. It may be necessary to revise proposed applications before filing, or even consider filing additional applications, based on ongoing developments.

Possible further patent applications should always be considered by your team, as ongoing problems give way to their solutions.

When Developing Technology in Conjunction with others

Co-development is often necessary these days. Developing a new product may be too costly for you or your company to do solely. The costs associated with meeting regulatory requirements, such as those encountered in the pharmaceutical or biomedical areas, may prevent you from being able to introduce a product, no matter how innovative or beneficial that product is. And, you simply may not have the expertise to solve all the technical problems envisioned.

It should be recognized that, if someone outside of your company invents a patentable solution to a technical problem, that person is an inventor. It does not matter whether the individual is the inventor of the first independent claim or the one who proposed the 15th dependent claim. That person is an inventor. As such, the patent may have rights assigned to a company other than yours. The rights may be limited, such as that company not being able to sell to your competitors, or they may, in a worst case scenario, give the other company complete control of the technology. Your company may have to buy subsystems or licenses from that company, irrespective of the price, or you may have to share your profits in a manner that was unforeseen. It is desirable to prevent this to the extent possible.

The easiest way to address this concern is to file applications on those problems for which you envision solutions before entering into any technical discussions with your collaborator. If the applications were filed in advance to such discussions, there is no question as to how and when an invention arose. Alternatively, if a solution occurs after discussions have commenced, it becomes questionable as to whom the inventor is. Yes, this can lead to premature disclosures if not done carefully. You will have to carefully balance the risks of disclosing otherwise patentable information before you are fully ready to do so with setting up circumstances that allow someone else to exercise control over your technology.

Concluding Remarks

Addressing solutions to ongoing or future problems while implementing a holistic patent strategy is challenging. To successfully do so requires that you constantly monitor what problems are being addressed and how they are being solved. It also requires that you be aware of problems that arise of which you were not previously cognizant.

You may have to revise your proposed applications in light of ongoing developments. However, remember that patents are issued to the first to file, not the first to invent. Time is not on your side. You must act in a timely manner and accept the fact that you will probably not be able to get patents on all your inventions. However, by implementing a well-designed patent strategy, you should be able to protect your technology and your place in the market.

References

1. R. Kuykendal and R. Deichmann, U. S. Patent #5,678,617 (1997).
2. E. M . Williams, *The Physics and Technology of the Xerographic Processes*, Wiley-Interscience, New York City (1984).
3. D. S. Rimai, D. J. Quesnel, L. P. DeMejo, and M. T. Regan, "Toner to Photoconductor Adhesion", *J. Imag. Sci. Technol.* 45, 179 (2001).
4. D. S. Rimai, D. S. Weiss, and D. J. Quesnel, "Particle Adhesion and Removal in Electrophotography", *J. Adhesion Sci. Technol.*, 17, 917 (2003).
5. D. S. Rimai, D. S. Weiss, and D. J. Quesnel, "Particle Adhesion and Removal in Electrophotography", *J. Adhesion Sci. Technol.*, 17, 917 (2003).
6. D. S. Rimai, P. Alexandrovich, and D. J. Quesnel, "Effects of Silica on the Adhesion of Toner to a Composite Photoconductor", J. Imag. Sci. Technol. 47, 1 (2003).

7. D. S. Rimai and C. Sreekumar, U. S. Patent #4,927,727 (1990).

8. W. A. Light, D. S. Rimai, and L. J. Sorriero, U.S. Patent #4,968,578 (1990).

9. W. A. Light, D. S. Rimai, and L. J. Sorriero, U.S. Patent #5,037,718 (1991).

10. W. A. Light, D. S. Rimai, and L. J. Sorriero, U.S. Patent #5,043,242 (1991).

11. D. S. Rimai, L. J. Sorriero, and D. Tyagi, U. S. Patent #5,045,424 (1991).

12. D. S. Rimai, M. Aslam, C. D. Baxter, K. M. Johnson, E. J. Tamary, J. E. Laukaitis, H. E. Wright, T. J. Chen, and W. J. Staudenmayer, U.S. Patent #5,089,363 (1992).

13. D. S. Rimai and M. Aslam, U.S. Patent #5,516,394 (1996).

14. D. S. Rimai and M. Aslam, U.S. Patent #5,691,039 (1997).

6

Prioritizing the Inventions

What Does Prioritizing Inventions Mean?

Isn't the concept of prioritizing inventions oxymoronic? After all, doesn't an invention have to be novel and nonobvious? In short, in order to be patentable, doesn't the solution to the problem have to be unanticipated? As such, how can you prioritize when you will have unanticipated results?

In fact, the process of prioritizing inventions is extremely important if you are going to introduce your product on time that has all the critical features at a price that customers would be willing to pay.

When prioritizing inventions, it is important to consider several factors. First, how critical is it for the project that a specific problem be solved? If the project cannot advance at all until a problem is solved, obtaining the solution to that problem has to be given a top priority. As discussed earlier in this book, the ability to completely transfer electrophotographic prints, made using toner particles having diameters of approximately 3 μm, from the photoreceptor to a receiver was absolutely crucial in order to use this technology for photofinishing applications. Being able to fix the toner image and obtain a gloss level that matched photographs, although critical to the project, did not have to be accomplished until after a method of transferring the image was discovered. Thus, solving the problems of fusing and glossing the print were postponed until after the transfer problem was solved.

Alternatively, if multiple solutions to a problem are envisioned, it may not be necessary to immediately solve that problem. Its solution can be worked on at a slower pace, giving priority to the more critical issues.

Problems associated with adding features to a proposed product, unless they represent critical challenges, can also be delayed. These can possibly form seeds for subsequent generations of the product.

Regulatory challenges should be addressed with the same priority as customer-driven features, using the same principles as just discussed.

And, of course, creative people tend to be creative, but not necessarily focused on the project at hand. Care should be taken to not unnecessarily discourage such creativity, as that creativity can give rise to very profitable future products. However, it should not distract from your accomplishing your goals. Whenever you determine the timetable for a product introduction, you inherently recognize that 1) time is money and the faster you can go to market, the greater your profits are likely to be; and 2) market windows open and close rapidly and a delay can result in your product being too late and not competitive. Clearly, you want to determine as accurately as possible how long it would take you to develop your product so that it can be released into the marketplace. And, in addition to criticality, you should consider risk factors when prioritizing inventions. These are factors that affect the probability of a project being completed on time and on budget.

During the course of developing a product, there are three broad classifications of risk factors. The first and lowest level of risk is associated with being able to complete well-defined and executable tasks within a prescribed period of time. These may include, for example, obtaining a machine that can produce a specific component that is envisioned for your product, lining up and contracting with suppliers who will provide various necessary subassemblies, ensuring that distribution channels are in place, and educating your salesforce so that they can explain and demonstrate the benefits of your product to potential customers. Each of these tasks takes time and resources to complete and has to be done in a timely manner, as your product cannot be marketed without them. However, the associated risk level is relatively low as there are few unanticipated issues that might arise. Sure, it is possible that your prospective suppliers simply cannot or are unwilling to commit to provide the enormous number of subassemblies that you envision needing or that there are simply not enough trucks available to take your product to the far-reaches of the globe. However, in general, addressing low-risk items is something that, based on past experiences (which can be either yours or from knowledge gained from discussions with suppliers or consultants or from any other source of reliable information) should be determinable within well-defined limits of time and resources available. The key basis here is that the issues are well-defined.*

The second level of risk involves many issues such as integrating all the subassemblies into a robust and well-functioning product. This may include the use of statistically designed experiments [1], such as those exemplified by the Taguchi robustness analyses and methods described by Phadke [2], Fowlkes and Creveling [3], Launsby and Weese [4], and Schmidt and Launsby [5]. However, this phase and risk level can also include problems associated with combining nominally known technologies in a novel fashion. An example of this is the combining serially of two electrophotographic printers to increase productivity, as described in Chapter 4.

Risks are present in either situation discussed above. For integrating known technologies to yield a product with new capabilities, problems can and do arise that may require novel engineering solutions. And in simple robustness evaluation, there may be limited or even no conditions that allow the subsystems to be integrated in a functional and/or sufficiently robust manner.

It should be apparent from the example of combining the two printers, discussed in Chapter 4, that solving problems related to integrating known components may give rise to significant patentable inventions. However, it should also be recognized that even robustness analysis, where the use of novel engineering is not anticipated, can also present patent opportunities. Specifically, if a narrow but well-defined set of operating parameters are found to work, whereas attempting to use values outside that range result in a less satisfactory performance, the narrower range may be patentable. These patents may be valuable if they preclude a competitor from marketing a similar device.

The third and highest level of risk is associated with the implementation of unknown or invention-stage† technologies for use in a proposed

---

* It should be noted that the discussion in this paragraph is confined to commercially available subsystems that can be purchased from a supplier. If a component has to be developed specifically for use in a product, it raises the risk level and may also involve patentability concerns that need to be addressed.

† "Invention-stage technology" refers to technology for which there are no known solutions, thus requiring at least one invention. This greatly increases the risk to a project, not just because solutions to the problems are unknown, but also because, assuming that a solution is found (i.e., an invention), unknown problems interfacing that invention with other components are likely to occur and will have to be solved for the project to advance.

product. While some problems may be known, others that might arise are not. Moreover, solutions that would appropriately address even those problems that are recognized are not known. These technologies are vital for the long-term growth of your business, but it is generally unwise to bet your immediate profitability on their success.

With this introduction, let us specifically address what is meant by prioritizing inventions. Prioritizing inventions involves identifying critical and noncritical challenges, generally giving priority to the critical challenges. This often includes both fundamental problems and necessary enabling technologies. It includes formulating a time line that identifies by what dates problems must be solved in order to meet the product introduction or market date.

Prioritizing inventions can also include identifying opportunities to solve critical challenges that your competitors may have in their products. This can give you leverage should you need a license to practice some components of their patented technologies or, alternatively, extract licensing fees from other companies. In other words, if you see a problem or limitation that your competitor's product has and that you can solve and for which you can file suitable patent applications, it may be worthwhile for you to do so.

An important consideration of prioritizing inventions is to focus the technical team members on solving problems related to the project under consideration according to their priority, as discuss previously. Members of the technical community tend to be very creative and focusing their activities has often been described as akin to herding cats. While one does not wish to overly restrict creativity, as that is often the source of your future products, it is important that such creativity not distract from your project goals. Adequate and appropriate time for unstructured creativity is valuable and should be encouraged, but only to the extent that it does not endanger your project.

Why is it Necessary to Prioritize Inventions?

Prioritizing inventions is important for several reasons that are associated with both building a solid patent portfolio and being able to introduce a successful product in a timely manner. Among the reasons prioritization is important are:

1. Prioritization allows you to continually assess whether or not your high risk tasks of a project are being addressed in a timely manner.

2. The prioritization process encourages you to continually assess how your competition is addressing similar problems and what their competing products are likely to look like.
3. Prioritization forces you to closely examine your proposed solutions to your technical problems and determine whether or not you can solve them in a timely and cost-effective manner. In the worst case scenario, you may determine that the project should be cancelled because you do not have a viable path forward, either because you cannot solve a problem or because implementation of an appropriate solution would infringe on patents to which you do not have access.
4. Prioritization may enable you to obtain patents that would enable you to enter into essential patent exchange agreements.
5. Prioritizing inventions is important because it identifies problems up front and imposes a time frame by which the problems have to be solved if the envisioned product is to be introduced on time.

Prioritizing inventions is important for yet another reason. Remember that your goal is to build a patent portfolio that protects your products' positions in the marketplace by allowing you to own the problem rather than just specific solutions to specific problems. The prioritization process requires that you look beyond individual inventions and patent applications and consider the advancing technology (both yours and that of your competition) as a whole and to develop a patent portfolio based on the resulting analysis.

During the prioritization process, the identified problems that need to be solved can be broken down into one of three categories: 1) those problems whose solutions will constitute inventions; 2) those problems whose solutions are in the public domain (i.e. the solutions are not protected by currently active patents); and 3) those problems whose solutions are protected by patents owned by others.

Let us consider each of these cases. It is fairly obvious that a strong patent strategy starts with having valuable[‡] inventions. As such, it is always necessary to keep in mind potential patenting opportunities. This starts with recognizing which solutions to your problems are novel and non-obvious. The list of potentially patentable inventions will change as your team's progress advances. Some solutions may not be as viable, broad, or

---

‡ Valuable refers to the necessity of another company to have access to your patents.

as appropriate as originally conceived. Still others may present themselves as new problems arise or anticipated problems, such as the case of the fusing and glossing of high quality electrophotographic prints, as discussed in Chapter 5, ripen to the point that they are being seriously addressed.

The second category, wherein the solutions to problems are found using art that is totally within the public domain, can certainly advance your program. It, again, should be emphasized that combining pieces of known art to solve a problem, with each component functioning as expected, does not make for a patentable invention even if that particular problem had not been previously solved. For a combination of known art to be patentable, the discovered solution must be unanticipated or there must be no reason why one would consider combining the prior art. Patenting opportunities do exist, but they may be limited. In any event, if a solution to a problem is found in the public domain, it is generally not patentable. You can use that solution, but so can anyone else who reverse engineers or copies your product.

The third category comprises the situation(s) in which someone else owns the patented technology that you need. It should be noted that the specific patent may not even be used by the owner at all, as may be the case of a patent troll, or may be used in a product that is totally different from the one that you conceived. It does not matter. You cannot use that technology without first obtaining permission from the owner.

Within this third category you have several paths you can pursue related to patents owned by others that you need. The first is to simply give up and not pursue your revolutionary product. A recent example of this came about when several states banned semiautomatic rifles with detachable magazines. Two companies began to manufacture and market similar devices that converted the detachable magazines used in AR-style rifles into fixed magazine rifles. However, one company had applied for a patent that was ultimately issued [6]. Once the patent was issued, the other company stopped producing and marketing its product.

A second path is to try to alter the design your product so that it does not infringe§ on someone else's patent. This may be simple to do or it may involve serious design modifications, possibly adding costs or reducing functionality. It is likely that a redesign will cause product introduction delays.

---

§ The legal terminology is that "a product reads on the claims" of a patent owned by someone else.

A third viable path requires that you pay licensing fees to the owner of the patent. Such fees can seriously cut into your profitability and may impose additional limitations, such as how many devices you can produce, what your product can do, and where you can market your goods or services. In some instances, the owner of the patent may view your entry into the marketplace as strategically unpalatable and may refuse to grant you a license, forcing you back to the first or second options. If the owner of the patent is a patent troll, buying a license may be the most viable option for you¶.

A fourth path is to recognize critical challenges faced by the owner of the patent(s) that you need and to address those challenges by solving those problems and obtaining patents on them. Those challenges do not have to be in competitive products. They merely have to be strategic to the owner of the patent that you need. Moreover, your patents on those challenges have to be sufficiently broad so as to preclude easy work-arounds. Recognizing such opportunities should be part of prioritizing your inventions. If you own patents that another company needs, that company may be very willing to enter into cross-licensing agreements that are quite favorable to you, thereby allowing you access to the their technology for your product.

How to Prioritize Inventions

As previously discussed, a valuable patent portfolio starts by first having valuable inventions. What constitutes a valuable invention? Unfortunately, that is not easy to recognize a priori. Patents are legal documents designed to protect a company's intellectual property by giving the company the right to exclude others from practicing the invention described in the claims of the patent. A patent is not a scientific paper per se, although it does describe the invention and how the invention is practiced. Moreover, a patent does not give the owner any right to practice the invention. Your ability to practice your invention may be blocked by someone else's patents. With the above discussion in mind, let us briefly discuss some errors that are all too commonly made when prioritizing inventions. These are,

---

¶ Patent trolls used to preferentially go after larger companies that were allegedly infringing their patents because the larger companies had deeper pockets. However, this has recently changed. Patent trolls are now often targeting smaller companies, knowing that defending a patent infringement suit can cost a company millions of dollars, whereas forcing a targeted company to pay a licensing fee in the range of tens to hundreds of thousands of dollars is often easier for the troll.

specifically, confusing fundamental advances in technology with critical challenges and, conversely, ignoring critical challenges that occur in required enabling technology because they are not fundamental technological advances.

As an example of the above, let us revisit Polaroid's assertion against Kodak for allegedly infringing on Polaroid's instant photography patents. Both companies had invented and patented distinct chemistry that enabled them to produce instant silver halide photographs. These chemistries were both fundamental and critical challenges. However, Polaroid recognized that the chemistry, by itself, was not sufficient to produce the photographs. Rather, it also required solving problems that were not fundamental, but still represented critical challenges. These included, for example, the use of a pair of rollers to squeeze the chemicals into the packet that contained the latent image once the silver halide emulsion was exposed to light. Kodak failed to recognized the importance of such enabling patents and argued that such patents were obvious and, therefore, not valid. In fact, being able to spread the development chemicals that allowed the consumer to immediately view photographs drove a marketing decision and, therefore, represented a critical challenge although it was unrelated to the fundamental chemistry of instant photography.

Polaroid asserted 9 patents against Kodak and the court ruled that, indeed, Kodak was correct regarding the invalidity of 2 of the 9 patents. However, the court ruled that the other 7 patents, each of which claimed rather simple enabling technology that was crucial to the functioning of the instant photographic process, were, in fact valid. This ruling forced Kodak to pay over $900 million in damages to Polaroid, exit the instant photography market, and buy back the cameras that had been sold.

The results of this patent infringement suit are made more poignant by the fact that Kodak was under contract by Polaroid to manufacture the Polaroid film packets. Kodak presumably had opportunities to develop and patent technology that Polaroid needed, but failed to do so. Had Kodak owned any patents that Polaroid needed, the results may have been far different.

Both companies had obtained patents on their own fundamental critical challenges related to instant photographic chemistry. However, Kodak did not pursue patenting critical challenges surrounding the enabling technology whereas Polaroid did. In effect, Polaroid executed a patent strategy aimed at protecting its technology, whereas Kodak did not do so.

It is apparent that the enabling patents owned by Polaroid were very valuable. But were the fundamental chemistry patents also valuable? In so far as those patents, presumably, required that Kodak invest heavily in developing its own chemistry, rather than just copying Polaroid's, the answer is yes. Were Kodak's chemistry patents valuable? Probably not. Patents are valuable only if someone else needs them. It became apparent that the instant photography market was sufficiently large for one company, but not large enough for a second. The author is unaware of any credible evidence suggesting that a third company desired to enter this market. It should be clear that, whereas the earlier fundamental chemistry patents of Polaroid, as part of their patent strategy, protected critical challenges, the later chemistry patents of Kodak did not. As discussed earlier in this book, Kodak did not pursue patents in the technology that would have driven customer buying decisions.

The above discussion was presented to illustrate the point that even modest inventions can lead to valuable patents if the inventions address critical challenges.

It should be noted that, in the following discussion of factors to consider when prioritizing inventions, the term "invention" may refer to either an actual invention (i.e., one in which you determined a novel and nonobvious solution to technical problem) or, as is likely to be the case as a project advances, a situation where an invention is needed to solve a problem. The following discussion assumes that work will often be required to complete each invention.

1. Whether or not an anticipated invention addresses a critical challenge for you is the first consideration in prioritizing inventions. If the invention addresses a critical challenge, is it timely to focus on solving the problem? As previously discussed, technology has to advance in a serial fashion as the solution to an earlier problem can lead to both opportunities and constraints in solving a subsequent problem.

2. Perhaps the next consideration is whether or not an invention represents a critical challenge for a competitor or for a company whose intellectual property you may need to access. In today's competitive world, it is highly likely that you will either need access to your competitor's technology or that your competitor will be able to make a reasonable case that your product is infringing on your competitor's patents. Presumably, in the course of your product development activities, you are planning to offer features that allow customers to traverse the limitation or problems of those products. The solutions to your competitors' problems, accordingly, can allow you to obtain patents that your

competitor needs and may allow you to obtain a better cross licensing agreement, force your competitor to pay you royalties, or prevent the introduction of a product that would be able to more effectively compete with yours.

3. Yet another factor is the ease with which alternative methods of achieving comparable results can be implemented. If at all possible, you will want to patent those alternatives. Presumably, you have decided upon the design of your product because of certain assumptions. These can include factors such as cost, ease of use, avoiding patents owned by others, etc. There may be other considerations such as present technological viability. Remember that the automotive distributor was a great invention until computer technology became sufficiently robust, fast, and inexpensive to eliminate the need for a mechanical switching device. A patent has a life of as long as twenty years. What will be the technology of the future? It is vital that you question your assumptions when prioritizing inventions to make sure that you have not left a valuable opening for someone else.

4. You should also consider whether or not an invention is ripe for filing. As an example, consider the fusing and glossing system discussed in Chapter 5. It may have been possible to file an application concurrently with the thermal assisted transfer process, but that would have been premature and may merely have disclosed material that would have made obtaining stronger patents later on problematic.

5. With that being said, there are times when urgency trumps completeness. If a competitor is filing on similar technology or if you are entering into a joint development program with another company or if you are going to disclose your technology, perhaps at a trade show, you may have to file earlier than desired, thereby elevating the priority of the patents. It may even be necessary to call together the technical team members to address the foreseen problems and pose solutions so that appropriate applications can be filed. Care should be taken, however, to disclose as little as possible to maximize the chance of filing more complete applications protecting further inventions in the future.

6. One issue that should be considered is whether or not an invention is detectable. Remember that you are teaching the world about your invention when you file an application.

Patents ultimately expire and may not even be allowed. Items such as the formulation of Coca-Cola syrup have not been patented. There is a place for trade secrets. An invention may be very valuable, but it may be better, in some instances, to keep it a secret.

7. There are inventions whose product life may be anticipated to be too short or whose uses have already become antiquated. It is generally not worth filing patent applications on these inventions, as such application would unnecessarily add to your product development costs and any resulting patents would generally be of very little value. Accordingly, these should be given a low priority.

8. Additionally, creative people often propose inventions that do not represent critical challenges. While building a patent portfolio may be gratifying for both your company and the inventors, it can be costly and distract from a focused development on your product and the marketplace. That is not to say that innovations should be discouraged. We have already discussed the importance of such innovations and the development of invention-stage technologies. Your future may be based on having that intellectual property in your portfolio. However, discretion should be carefully exercised when supporting such development.

9. If an alternative to your invention is proposed and it is simply an alternative, it may still be of value. However, if it is not viable, perhaps a Rube Goldberg device or something that is hopelessly complex and costly, it may not be worth pursuing. Caution should be exercised here, however, before discarding such alternative inventions. The reader is urged to reexamine the fundamental assumptions and determine if changes in those assumptions would make the proposed alternative viable.

As an example of the above, let us consider automotive technology. Many of us remember when carburetors and distributors were used to power cars. Steering and braking were accomplished using hydraulic pumps. And, if you stepped too hard on your brake pedal while on icy roads, you skidded. Advances in the automobile industry included substituting rack and pinion steering for recirculating balls and disk brakes for drum brakes. Electronic ignitions replaced points, rotors, and condensers. As computers were large and operated too slowly to properly control subsystems in a car, few individuals, if any, envisioned controlling the electronic ignition, steering (drive by wire) or braking (ABS) with a computer. In other words, there would have been few, if any, claims in the patents covering the advancing automotive technology to include microprocessor control. The assumption was that computers were never going to be used in cars. That assumption was obviously in error. Can you imagine how much claims for the use of computer technology in the automotive industry would have been worth? You really need to constantly examine your fundamental assumptions. The life of a patent is twenty years from the date of filing. What will technology look like twenty years from now?

Concluding Remarks

The value of an invention, aside from its immediate use in your proposed product, is often very hard to determine. Seemingly fundamental inventions can be worthless, whereas trivial ones can be very valuable and vice versa. Specific applications can be short-lived these days, but an invention can be valuable for other uses long after its initial use has died.

Prioritization should be an on-going process. As you develop technology, previously proposed solutions that contained new, important inventions may evolve into other inventions. Others may become less significant as you learn more.

Throughout all this, time is not on your side. The first to file an application is construed as the inventor. In addition, the world does not stand still and advances are being made in other companies that can impact both your specific product and the market in general. Typewriters and slide rules have all but disappeared, having given way to word processers and calculators. Silver halide photography has been supplanted by digital cameras which, in turn, have lost their market share to smart phones. These advances often occur in industries that you would not consider competitive with yours. The products they introduce can quickly disrupt your market. However, your inventions can live on and generate revenue long after the initial product has become obsolete.

References

1. G. E. P. Box, W. G. Hunter, and J. S. Hunter, *Statistics for Experimenters*, Wiley-Interscience, New York, NY (1978).

2. M. S. Phadke, *Quality Engineering Using Robust Design*, Prentice Hall, Englewood Cliffs, NJ (1989).
3. W. Y. Fowlkes and C. M. Creveling, *Engineering Methods for Robust Product Design*, Addison Wesley, Reading, MA (1995).
4. R. G. Launsby and D. L. Weese, *Straight Talk on Designing Experiments*, Launsby Consulting, Colorado Springs, CO (1993).
5. S. R. Schmidt and R. G. Launsby, *Understanding Industrial Designed Experiments*, Air Academy Press, Colorado Springs, CO (1994).
6. C. Harris, S. Thomas, and R. Bernard, U.S. Patent #8,756,845 (1014).

7

Prioritizing Your Patent Applications

What is the Difference between Prioritizing Inventions and Prioritizing Patent Applications?

In Chapter 6 we discussed the value of and factors involved in prioritizing inventions. In this chapter we will be discussing prioritizing patent applications. Are these not one and the same? The answer is that they are not, and, while there is some overlap between both prioritizations, they are distinct and done for different reasons. To understand this, let us review what is meant by an invention and a patent.

When developing a product you have to solve numerous problems. Some solutions involve integrating commonly held pieces of information. That information may be totally in the public domain or it may be protected by patents owned by others. Other solutions are novel and nonobvious and constitute inventions. Some problems are more significant than others. For example, a problem for which there appears to be only a single solution that is critical to the customer acceptance of your product, drives costs, or is mandated by regulations, is extremely important and constitutes a critical challenge. Other problems may be less pressing or may have multiple viable solutions.

In yet other instances, it may simply be premature to attempt to solve a problem. Even in cases where the problem is anticipated, specific underlying factors that may impact its solution may not yet have been determined. In other instances it may not be the best use of resources to address a problem at the present, but may be better to postpone solving it.

In all cases, it is important to lay out a roadmap of when problems must be solved if, for no other reason, than to ensure that the project is progressing in a time frame that makes business sense. An additional benefit is that it allows you to repeatedly assess the environment in which your product will compete and to fine tune its attributes, or even totally abandon it, as market forces dictate.

In other words, prioritizing inventions is a way of tracking what has to be accomplished and by when. It is part of the technological development roadmap that needs to be implemented to ensure success.

In contrast to an invention, which is a technical solution to a problem, a patent is a legal document, granted by a government issuing authority that provides legal protection to the owner of the patent. In itself it does not comment on the importance or significance of the invention. A patent merely states that the invention described therein is a technical solution that is nonobvious and novel to a problem. In contrast to an invention, which presumably is directly related to the value of your proposed product, a patent's value is determined by how much someone else needs access to the claimed technology. A patent does not, in itself, determine the marketability of a product.* In fact many highly successful products, such as Coca Cola syrup, are not covered by patents. You do not need a patent in order to market a product. Conversely, as previously stated, having a patent does not grant you the right to market your product.

With that being said, a properly constructed patent portfolio can add a lot of value to your company. Specifically, it can give you a monopolistic or technologically advantageous position for marketing your product. It can also generate revenues for your company through licensing fees obtained

---

* It is a well-known marketing ploy to describe something as so significant or innovative or superlative as to be awarded a patent. That is, of course, strictly for public consumption and is irrelevant to the importance of the proposed product.

from others and facilitate your entering into cross-licensing agreements that give you access to needed technology owned by others.

It is obvious that a solid patent portfolio starts with inventions that encompass the technology used in your perceived product. But it goes beyond that. Thus, prioritizing inventions is just the beginning of prioritizing your patent applications. Again, the reader is reminded that the goal is to generate a coherent patent portfolio and not just a collection of individual patents that protect specific solutions to specific problems. The goal of prioritizing your patent applications is to ensure that you generate an appropriate portfolio that protects your intellectual property and adds value to your company, rather than just being an expense. And, again, it should be emphasized that it is very difficult, at best, to determine how valuable specific patents will be.

Many individuals and companies often mistake advances in their fundamental technology for how valuable a patent, if obtained, would be. "Fundamental", as related to the innovation of the basic technology (e.g., how ground breaking that particular advancement is) and "valuable", as related to how blocking some patents would be in preventing others from competing with your products, have distinct meanings and, while not necessarily either inclusive or exclusive, should not be confused. The reader is cautioned that, while fundamental technological advances are often easy to discern at the time of invention, the value of patents is often recognized long after the patents are issued.

You also need to remember that you will not receive every patent for which you apply. If you carefully define the problem and elucidate how you solved that problem, taking care to discuss why the prior art, either as individual pieces or in combination, does not solve your problem, you stand an excellent chance of being awarded a patent. However, if you are having a success rate of greater than about 90%, you may be presenting claims that are too narrow to give you adequate legal protection or you might be operating in "white space" [1] where there is little commercial activity resulting in little interest by others in pursuing patents. Alternatively, if your success rate is less than about 70%, you may be trying to claim too much, not carefully defining your problem or its solution, or not sufficiently addressing the prior art.

In all instances you should remember that your application will become public knowledge after about eighteen months, irrespective of whether or not a patent is ultimately issued. When implementing your patent strategy, you should design it so that you will protect your intellectual property despite the fact that you will not be 100% successful in obtaining patents.

Types of Factors Determining Patent Application Priority

Factors affecting the priority of filing applications can be broadly classified according to technological impact or temporal considerations. In other words, there are both perceived technological importance and urgency factors that must be considered.

Urgency or temporal factors include anything that affects the timing of filing applications. These include the necessity of disclosing the invention at a certain time; knowledge of related activities being performed by competitors or other individuals; necessary coherence in the disclosures of your applications related to building your portfolio; the approach of the date when a previously filed application becomes public knowledge and, thus, prior art, and; of course, the legal requirement that patents are awarded to the first to file an application.

Factors affecting technological impacts include whether or not an invention addresses a critical challenge, whether the invention is important to another company, whether the invention builds upon other inventions within your portfolio, and whether the proposed patent for which an application is being filed is enforceable. We will now address both temporal and technological factors.

Technological Considerations

Let us first consider the technological factors that affect patent application prioritization for the obvious reason that, if an application is not worthy of filing for technical reasons, there is no sense being concerned with its timing.

Although, in an ideal world, one could file an application for every invention, resource limitations generally preclude this. Stated another way, costs and the ability to commit the time of the team members in filing activities generally limit the number of applications that can be filed. Accordingly, you generally have to be selective regarding for which inventions you will choose to file applications. Let us now consider technological factors that would give an application a high priority for you to file.

Paramount among the considerations is whether or not a potential patent application addresses a critical challenge. Considering that the critical challenges are those that drive customer purchase decisions, address regulatory requirements, or impact cost factors, such applications may be of considerable importance. However, depending on other factors, just because the application claims the solution to a critical challenge is not sufficient to elevate the application to the highest priority. This will be discussed in more detail as we progress through the present discourse.

It should be noted that a solution to a critical challenge does not necessarily mean that it is *the* solution that you intend to implement in your product. It should be remembered that the goal of a patent strategy is to protect your marketplace and to build a portfolio that adds value to your company. It is not sufficient to file applications that represent only the solutions to problems that you are planning to implement. Presumably, during the engineering of your project, your team had to consider multiple solutions to each problem and selected those solutions that were deemed most advantageous. However, those selections are based on assumptions that may not hold for an alternative strategy being implemented by another company in their competitive product. You need to question your assumptions.

Obviously, you do not want to waste resources pursuing patents on impractical or unfeasible alternatives to the solutions that you are pursuing. However, just because you chose an alternative that matched your needs more advantageously does not mean that a competitor may not perceive an alternative solution as being preferential. Moreover, even if the path that you have chosen is the better one all around, you need to ask if the alternatives would still present a viable option if you are successful in obtaining patent coverage on your chosen technological path. In other words, are there reasonable work-arounds that can be pursued by competitors? If so, it is important that you own that intellectual property along with the specific solutions that you intend to implement.

Finally, as you develop your product, it may become apparent that the solution that you thought was preferred at an earlier stage may present some challenges. It may not, for example, integrate well with other subsystems or product requirements or it may not allow leveraging of your technology into a family of products as well as an alternative that was previously discarded. You want to own the problem, as discussed in *Patent Engineering* [1], rather than just a specific solution to a problem. Also, please remember that whenever you file a patent application, you are teaching about the problem and how you solved it. An individual application can instruct a competitor on how to address the problem while circumventing your patent. It is important to try to block such viable alternatives that would remain open to your competition, by your owning patents covering alternative solutions in addition to the solutions that you are planning to implement.

When prioritizing potential patent applications, you should ask if an infringement of the proposed claims could be detected. In other words, would you positively know that someone was infringing on your patent? If you cannot demonstrate infringement, why would you want to teach about your product or process? There are valid reasons for wanting to augment a patent portfolio with patents claiming undetectable inventions, but such patents should not be at the forefront of your portfolio and generally should only considered as part of a broader and more encompassing portfolio in which infringements of the other patents are readily detectable.

At one time industrial processes were often considered as undetectable, as it would require your entering your competitor's plant for you to observe its processes. That was in the day when employees often stayed with a single company for life and employee-company loyalty was the norm. Today, that has changed. Individuals will generally hold multiple positions over the course of their careers and, when transitioning from one employer to another, take with them the knowledge garnered at their previous places of employment. Moreover, some individuals embark on careers as consultants, migrating from one client to the next, selling their knowledge along the way. Suffice-it to say, corporate secrets are no longer as secure as they once were and it is possible to gather enough knowledge of a company's internal processes to allow a patent infringement suit to be launched.[†]

As an advisory note, it is suggested that you include, in your disclosure, the method of how you would detect an infringement. For example, if the claims include a specific physical parameter such as a Young's modulus or surface energy, it would be valuable to include exactly how that parameter would be determined. This is because, as often as not, different measurement techniques would result in differing values of the parameter. If the technique is not specified, alleged infringers could claim that there is no infringement if their measurement methods give values of the parameters that are outside of the limits of your claims. If the measurement techniques are specified in the patent, then alternative methods become moot. With this in mind, when specifying how the value of a parameter is determined, it is better to describe a single technique rather than presenting several alternatives. It should be remembered that someone's product either reads on your claims or doesn't and it is up to you to prove infringement. If a defendant can choose the measurement methods to be employed, especially if

---

[†] The information gathered from the above sources would be augmented in the process known as "discovery", in which a court orders relevant documents to be produced. You would most likely not be relying solely on the reports of previous employees and consultants when making your infringement case, but would also be using a company's documentation. This, of course, cuts two ways and a defendant can use your documentation to discredit your patents. Be careful what documentation you create.

they are one of the various methods that you have suggested, and their product according to that method does not read on your claims, it may be difficult to convince a jury that the product does infringe your patent.

Closely related to whether or not an infringement can be detected is whether or not you could explain to a jury the invention(s), i.e., the claim(s) in your patent(s), and how what the competitor is practicing reads on your claim(s). It is important to recognize that a jury is composed of individuals who are lay people. They will not have expertise in your field and probably are not technical experts at all. They will need to understand your invention, as it is claimed in the patents that you are asserting, and how what the alleged infringer is practicing reads on your claims.

With this in mind, it is often easiest to demonstrate a mechanical invention, whereby the components and workings can be laid out and shown to the members of the jury. Alternatively, claims based on complex mathematical algorithms can be quite difficult to explain in lay terms.

As an example, the author of this book was involved in the determination of whether or not an algorithm for producing electrostatic latent images of fonts in an electrophotographic printer‡ was being infringed upon by the manufacturer of another printer [2].

In an electrophotographic printer, a photoreceptive element, also often referred to as a primary imaging member, is initially electrostatically charged uniformly. An electrostatic latent image is then created by image-wise exposing the element to light using either a laser scanner or an LED array, generally referred to as a "writer". A visible image is then created by bringing the latent image into contact with charged marking particles, generally referred to as toner particles, which adhere to the element in the exposed regions.

The laser or LED array is pulsed in a manner so as to create the desired electrostatic latent image and many pulses of varying intensity and location are required to form a single character. Each of these pulses corresponds to a "picture element" or "pixel". Most readers are familiar with terms such as 600 x 600 dpi resolution, which refers to the spatial resolution of the writer.

The writer is driven by complex mathematical algorithms that determine properties such as sharpness, contrast, and resolution of the electrostatic latent image. Not only is the quality of the printed page affected by the location and intensity of the exposure of the photoconductive member, but also by the sequence of when a particular pixel was exposed relative

---

‡ The electrophotographic process is discussed in detail in Appendix 1. The reader is invited to see the technical discussion of this topic in that section of the book.

to the other pixels. Indeed, the mathematical algorithm driving the writer has to be complex, taking into account the responses of the writer and the photoconductive member, but also utilizing human perceptive capabilities that factor in how the human eye perceives images. It is very clear that the algorithm used is quite complex.

There is no question that the invention, per se, was extremely important and worthy of receiving a high priority according to the guidelines presented in Chapter 6. Specifically, the resulting image quality obtained using this invention drove customer buying decisions. However, caution should be exercised when prioritizing patent applications as the patent resulting from this application, for example, presented challenges that should have been foreseen. Specifically, when we were attempting to decide whether or not to assert this patent, it took us several days of intense discussions with the inventor and another technical expert to understand the algorithm being claimed. Being able to explain that algorithm to members of a perspective jury would have been most challenging. In addition, analyzing the software used by the competitor would not have been possible. As a result, any infringement would have to have been detected just from printed documents made on the suspected printer. Granted, we could use test targets to produce documents that would highlight the suspected infringements, but even so, any infringement would have to be demonstrated just from the documents. This would have been made more complicated as, following the formation of the electrostatic latent image, the printed document would have been produced by first developing the latent image by depositing toner onto the photoreceptor (the development process), transferring the toner to paper (transfer step) and fixing the toned image to the paper (fusing step). Each step alters the printed image from that produced during exposure, when the latent image is formed.

In addition, it would not have been sufficient to identify the shapes or other characteristics of the pixels that were consistent with the images produced using this writing algorithm, as presented in the claims. It would have to be demonstrated that the specific timing of the formation of the pixels, as also spelled out in the claims, was being performed. Finally, it would have had to have been proven that there was no other way that comparable characteristics of the image could have been produced. Suffice-it to say, the decision was made not to assert this patent.

Does this mean that a patent application covering this invention should not have been pursued? It certainly suffered from significant difficulties associated with both detecting infringements and describing the invention to a jury. However, despite these shortcomings, it probably would have been worth pursuing as part of an entire patent portfolio, recognizing that the patent taught a lot about the formation of the pixels. Its value also lies in the fact that it does prevent a competitor from patenting this invention, remembering that the patent goes to the first to file. However, as a stand-alone invention, it probably would not have been worth filing. Making these decisions is part of the evaluation process and is unique to every circumstance. Falling short on some evaluation metrics is not necessarily grounds for not filing. Rather, the metrics are tools to aid your decisions.

Yet another factor to consider when prioritizing patent applications is what your competitors are doing. Specifically, are any other companies interested in your technology? These can include companies that either have or plan to introduce products that will directly compete with yours. Alternatively, they can include companies whose products do not compete with yours, but whose market offerings might benefit from your intellectual property. It should always be remembered that patents are valuable only if someone else needs to use the claimed intellectual property. If no one is interested, obtaining a patent is merely an expense that teaches others about a problem and a specific solution to that problem. However, just because an outside interested party cannot be identified does not mean that an application should not be filed. Your product may be so innovative that you are ahead of the market, which will rapidly strive to copy you once your technology is known. However, be realistic in your evaluation. Is your product so valuable or are you simply in "white space" – an area devoid of any interest because there is and will be no significant market?

With the above discussion in mind, it is worthwhile for you to estimate the size of the market. This may not be easy. Your product may be innovative and competition may arise once your product has been marketed. Alternatively, your invention may be in "white space" [1] as noted above. An example of the former is the invention of the electrophotographic printer by Chester Carlson [3–5]. In fact, a more detailed discussion of Carlson's invention is illustrative of just how difficult determining the priority of patent applications can be when the technology is sufficiently novel.

Prior to Carlson's invention, the ability to make a limited numbers of copies of a document was restricted and difficult.§ Small numbers of multiple copies could be made while producing an original document using devices such as carbon paper inserted between sheets of paper. Thomas Jefferson, a prolific writer, was known to use a device called a "polygraph",

---

§ Larger numbers of copies could be produced using devices such as printing presses. However, the need to typeset or produce a lithoplate renders this technology unfeasible for fewer than several hundred copies.

(similar to a pantograph) invented by John Isaac Hawkins [6], whereby an original document and a copy could be written in the author's hand at one time. Other devices such as a mimeograph or a ditto machine, both of which relied on the original production of a master, could be used to print multiple copies of a document. Alternatively, multiple copies could be made using lithographic techniques such as an offset press. However, typesetting or the production of press plates was time consuming, and hence expensive, and limited the use of such devices to instances where many copies had to be made.

Methods of copying preexisting documents were limited to techniques such as the Kodak Verifax [7]. This technique relied on the transfer of a colloidal dye from a donor sheet to the paper receiver. While inexpensive and simple to produce‡, it was slow and messy and the resulting image quality, although quite legible, was marginal.

The history of Carlson's photocopier is well known. At first he tried unsuccessfully to sell his patent rights to companies such as Kodak and IBM, among many others. Ultimately, he was able to get Joseph Wilson, the CEO of a failing photographic company named Haloid to literally bet the company's continued existence on this technology. That company ultimately changed its name to Xerox. Electrophotographic copiers became the dominant technology for making short-run duplicates of documents quickly. Today, electrophotography is commonly used in digital printing technologies ranging from desk-top printers to commercial presses. Electrophotography was, indeed, a valuable technology that few, at the time of Carlson's invention, appreciated.

The lesson here was that no one wanted Carlson's patent rights. The companies Carlson approached assumed that there would be no market for such products. Today, electrophotography is the mainstay of many companies and generates hundreds of billions of dollars in revenue each year. Clearly, the lack of interest by other companies in this technology did not negate its ultimate value. However, such situations have to be approached with due caution as there, indeed, may not be a market for the products that use that technology. There may be good reasons why no other company is interested in your technology. Then, again, there may not be.

Closely aligned with other companies needing your technology is the question of how limiting a lack of access to your intellectual property would be. If the claims are sufficiently broad and alternatives are not readily available, your patents may be more valuable. However, even narrowly

---

‡ The author actually built one of these devices for a high school science project.

defined claims can be valuable if there are no suitable alternatives, as was demonstrated in the Kodak-Polaroid instant photography lawsuit, discussed in Chapter 4.

How do you know if and which other companies would be interested in your patents? The first indication is which other companies are making competitive products. Also pertinent is what products are about to be introduced by these companies. Trade shows and scientific conferences are often great sources of information on this topic. In addition, what patent applications have been filed by other companies and what patents have been issued?

When conducting your prior art searches, to be discussed in more detail in Chapter 9, see which companies have cited your patents. If they are citing your patents, it is a good indication that they are interested in your intellectual property. Have you entered into cross-licensing agreements or obtained licensing fees from other companies? They may be interested. Finally, what art have examiners cited in their office actions on your previous applications? Those may also reflect companies that may be interested in your technology, even if they are not direct competitors.

Yet another consideration when prioritizing potential patent applications is whether the proposed patent would be one of a series or a stand-alone invention. The simple rule of thumb is that there is strength in numbers and having multiple patents protecting related technological solutions presents a greater hurdle for a competitor to overcome and it is easier for you to assert.

Temporal Considerations

As mentioned earlier in this chapter, technological advances are not the only factors to be considered when prioritizing potential patent applications. There are temporal, or timing, factors that also should be considered. In some ways temporal considerations are even more important than are technical concerns when prioritizing potential patent applications. Improperly assigning too high a priority to an application because of technical reasons can result in generating a portfolio that may be weaker and more expensive than desired. However, improper assignment of priorities for temporal reasons may prevent you from even obtaining patents. Moreover, even if you do obtain patents, your ownership may be compromised by others having assignee rights to those patents. Let us examine the timing factors that should be considered when prioritizing patent applications.

First, it should be recognized that under GATT** patents are granted to the first to file. Previously, the United States granted patents to the first to invent. The requirement of the first to invent could set off legal battles, with each side producing evidence, such as witnessed and dated laboratory notebooks describing the invention, in order to demonstrate that their side came up with the invention first. While recognizing the importance of when an invention occurred, this resulted in costly legal battles. Today, it is assumed that the first to file is the legitimate inventor. In other words, time is not on your side. If you delay filing, you may lose your ability to protect your invention. That said, however, filing applications prematurely can preclude your ability to obtain stronger coverage and may adversely affect your ability to optimize your patent portfolio. This is because, by filing prematurely, you risk disclosing information that may either disclose future inventions or serve as prior art that can be combined with other prior art. In either case your ability to patent your more fully developed inventions and develop a more valuable and solid patent portfolio that properly protects your technology can be adversely impacted by prematurely filing patent applications

Timing can be a factor when there are disclosures that you or others may make that do not precisely teach your invention and may not, in fact, even be in the same technological area. Why should the timing of these disclosures be of concern to you? Within one year of disclosure, the information disclosed is not yet considered prior art. However, if one year after disclosure such information can be used in conjunction with other publically available information allowing someone, in the opinion of the examiner, to come up with your invention, you may lose your ability to obtain a patent. Even your own disclosures are subject to the one-year time line.††
Simply stated, if a combination of information is available to the public that can lead someone to your solution to a technical problem, your solution becomes obvious and loses novelty.

Demonstrating your inventions in a trade show or publication establishes prior art. Again, once this is done, you have one year in which to file your patent applications. Similarly, any sort of disclosure, such as showing your inventions to a consultant, an outside contractor, or a customer may

---

** Global Agreement on Tariffs and Trade
†† There often are legal ways by which you can circumvent your prior disclosures from being construed as prior art. For example, if you can swear in an affidavit that your invention predates the previously disclosed material, you may be able to avoid having the earlier material considered to be prior art. However, this requires legal intervention and is not always successful. It is better to avoid such situations if possible.

start the timing clock for filing applications. You can, of course, insist that whomever is shown the inventions first sign a nondisclosure or confidentiality agreement. That does preclude that particular disclosure from being construed as prior art. But, suppose the individual to whom the invention is shown subsequently discloses it to a third party, either inadvertently or deliberately. You now have a disclosure and the clock starts ticking, even if you were not aware of that disclosure. Sure, you can sue the signer of the confidentiality agreement for damages, but the amount you may be able to ultimately collect, after subtracting legal costs, may pale compared to the damage that you suffered. It is far better to file as quickly as possible, bearing in mind the general one-year period.

The above discussion also applies when you are about to engage an outside contractor to help develop a product. It is beneficial for you to file whatever patent applications you can prior to entering into technical discussions with members of the other company. Failure to do so may result in the other company believing that they came up with the inventions that you need. They may file and obtain the patents. Even if your contract with the contractual company spells out that you have exclusive rights to use that technology, they can still stop you from bidding out the protected components. It is far better if you file your applications prior to the commencement of discussions.

Similarly, trade shows are valuable venues that afford you the opportunity to demonstrate your new or developing products, but can also result in premature disclosures. This is another temporal consideration that must be addressed, as the deadlines imposed by trade shows may create an urgency for the filing of your patent applications, according to your strategy. It is important to protect your ability to patent your technology by filing your applications, to the extent possible, prior to the trade show. How do you do this when you may not have the invention sufficiently defined to allow the drafting of claims? One method is to file the necessary disclosures without claims as provisional patent applications. However, even though you do not need claims to file provisional applications, you still need a complete disclosure that will support all subsequently filed claims. With that in mind, care must be taken not to disclose more information than is absolutely required for the present application and for which you may desire to file patent applications in the future, but are not yet ready.

An advantage of filing provisional applications is that a single disclosure can be used on which to base your final applications that include the claims. The disadvantages include the fact that provisional applications do constitute disclosures of the inventions and, accordingly, must be finalized within one year to avoid their constituting prior art. In addition, the claims must be anticipated to ensure that there is technical disclosure that supports those claims without disclosing more material than is necessary. Finally, the filing of provisional applications does incur additional legal and filing costs. And, to reiterate, the filing of provisional applications does elevate the temporal priorities on the filing of the final applications.

Another consideration that can elevate the temporal priority of patent applications is whether or not someone else, be it a competitor, a non-competitive entity (including patent trolls or universities) or individuals, are planning to file applications. How can you tell? Perhaps information obtained at a scientific conference or trade show can lead you to that conclusion. Also, when searching published applications, you may find a trend that suggests someone is conducting research in a similar area. If you believe that someone else is about to file, it behooves you to file first.

There is yet another situation that can elevate the temporal priorities – the decision to file a continuation or a continuation-in-part. What are these?

There are occasions that, upon reflection and additional technological developments, you decide that you can really use some additional protection for your intellectual property. In other words, there are additional inventions that are totally or partially disclosed in your applications that you have not yet claimed. Under certain circumstances you can do so. This amounts to using the same disclosure and filing a new patent application with new claims. This is called a continuation. Alternatively, you may be able to use the existing disclosure provided that you add additional material to cover the new claims. This is a continuation-in-part. In either instance, you generally have one year from the date of issuance of the patent to file continuations or continuations-in-part.

There are cautionary notes, however, should you decide to pursue either of these options. While either affords you the opportunity to increase the strength of your patent protections around your inventions, both are considered to be new applications. Just because you received a patent for your earlier claimed invention does not mean that you will be allowed further coverage. Moreover, each application creates a file history that is open for discovery should you choose to assert your patent. Again, this is the case whether or not your continuations or continuations-in-part result in issued patents. The danger is that an examiner may argue against the inventions claimed in the new applications. Your discussions with the examiner lengthen a file history that can be used against you in an assertion. Whether or not the additional risks (and expenses) warrant the attempt to enhance your protection is a topic that you should discuss with your legal counsel.

Thus far, we have presented a case for urgency in prioritizing and filing applications. However, there are times that restraint may be the preferred course of action. Please remember that the goal of a patent strategy is to develop a valuable and powerful patent portfolio, rather than just a collection of individual patents.

In Chapter 6 we discussed prioritizing your inventions. It should be apparent that you will have to formulate an R&D plan that includes prioritizing your inventions so that you will be able to achieve your technological goals, develop your patent strategy, and build your patent portfolio. This requires working closely with your teammates and constantly evaluating the state of your progress.

Questions that you must consider when implementing your patent strategy include whether or not an invention is sufficiently ripe for filing a patent application and whether or not filing an application now would significantly and adversely impact the filings on future developments.

It is recognized that every answer in a research setting yields about a dozen new problems and, were you to wait to obtain the answers to all problems before you file, you would never file a single application. That being said, you do need to exercise due caution so that you do not prematurely disclose material. This requires closely working with your teammates and constantly evaluating the state of your progress. Again, you are reminded that a goal of a patent strategy is to build an impenetrable wall around your technology. This can only be done by carefully considering and advancing your patent applications with the entire project constantly in mind.

Concluding Remarks

As stressed throughout this book, your goal should be to implement a strong patent strategy in order to build a solid patent portfolio rather than just a collection of individual patents that claim inventions representing specific solutions to specific problems. You should strive to own the problem rather than just individual solutions. To do so requires that you prioritize potential patent applications according to both technological advances and temporal considerations.

In some ways, prioritizing patent applications according to the technological problems solved may seem simpler. If you had unlimited funds and time, you could file on all inventions. However, those conditions are unlikely. You will need to choose. When prioritizing, please bear in mind that it is impossible to a priori determine which patents would be valuable and which would not. We have presented guidelines that should help you, however, in your decision process.

Temporal factors are often more difficult to address because it is a risk-benefit analysis must be considered when determining what applications need to be filed in short order, what can be postponed, and what should be postponed.

When considering both technological and temporal factors, you need to keep in mind the goals and progress of your project. You need to constantly evaluate how filing on your advances on certain problems will impact your filings in other areas. In other words, you need to think strategically about patents, remembering the entire picture of where you are and where you are going. If you lose sight of this, you will merely file on specific inventions. While patents thus obtained can be valuable, it is unlikely that they will give you the value of protection you seek from your patent portfolio.

References

1. D. S. Rimai, *Patent Engineering*, Scrivener Publishing, Beverly, MA (2016).
2. JH.-T. Tai, C.-H. Kuo, and D. A. Gusev, U. S. Patent #7,626,730 (2009).
3. C. F. Carlson, U. S. Patent # 2,221,776 (1940).
4. C. F. Carlson, U. S. Patent #2,297,691 (1942).
5. C. F. Carlson, U. S. Patent #2,357,809 (1944).
6. https://en.wikipedia.org/wiki/Polygraph_(duplicating_device)
7. H. C. Yutzy and E. C. Yackel, U. S. Patent #2,596,756 (1952).

8

Proposing and Writing Claims

Why Should Inventors Write Claims?

The claims are the backbone of a patent. They are what give you the legal rights to exclude others from practicing your invention. Should not, therefore, the attorneys write the claims? If inventors are writing the claims, what is left for the attorneys to do? Let us address these issues before delving into what to include in claims and how to write them.

Yes, your attorney will ultimately write the claims that are submitted in your patent applications and will most likely significantly revise those that you have proposed. In fact, it is likely that your attorney will propose revisions throughout your proposed application. But, as previously discussed, your attorney is a legal expert, not a technical expert. Even attorneys who are part of an in-house legal team will not have your expert knowledge of the problems encountered and their solutions. Nor would they necessarily know what is in the related art. It is really up to the inventors to describe the problem and its solution. That is what constitutes the invention. And, as a reminder, the claims, especially the first independent claim, is the description of the invention. In other words, for your patent to be of value, you need to convey to your attorney an accurate description of the invention. The best way to do that is to write the claims. Do not worry about getting all the legalities in order. That is the job for your legal counsel. However, you need to provide an accurate and exact description of the invention in the claims.

There are other reasons why it is important for you, the inventor, to write the claims. Over the years that I have worked with inventors, I have heard the refrain many times that they described the invention to the attorneys, but could not understand what the attorneys actually wrote. They could not see the connection between their inventions and the patent application in general and the claims in particular. This is a serious issue as the inventors, upon signing the application, are swearing, under penalty of law, that they have read and understood the application.

At other times, attorneys have misinterpreted the information conveyed to them by the inventors or have tried, on their own, to circumvent prior art. Sometimes these situations are rectified. At other times, the inventors just get frustrated with the entire patenting process, sign the required affidavits, and walk away. And, on still other occasions, the inventors simply give up trying to understand the claims as written. None of these scenarios are good.

Now let us fast forward to sometime after your patent has issued and you or your company decide to assert it against an alleged infringer. You will likely be called to the witness stand to explain to the members of a jury your invention and why the prior art did not anticipate your invention. You will have to explain it in sufficient clarity that lay people will not just understand your invention, but will also appreciate why the solution that you proposed to the technical problem that you solved was not obvious. There is no better way to feel comfortable with your claims than writing them yourself.

Finally, you need to discuss your invention and its relationship to the prior art in your disclosure without discussing material that is not directly related to your invention. In other words, as previously discussed, everything presented in your disclosure is there to support your claims and establish their novelty and non-obviousness. This is particularly important when your disclosure is part of an overarching patent strategy aimed at obtaining a holistic patent portfolio. Along with this you will have to prioritize your proposed applications so that they do not conflict with the disclosures and claims of the other forthcoming applications. The easiest way to achieve these objectives is to write the claims.

Yes, writing claims and, after that, the disclosure is time consuming. Moreover, many technically-oriented people do not care for writing. That being said, submitting a relatively complete description of the invention, the suggested claims, and the background of the problem to your legal expert will save you time and effort correcting applications written by attorneys and will let your attorneys focus on what they do best – applying their legal expertise to obtain for you the best patents.

Do You Have More than a Single Invention?

Years ago, what today is considered multiple inventions could be covered with a single patent. That is no longer the case. Patents today are issued to what is fairly strictly construed as a single invention. What does that mean? As an example, consider a patentable apparatus that, when used in a pre-scribed manner, is able to accomplish a task in a novel fashion. In the past, the apparatus and the method of using that apparatus could probably be covered in a single patent. Today it is much more likely that an examiner would decide that the method and the apparatus consist of two distinct inventions, as the method could be employed using a different type of apparatus and the apparatus could be used in a manner other than that described by the method.* If you attempt to patent both in a single application, the examiner would likely reject the application and inform you that you would have to select a set of distinct claims to prosecute at this time. All this occurs before the examiner has even searched the claims and has made any decision on whether or not the application contains a patentable invention!

If the above were to occur, the inventor would have to sort out which claims to initially pursue and which to forgo pursuing until a later time. The disclosure may be the same, but the patent applications, because of the claims, would be different. The resulting applications are called "division-als". It should be noted that the examiner may require multiple divisionals – not just splitting the patent application into two.

An examiner's divisional requirements will not always be clear prior to the filing of a patent application. There are, in fact, occasions when the applicants may know that they have multiple inventions but cannot, by themselves, appropriately separate the inventions into individual applications. When that occurs, the inventors may decide to submit one application and allow the examiner to divide it. However, in general, it is better if the applicants appro-priately separate the inventions and file the appropriate applications for each

---

* It should be noted that if the apparatus and the method were sufficiently linked so that one could not be practiced without employing the other, the examiner might consider that to be a single invention. Similarly, a novel material may or may not be considered to be a distinct invention from an apparatus or a method.

invention, as doing so will result in a smaller case history and will allow the inventors to better control the prosecution of the applications.

Types of Claims and Inventions

For the sake of this book, we will only consider the utility patents, which are the most common type of patents.[†] Unless otherwise specified, the term "patent" used in this book refers to utility patents.

Patents are broadly classified as apparatus patents, whereby a novel piece of equipment is disclosed; materials patents, in which a novel material is presented; or method patents, in which a novel way of doing something is taught.

As previously discussed, the key component of a patent is its claims. Claims serve two purposes. First and foremost is that they precisely define what is legally protected. The second purpose, which is closely aligned with the first, is that the claims define the invention. All other information presented in a patent should be there to support the claims. In other words, if material is proposed that is not needed to support the claims, either by stating the problem, how others have attempted to address the problem or the background of the problem, including the prior art, and how you, the inventor, solved the problem, that information generally does not belong in the disclosure. Yes, there will be times when you may desire to include information that is not directly related to the claims. Such information could be included to prevent others from obtaining additional patents or to give supporting documentation to support a narrower set of claims should your proposed claims be rejected. These should be conscientious decisions. Information should not be included that does not serve a strategic purpose. You do not want to just educate people.

Claims are classified as being either independent or dependent. Independent claims define the basic invention, whereas dependent claims augment either independent claims or other dependent ones. For example, a dependent claim may relate to a preferred way in which the independent claim is practiced. Dependent claims will relate back, within the wording of the claim, to the prior claim on which it is dependent. In all instances, the claims serve as warning signs that say to everyone that the property described therein is protected and that no trespassing is allowed. It is vital

---

† There are also design patents whereby the design or "look" of an item is considered to be distinct; and plant patents that are concerned with genetic material. These will not be discussed in this book.

that everything required to practice the invention be stated in the independent claims. Alternatively, if something is not necessary in order to practice the invention, it should not be included in the independent claims.

A typical U.S. patent contains between one and three independent claims and up to a total of 20 claims. A patent can contain additional claims, if necessary. However, the reader is cautioned against having an excessive number of claims. First, the United States Patent and Trademark Office (www.uspto.gov) charges additional fees for more than twenty claims. Second, the prosecution of the additional claims may lengthen the file history, which can be used against you when asserting. Third, it is unusual that claims in excess of twenty will afford you much additional protection. If you really need that many, perhaps you have more than a single invention and should file multiple applications. Remember that you are trying to implement a patent strategy and not just obtain a single patent that protects a single solution to a particular problem. Let us now further elucidate the above discussion with three actual examples.

1.   An Electrophotographic Printer Patent:
The first example relates to an electrophotographic printer. As discussed in Appendix 1, a toner image is formed on a photoreceptive element and transferred to a receiver such as paper. However, not all toner is transferred due to inefficiencies in the transfer process. In order to be able to reuse the photoreceptive member, the residual toner must be removed in a cleaning process and that toner must be stored somehow until it is ready to be removed from the printer. Generally, the reservoir containing unused toner and residual toner are separate, and the residual toner is disposed of during a service process.

In a patent assigned to Lexmark International, Inc. [1] entitled "Systems and Methods for Reincorporating Waste Toner with Fresh Toner" the residual toner is stored in the same container but in a separate compartment from the fresh toner. However, the residual toner is mixed upon occasion with the fresh toner, thereby reducing or eliminating waste. The patent contains a total of fifteen claims, of which three are independent and twelve are dependent claims. Let us examine several of the claims. The first independent claim states:

> "*A toner cartridge for an electrophotographic image forming device, comprising: a housing having a reservoir for storing toner, the housing having an exit for exiting toner from the housing and an entry port for receiving waste toner into the housing; and a partition dividing the reservoir into a first compartment for storing fresh toner and a second compartment for storing waste toner,*

> *the first compartment is in fluid communication with the exit, the partition is movable within the reservoir between a first position and a second position, wherein the entry port is in fluid communication with the first compartment when the partition is in the first position such that waste toner received through the entry port is deposited into the first compartment when the partition is in the first position and the entry port is in fluid communication with the second compartment but closed off from the first compartment when the partition is in the second position such that waste toner received through the entry port is deposited into the second compartment but blocked from entering the first compartment when the partition is in the second position."*

Key provisions of this claim worth noting include the preamble to the claim, ending in the word "comprising". This preamble, although quite important and relevant when asserting a patent, is ignored by the examiner during prosecution. If the examiner finds a similar solution to a problem, irrelevant to the technical area in which it is employed, he or she will argue that the solution is obvious and is not patentable. In other words, if someone used a similar device to recycle flour used as a release aid when rolling dough in a bakery, the presently proposed use would have been considered to be lacking novelty.

It should also be noted that the word "comprises" has a specific meaning that differs from "consists". Specifically, "comprises" means that the device, process, or material described contains the features described in the claim. There may be additional components present. If someone were producing a device that contained the features described in the claim plus additional features or components, that device would still read on the claim and the producer would be infringing the patent. However, if the patent applicant used the word "consists" instead of "comprises", the patent would be applicable only in instances where there were no additional features or components.

It should be noted that the cartridge claim contains a number of elements that are necessary for the practicing of this particular invention but, by themselves, would not be novel. For example, claim 1 includes "a housing having a reservoir for storing toner". As virtually every toner replenishment bottle contains a toner reservoir, that component, by itself, would not be novel. However, that component is required for the implementation of the present invention, so it must be contained within the claim. If that feature were missing from the claim, the device would not work. Similarly, every toner reservoir must contain an exit to allow toner to enter the development station and every waste toner collection bottle must contain an entry port for the waste toner to enter the bottle. The novelty in this patent is the communication between the two portions of the bottle.

Claims 2 through 4[‡] are dependent claims that describe how the partition is moved. It should be noted that claims 2 and 4 refer back to the independent claim 1, whereas claim 3 refers back to dependent claim 2.

Claims 5 and 12 are independent claims that describe a system and a method for reclaiming recycled toner. As these claims use the same device described in claim 1 and, as written, cannot be practiced in another fashion, the examiner appears to have decided that these are one invention, despite having independent claims, and thus can be awarded a single patent, rather than requiring a divisional. The remaining claims are dependent claims.

The dependent claims describe specific components or methods that allow the recycled and fresh toner to be combined. As these are not required to practice the described invention in its broadest form, but are preferred modes and important, they were added as dependent claims. It should be noted that, had the examiner decided that the independent claims, as written, were too broad, a patent may have been allowed that restricted the independent claims by revising them to include one or more dependent claims. However, that would narrow the range of validity of the patent and make it easier to circumvent.[§] Whether or not a patent is worth pursuing if the examiner restricts the claims is a decision you will have to make.

2. A Glock Pistol Patent:

A second example is the patent for a semiautomatic handgun[¶] introduced by Gaston Glock in the early 1980s [2].

The Glock Model 17 handgun is, perhaps, best known to the general public because of its use of a polymer, rather than steel, in the fabrication

---

‡ 2. *The toner cartridge of claim 1, further comprising a rotatable shaft positioned within the reservoir, wherein the partition is moveable by rotation of the shaft.*

3. The toner cartridge of claim 2, wherein the partition is mounted on the shaft and moveable axially along the shaft.

4. The toner cartridge of claim 1, further comprising a paddle assembly positioned within the first compartment for mixing waste toner with fresh toner within the first compartment.

§ The reader should note that the author is not commenting on the validity, importance, or value of any patent discussed in this chapter. They are being used strictly for exemplary information.

¶ Semiautomatic firearms are frequently mischaracterized as automatic firearms. Semiautomatic firearms fire a single shot and load a new cartridge into a firing chamber every time the trigger is pulled. In contrast, automatic firearms continuously fire and load until the trigger is released.

of the frame of the gun**. While the use of a polymer was a notable advancement, reducing the weight of the firearm and improving its longevity, it was only one of a series of innovations introduced by Gaston Glock. To understand these advancements and the claims in the relevant patents, it is worthwhile to first present an overview of the technology used in semiautomatic pistols available at that time.

Handguns are broadly classified as either "single action" (SA) or "double action" (DA). In a single action handgun, a hammer, which is used to strike a firing pin, must first be cocked by hand. Pulling the trigger only releases the hammer and fires the gun. Because the hammer had been manually cocked, the distance that the trigger must be pulled and the force needed do so in order to fire the gun is relatively small, typically only a pound or two. Because of the small distance and force required to fire the gun, it is relatively easy for someone to shoot accurately. However, leaving the gun in a cocked position is dangerous.

In contrast to a single action firearm, pulling the trigger in a double action handgun first cocks and then releases the hammer. Pulling the trigger, then, serves two functions. This requires a much longer and harder trigger pull, making the gun safer, but harder to shoot accurately.

Both single action and double action revolvers and semiautomatic pistols are made. As this discussion will focus on patents held by Glock, we will focus strictly on semiautomatic pistols. Moreover, semiautomatic pistols are often (although erroneously) referred to as "automatics" and, as that terminology has crept into the popular vernacular, we will also adopt it. The reader should bear in mind that, from this point, when we refer to a handgun as an automatic, we are really describing a semiautomatic, i.e. a handgun that fires one bullet each time the trigger is pulled, while chambering the next round.

All automatic handguns comprise a frame to which all components of the firearm are attached and a barrel through which a fired bullet passes on its way to the target. The barrel has a muzzle and a breach end, the muzzle being the portion of the barrel through which the bullet passes when it exits the firearm and the breach end being at the opposite end of the barrel to the muzzle.

A cartridge typically comprises a casing that holds a projectile or bullet. Within the casing is a fast burning propellant. At the end of the casing

---

** The polymer frame caused much consternation with the general public over fears that the gun could not be detected using conventional magnetometers. In fact, the gun, while much lighter than comparable pistols, still contained over a pound of steel in its other components and was, therefore, readily detectable.

opposite to the end holding the bullet is a primer that, when struck, generates a spark that ignites the propellant. The gases released when the propellant burns propel the bullet down the barrel and out the muzzle on its way to the target.

In an automatic handgun, the cartridges are contained in an ammunition feeding device called a magazine. The magazine is affixed to the frame of the firearm. Most often it is inserted into the portion of the frame known as the grip that the shooter's hand encompasses.

At the breach end of the barrel is the chamber, whose function is to precisely hold the cartridge at the moment of firing. Cartridges are fed into the chamber from the magazine.

The barrel is encompassed by a member known as the slide. The slide is affixed to the frame so that it can articulate between a closed position that will cover the primer end of the cartridge and an open position that allows the spent casing to be ejected through the ejection port located on the slide.

When the firearm is fired, the slide articulates rearwards, ejecting the spent casing, chambering a fresh cartridge, and, depending on the design of the firearm, cocking the handgun in preparation for firing a subsequent shot. All this has to be precisely accomplished within milliseconds if the firearm is to function properly.

Now let us look at the two common designs of automatics that were available at the time of Glock's inventions. The first was the single action handgun such as the Colt Model 1911. This type of firearm is cocked when, after inserting a loaded magazine, the shooter pulls the slide all the way back and releases it in a process known as "racking". As discussed previously, being a single action firearm, the 1911 would only require a light touch on the trigger to pull it back the short distance required to fire it. This is obviously not safe. To remedy this situation, 1911s generally employ two safeties. The first, known as the grip safety, must be depressed by the shooter's hand when the gun is properly gripped. The second, known as the thumb safety, comprises a lever that must be manually depressed by the shooter's thumb. Both safeties must be disengaged to enable the firearm to fire and both must be engaged to enable the gun to be safely transported.

In addition to single action automatic handguns[††], there are, and were at the time that the Glock 17 was introduced, double action handguns such as the Walther P38. These are often designated as DA, although this has, since

---

[††] The reader is reminded that the term "automatic handgun" is a misnomer, as the firearms being discussed are semiautomatic. However, as this term is commonly used to designate semiautomatic firearms, it is being presently used for the same purpose.

the introduction of the Glock 17 and other firearms with a similar trigger design, become somewhat confusing.‡‡ The source of this confusion will be discussed forthwith. However, to avoid confusion, firearms employing actions such as the Walther P38 will be designated as DA/SA. In contrast, firearms employing actions that require the pressing of the trigger to both cock and fire the gun for each shot will be designated as double action only or DAO.

In DA/SA automatic firearms, the slide cocks the gun. This is automatically accomplished when the gun is fired, as the rearwards motion of the slide, in addition to ejecting the spent casing and chambering a fresh cartridge, also serves to cock the firearm. Under these circumstances, pulling the trigger only releases the hammer. The gun is, therefore, acting in a single action mode. In other words, after the first shot has been fired, the gun is, essentially, a single action firearm, complete with a short, light force applied to the trigger that that would be required to fire the next round. This also occurs when the shooter manually chambers the first round, which requires the manual racking of the slide. However, as discussed previously, a gun in this condition is not safe to carry.

To remedy this situation requires that a means to lower the hammer, or decock the handgun, has to be incorporated into the firearm. The decocking mechanism, obviously, must be able to lower the hammer without requiring that the pressing of the trigger.

After decocking, the firing of a DA/SA handgun would either require the manual cocking of the hammer so that the firearm is in the single action mode, or that a long, hard press of the trigger be applied to first cock and then fire the gun. After the first shot is fired, the gun would be in the SA mode for all subsequent shots. Thus, the shooter would have to be prepared for different trigger pulls when using the gun.

In both the SA and DA/SA firearms, the shooter must render the firearm safe after shooting by either applying a manual safety or decocking the handgun. This may not always occur, especially if the shooter were to have to discharge the firearm in a stressful self-defense situation.

As in the case of the SA handgun, the DA/SA firearm must release the firing pin to fire the bullet, have the slide move back to eject the spent casing, and rechamber a fresh round in a precise position while re-cocking the gun. And all this must be reliably done in milliseconds.

It should be noted that the firearms discussed thus far are high quality and these, or other firearms employing similar mechanisms, are still commonly available and often preferred by many individuals.

---

‡‡ For the reasons discussed in the text, such firearms are often presently designated as DA/SA or "traditional double action" firearms.

The discussion of semiautomatic firearm mechanisms is not meant to provide a thorough understanding of every bit of technology that is employed in a quality firearm. Rather, the topic has been discussed to familiarize the reader with the immense complications in semiautomatic handguns, especially those prior to Glock's innovations. Specifically, a quality handgun must be able to function without failure for thousands of rounds fired, and the gun must be able to do so regardless of the environment or of the fouling that occurs within a firearm as a result of firing, with a variety of ammunition, and under the repeated shocks encountered when firing. These are not easy conditions to meet and have required handguns to be very complex and expensive, requiring many precisely machined components. And this is where Glock's innovations came in.

The story [2] is that, in 1980, Glock, the manager of an automotive radiator factory, having no firearms design or manufacturing experience, learned that the Austrian army was looking for bids to replace its aging Walther P38 handguns. He requested and received the army's requirements for the gun and decided to bid for the contract. Studying the firearms produced by other highly reputable manufacturers, Glock decided that he could build a highly reliable handgun at a much lower cost that also had a number of technological improvements.

Glock began his development by obtaining a number of high quality firearms that were available at that time and disassembling, reassembling, and contrasting the methods used to manufacture them [2]. In effect, he was conducting a prior art search, thereby obtaining direct knowledge of the competitive products. Using this knowledge, he was able to design the firearm that bears his name – the Glock Model 17.

His innovations were numerous. Not only did he replace the steel frame that was in common usage at the time with one made of a polymer, thereby making a lighter weight firearm, but he changed the entire firing mechanism, reducing the numerous parts to just thirty-four, and eliminated the need to activate manually controlled safeties and/or decockers. While his design was for a double action handgun, it also eliminated the long, hard trigger pull characteristic of the first shot and the single action trigger generally employed for subsequent shots. In effect, each shot required the same trigger pull. Glock's innovations, besides reducing the complexity of handguns, allowed him to produce firearms at a much lower cost. Glock was awarded three patents for his innovations [3–5]. It should be noted that none of the three patents claim the polymer frame[§§], which is probably

---

§§ The reader should note that probably the first firearm comprising a polymer receiver was the Remington Nylon 66, chambered in the relatively low power .22 long rifle and first sold

the characteristic most notable to the general public. Rather, the patents focus on the inventions that enabled Glock to achieve his technical aims.

We will consider, as an example, Glock's second cited patent entitled simply "Automatic Pistol" [4]. As discussed in Chapter 2, the title of a patent is short and rarely descriptive. This is certainly the case here as the title conveys little meaningful information and may be, in fact, misleading as the pistol described is actually a semiautomatic, rather than an automatic, pistol. However, in view of the vernacular usage of the term "automatic", that term would be acceptable here. In fact, this patent describes and claims the mechanism by which the trigger designed by Glock works.

The disclosure contains thirty-nine figures, with each component of each figure carefully enumerated. Absent from this patent is a section entitled "List of Parts", which is commonly included in current patents and lists, by number called out in the figures, each part with its title.

The background section of Glock's patent carefully describes the limitations of automatic pistols, as they existed at the time. This is important, as the Swiss Parabellum 1900, the Luger Pistole Parabellum 1908, and the Colt Model 1911 were semiautomatic pistols that had been around for over 70 years and other manufacturers, such as Steyr, Beretta, and Walther, were also manufacturing semiautomatic handguns. The reader is cautioned, however, that, presently, background sections must be more detailed in light of KSR International Co. v. Teleflex, Inc. [6]** Please keep in mind that the background section in Glock's patent had been written and submitted to the USPTO several decades prior to the KSR decision and was subject to the requirements in place at the time of its submission.

It should be noted that, in this particular Glock patent, information was also included in the background section that was not directly related to the claims. For example, the background section discusses the need for tools to disassemble some semiautomatic firearms. While this comment is correct per se, there is nothing in the claims relevant to eliminating the need for a tool. Moreover, not all firearms in existence at the time required tools for routine cleaning and maintenance. Although discussion about the

---

in 1959. Heckler and Koch introduced the VP 70 selective fire machine pistol in 1970. Both would serve as prior art that teaches the use of a polymer frame, thus precluding Glock's ability to patent, perhaps, its most renowned feature.

** In this case, the Supreme Court expanded the extent of prior art that can be considered and restricted arguments as to why that art should be excluded. Moreover, the Court also ruled that one of ordinary skill in the art did not imply an automaton, but allowed testing to select among alternatives. This ruling greatly expanded what would be considered obvious, thereby not inventive. A detailed discussion of this case is beyond the scope of this book and the reader is urged to discuss its relevance with legal counsel.

need for tools does not hurt this particular patent, it does not appear to be necessary. However, as this is in the background section, rather than in the description of the invention, it may help educate the examiner about the limitations encountered when practicing the related art.

With this discussion, let us now turn our attention back to the claims in this patent. Specifically, this patent has eight claims, the first being the independent claim and the other seven dependent claims relating back to claim 1. Let us now look at the details of the first claim, which states:

> *"In a pistol, including*
> *a frame having a longitudinal axis and a barrel mounted in the frame;*
> *a slide mounted on the frame so as to be slidable forwardly toward the barrel into a closed position in which the frame is in contact with the barrel and rearwardly out of a closed position, a recoil spring for biasing the slide into the closed position;*
> *the slide including a breech block, the breech block closing off a cartridge chamber in the closed position of the slide;*
> *a firing pin being mounted longitudinally movable in the breech block and having a nose projecting toward the frame, a firing pin spring for biasing the firing pin, the tension of the firing pin spring being releasable in a direction toward the barrel;*
> *the frame further including a trigger mechanism with a trigger means and an abutment, the abutment being movable by the trigger means from an initial position initially parallel to the firing pin so that the firing pin nose engages the abutment and is moved and the firing pin spring is tensioned, the abutment being further movable in release direction until the abutment and the nose are disengaged;*
> *the slide defining control means which during firing cause the abutment to be moved from the released position into the path of movement of the nose;*
> *the improvement comprising,*
> *a stop spring having first and second ends, the first end acting on the frame and the second end acting on the trigger means, wherein the stop spring acts on the trigger means in a direction which is opposite the direction of action of the firing pin spring by the nose of the firing pin on the abutment, the tension of the firing pin spring being greater than the tension of the stop spring."*

The last paragraph, beginning with *"the improvement comprising,..."* is clearly the invention. Why, then, are the first six paragraphs included in this claim? It is clear, upon a careful reading, that the described features such as a frame, a barrel mounted on the frame, a trigger, and a firing pin are present in virtually all semiautomatic handguns. The reason that these features are included in the claim is because they are crucial to the ability to practice the innovation described in the last paragraph. In other words, each of those elements must be present, even though they, by themselves, are not innovative. Absent those details, the present invention would not work. The lesson here is that every detail that is required to make an innovation work is part of the invention and must be included in the claim.

Conversely, anything that is not pertinent to practicing a claim should be omitted from the claim. The reader is reminded that an alleged infringer must be practicing every item in a claim in order to be reading on that claim. What this means is that pistol manufacturers, all of whom have barrels, triggers, and firing pins, are not infringing Glock's claim unless they are practicing all the above including the aspects described in the last paragraph. Conversely, the Ruger Mark IV pistol does not contain "*a slide mounted on the frame so as to be slidable forwardly toward the barrel into a closed position*". Rather, the barrel is held in a fixed position without a slide, but does have a bolt that articulates within the barrel. Accordingly, the Ruger Mark IV pistol could practice the innovation described in the last paragraph, but would probably not be judged to be infringing on this patent, as it does not appear to be practicing every word of the claim.

When reading this claim, you may find that the language appears somewhat stilted and difficult to follow. There are terms such as "*firing pin nose*" and "*slide defining control means*" that are not generally encountered in the firearms literature. Unusual terms can be used in a patent provided that they are properly defined within that patent. The writer of a patent application can be his own lexicographer, but must make sure that his nomenclature is understood. In addition, it is the role of the figures, including the called-out numbers in the disclosure, as well as both the detailed description of the invention and the parts list, to make sure that, with some effort, the terms can be understood. Indeed, this patent, with its thirty-nine figures, should be comprehensible to an examiner during prosecution and should be explainable to members of a jury during an assertion.

Finally, let us discuss some of the phrases used in this claim. The first is the phase "*In a pistol, including...*" The word "including" was used in lieu of "comprising". It is unlikely that the examiner will consider this phrase during prosecution. If any other art or combination of art describing a similar mechanism is found, the examiner will probably decide that the application lacks novelty. The specific use of the invention, i.e., in a pistol, will probably not be considered. However, this is not the case during an assertion. There, the use will most likely be taken into account so that someone employing similar technology for a totally different application would probably not be deemed to be infringing on this patent.

There are also specific requirements for the use of the indefinite article "a" and the definite article "the" when writing claims and the supporting disclosure. The first time an item is referenced, such as the word "frame" in the first paragraph, "*a frame having a longitudinal axis and a barrel mounted in **the** frame*", the indefinite article is used as there is no prior reference to any particular frame. However, subsequent use of the term "frame" uses the definite article because it refers back to the specific frame mentioned in the first paragraph. These are items of which you should be aware and your skills will develop with usage. However, your legal counsel will undoubtedly correct errors. It is far more important that you accurately and completely describe your invention.

3.   A Gray Scale Electrophotographic Printing Patent:
The third patent to be considered in the discussion of claims is entitled "Apparatus and Method for Gray Level Printing" [7]. It is related to a rendering algorithm used to control the writer in an electrophotographic printer. Before delving into this patent, it is worthwhile discussing how gray scales are produced and why they are important.

We see a world that has both very dark and very light regions, and all shades in between. The shades between the extreme light or white areas and the extreme dark or black regions contain information. For example, we recognize people by their facial tones. Information is also available in shadowy regions. The difference that can be resolved between the light and dark portions of a scene is called the contrast. If all that the human eye could process was limited to the dark or high density regions and the light or low density regions, we would lose much of our perceptive abilities.

When making prints that attempt to capture the information in a scene, it is important to control the contrast. In some applications, such as the printing of alpha-numeric documents, it is generally preferred to either have light (e.g., the bare paper of a page in a textual book) or dark, where a letter or number is printed, and little gray. This is referred to as a high contrast print, as there are few, if any, perceivable levels of gray. However, when printing documents with pictorial content, capturing as much of the gray scale as possible is very important for the esthetics and information contained in the print. This is a low contrast system.

Contrast is generally produced in printed documents using one of two methods. The first is what is known as continuous tone printing, such as is typified by silver halide photographic prints. These rely on generating levels of gray by either producing varying amounts of dye in the respective portions of a color print or by the amount of metallic silver present in a black and white photograph.

The second type of a gray scale in printed articles is known as a halftone, and is commonly used in conventional printing such as with offset presses and lithography. This is used because such presses cannot modulate the amount of ink deposited per unit area. Rather, ink is either deposited as a high density or not deposited at all, leaving that particular area bare.

When printing a gray scale using a halftone process, the page to be printed is divided into an imaginary grid of lines analogous to the real lines present in graph paper. For high quality printing, a fine ruling, perhaps 150 to greater than 200 lines per inch, is used. For lower quality printing, such as used in newspapers, typical rulings are between 66 and 80 lines per inch.

A dot of ink is deposited by the press at each vertex of the grid, with the size of the dot varying from little or no ink to the whole region incorporated within the grid lines covered. The gray scale is achieved by, in essence, an area modulation of the grid, with the human eye integrating the unmarked and marked portions of the grid.

Halftone printing is a binary process. There either is ink present on a particular area or there is not. Unlike the continuous tone printing of a silver halide photograph, there is no modulation of the density of the ink deposited. Rather, modulation and gray scale is achieved solely through an area modulation of the deposited ink.

The generation of gray scale in electrophotography is often a hybrid of continuous and halftone printing. In electrophotographic printing, as in lithography or off-set printing, an imaginary grid is formed that serves as the basis for a halftone printing. However, unlike conventional ink printing wherein the location of the center of an ink deposit and its shape are both fixed, electrophotography can deposit toner particles anywhere within the grid. This gives rise to the ability to vary the shape of a halftone dot, as well as the capability of depositing toner anywhere within the grid pattern. This allows printing of both halftone and continuous tone gray scales within a single print. This capability allows far more levels of gray to be printed. It also can reduce the apparent granularity[***] of a print. However, to do so

---

[***] Granularity is the noise that is generated by irregular and unintended variations in density. In continuous tone printing, it is due to unwanted variations in the optical density within an area. With halftone printing, it arises from unintended variations in the size and shape of the printed dots.

requires a sophisticated writing algorithm that produces the electrostatic latent image that is ultimately toned into a visible image. Typically, the writing algorithm addresses factors that cannot be controlled in either continuous or halftone printing, including the shape of halftone dots, how much toner gets deposited within a dot and how much outside the dot, and where and when components of the electrostatic latent image are actually formed or written.

It is with this background that we will discuss the first claim of U.S. Patent #6,538,677 (2003), entitled "Apparatus and Method for Gray Level Printing" which reads:

> "A method for generating variable density halftone images with electrography comprising the steps of: grouping sets of adjacent pixels into a set of adjacent cells where each cell corresponds to a halftone dot of an image; selectively setting exposure levels for a gray scale writer to grow halftone dots from zero size to a desired size equal to or less than a maximum size by increasing exposure of one pixel in the cell one exposure level at a time until the pixel reaches a first total level of exposure and selectively repeating this step for the rest of the pixels until the cell is at its desired size and at an initial density; selectively adjusting exposure of the initial density of cells at the maximum size by sequentially increasing the level of exposure of each pixel in the maximum size cell by one exposure level at a time for each pixel until all pixels are at the same next level of exposure and then repeating this step to further increase the density of the cell to desired density; discharging areas of a charged image member in accordance with the selected levels of exposure of the prior steps to form a latent image of variable density halftone dots on the image member; enclosing a cylindrical magnetic roller in a concentric sleeve; rotating the magnetic roller in a first direction; disposing the magnetic roller and the sleeve in a container holding a two-component toner comprising hard magnetic carrier particles and toner particles; rotating the concentric sleeve in a direction opposite to the direction of the magnetic roller and in a direction co-current with an imaging member; contacting the sleeve and the latent image on the image member; transferring toner particles from the sleeve to the latent image to develop the latent image; transferring the developed image to a copy sheet; fixing the developed image on the copy sheet."

An examination of the above claim quickly reveals its numerous aspects that undermine its value. In fact this patent seems to be a clear representation of why the priority of an invention or technological advancement, discussed in Chapter 6, may differ greatly from that of the corresponding patent application, which was discussed in Chapter 7. However, in order to fully understand the discrepancy between the value of the invention and that of the patent, it is first necessary to briefly describe the technology involved in this invention. The reader is referred to Appendix 1 for a more complete presentation.

With the intent of justifying the above assertions, let us review how toner particles are deposited onto a photoreceptor in an electrophotographic engine in order to create a visible image and how that process is related to the limitations of the patent under discussion.

At the beginning of a cycle aimed at producing a toner image, a photoreceptive member is uniformly electrically charged. An electrostatic latent image is then created by image-wise exposing the photoreceptor to light. In the days of copiers, exposure was often obtained by focusing the light from flash lamp that reflected off the original print onto the photoreceptor. Upon illumination, the photoreceptor discharges in the exposed regions, but remains electrically charged in the unexposed areas, thus creating the latent image.

With modern electrophotographic printers, the exposure is obtained using either a laser scanner or an LED array. This is known as a writer because it writes the electrostatic latent image. The intensity, duration, and timing of when the writer exposes the photoreceptor are accomplished using mathematical algorithms fed into a microprocessor that drives the writer.

Once the electrostatic latent image has been created, it is converted into a visible image by bringing electrically charged toner particles into operational proximity to the photoreceptor. This begs at least three questions. The first is what is meant by operational proximity. The second is how the toner particles become charged. The third question is how they are brought into operational proximity to the photoreceptor.

The term "operational proximity" means that the toner is sufficiently close to the photoreceptor so that it is attracted to and adheres to the electrostatic latent image. Typically, this means that the toner must be brought into contact with the photoreceptor.

Toner particles become electrically charged through triboelectrification. While this can be achieved by several means, it is most commonly accomplished by making a developer that comprises both the toner particles and larger magnetic carrier particles. At least one or both of these particles contain a suitable charge agent so that, upon mixing the toner and carrier particles, the toner particles tribocharge against the carrier particles, thereby obtaining the desired sign and magnitude of charge.

The magnetic carrier particles do more than just tribocharge the toner particles. The developer is loaded into a development station that contains an electrically conducting cylindrical shell and a coaxial magnetic core. By suitably rotating the appropriate components of the development station, the developer is brought into operational proximity to the photoreceptor. Most often, the carrier particles are approximately 100 to 200 µm in diameter, whereas the toner particles are typically between 3 and 12 µm. The development station is designed so that the shell rotates, while the magnetic core is stationary.

This system worked quite well when the role of the electrophotographic engine was relegated to reproducing alphanumeric documents. However, as demand for documents containing pictorial content increased, the image quality produced in this manner was not adequate. Specifically, the above technology was able to reproduce fine lines very well, but it was not able to appropriately print broader areas. This is because the leading edge of the latent image would take the toner that was being transported into the nip, thereby depleting the developer. The rate that the toner could be replenished was not adequate to allow the presence of sufficient toner particles to develop the interiors of broad areas.

In the early 1980s, scientists at Eastman Kodak [8, 9] devised a way to develop solid areas by reducing the diameters of the carrier particles from between 100 and 200 µm to between 20 and 30 µm and rotating the magnetic core, in addition to the shell, in the development station. This allowed more toner to be transported into the development area, thereby alleviating the toner depletion problem. Suffice-it to say, this advancement gave Eastman Kodak a decided technological advantage at that time in the marketplace.

With this discussion in mind, let us now return to the claim of U.S. Patent No. 6,538,677 (reference 7) and discuss its limitations and what could have been done to strengthen it. Let us consider these limitations in order of decreasing significance.

The first limitation is the apparently narrow range of coverage of the patent brought about by the seemingly unnecessary confounding of the writing algorithm with the use of a rotating magnetic core. By the date of issuance of this patent (2003), the earlier patent by Fritz et al. [8] was nineteen years old and had expired. It is clear that the rotating core was well known. Moreover, the writing algorithm was a distinct invention. There was no apparent need to tie it to the restriction of its use with a rotating magnetic core. The possible motivation of doing so will be discussed later in this chapter. But wait! Did not the three cited Glock patents also include older, well known, requirements within its first (the independent) claim? The answer is "yes". However, in the Glock patents, those restrictions were pertinent to the use of the improvement invented by Glock. In other words, Glock's solution to a technical problem would not function absent those restrictions. Therefore, they had to be within that claim.

In the present patent, the writing algorithm could have been implemented for use with other development systems. The use of the rotating magnetic core was irrelevant to the advancement. In other words, a patent that disclosed a significant technological advancement (the writing algorithm) was made much more restrictive than necessary for practicing what should have been the invention, as defined by the claim. Moreover, tying the writing algorithm to the requirement that it be used in conjunction with a rotating magnetic core made this patent worthless, as few companies, other than Eastman Kodak, use a development system comprising a rotating magnetic core. This patent taught much, but was not assertable because of this restriction.

The claim is further unnecessarily restricted by such requirements that it be used with a two-component developer[†††] and that the developer comprise "hard ferrite" particles. From a technical point of view, none of these restrictions were required to practice the advancement.

It is important to remember that, in order for a patent to be infringed, the allegedly infringing company's product must read on every phrase of the claim. If their product reads on 95% of a claim, but not on the other 5%, there is no infringement.

This may be an example of why it is important for the inventors to propose the claims themselves. In particular, the inventors need to clearly elucidate every aspect of what is required to practice the invention and eliminate all aspects that would not be required. In this invention, if there were a particular advantage to using this algorithm with a rotating magnetic core, that should have been included in a subsequent dependent claim.

The second limitation of this patent is its ability to be asserted. As an example of this, consider the phrase in the claim:

[†††] Not all electrophotographic developers comprise two components. There are development systems in which the developer comprises only marking particles and, in fact, the rotating magnetic core can be used with some of them. These are also so-called "liquid developers" comprising sub micrometer marking particles in a liquid carrier, such as some products produced by Hewlett Packard.

"selectively setting exposure levels for a gray scale writer to grow halftone dots from zero size to a desired size equal to or less than a maximum size by increasing exposure of one pixel in the cell one exposure level at a time..."

This phrase would apparently require that, during an assertion, it would have to be proved that the software driving a writer is exposing one pixel at a time within each cell in order to achieve a density within that cell. This would be extremely hard to do, as it would require a detailed knowledge of the competitor's software – something that is not likely to happen. Moreover, even if such information could be obtained, any slight modification of this algorithm by a competitor would result in the patent not being infringed. It would have been far better if the patent disclosed the use of certain test documents that could simulate the desired exposure of the pixels and write the claim in terms of an observable effect, rather than the result of a software-driven process.

The third limitation involves how readily the claims and evidence that a competitor's product reads on those claims could be explained to and understood by a jury. If a jury does not understand the patent or its claims, it is unlikely that the claimant will win the suit. It would have been far better if the patent disclosed the use of characteristic tests or prints that could have been used to define and elucidate the claim, rather than relying on explanations of complicated mathematical constructs.

Why did this patent suffer from the serious limitations discussed? We can only speculate. However, it seems likely that Eastman Kodak developed a patent strategy that was aimed at owning a particular solution to a problem instead of owning the problem itself. What does this mean?

The problem that Kodak should have attempted to own was the ability to convert electrostatic latent images into high quality electrophotographic prints. High quality includes metrics such as developing a uniform density in broad areas, maintaining high resolution, and minimizing granularity. Instead of that, they found that, by rotating both the core and shell in an electrophotographic development station and using smaller carrier particles, they could improve the uniformity of broad areas. From their first patent, issued in 1984, to the present, Kodak obtained 31 patents in which the phrase "rotating magnetic core" is used in the claims and 132 in which it appears in the disclosure. There are many additional patents focused on the carriers, toners, charge agents, background minimization, replenishment, etc., in their portfolio.

Eastman Kodak appears to have recognized their technological advancement and its value in the marketplace brought about by rotating the magnetic core, and aggressively protected their intellectual property with patents. As may be apparent, however, rotating both the core and shell in a development station is complex and expensive, requiring additional motors and motor controllers, as well as precision machining of components. These all add to manufacturing costs, resulting in expensive products.

Meanwhile, other companies recognized the ability to produce high quality prints using electrophotography would be of value to them. This recognition was, at least in part, brought about by the teachings in Kodak's patents and the products it marketed. Locked out of using rotating core technology, these companies developed alternatives that produced comparable images at much lower manufacturing costs. Meanwhile, Kodak, not having patents in these alternative technologies, found itself with patents that other companies did not need, and faced with stiff competition. And, with a lack of patents in alternative technologies, Kodak was in a weak position to enter into cross-licensing agreements with their competitors.

Concluding Remarks

The claims are the heart and soul of a patent. As they define the invention, they must be clearly and completely written, without including any superfluous material. They should be written with the idea of asserting them against alleged infringers. With this in mind, you are advised to avoid, to the extent possible, the following situations:

The first situation involves instances where more than a single entity is required to infringe a patent. Let us consider a hypothetical example. In this example, assume that you are living many centuries ago and earn your living as a carpenter. However, in the absence of stores, you must also make your own tools and fastening devices. Accordingly, you discover that you can facilitate construction of houses by fastening boards together by driving fastening devices that you refer to as "nails" through one board and into a second. Moreover, you have invented a driver of those devices that you call a "hammer". You want to give yourself a competitive advantage over other carpenters so you patent your invention. In the patent application, you claim:

"A method of fastening a plurality of boards comprising:

Making a hammer;
Using the hammer to drive nails through one board into a
second."

There are, of course, numerous problems with this hypothetical claim.
However, let us focus on one, which is who would be infringing the claim.

As written, the claim would require the same person or company to
both make and use a hammer. If the carpenter hires a blacksmith to make
a hammer and then uses the hammer to affix boards to each other, no one
is infringing the claim despite the fact that, in the end, the claim is being
infringed. It is important to always keep in mind the possibility of asserting
a patent when drafting an application.

The second cautionary note involves what is referred to as "means
plus function". This phrase denotes the situation in which a component and its function are defined within a claim. For example, consider an apparatus that must be contained in a vacuum. In order to
assemble the apparatus, it is necessary that the container be initially
open and subsequently, after inserting the apparatus, the parts of the
container affixed to each other and hermetically sealed. This is accomplished by sealing the portions of the container together with a continuous bead of an adhesive that both attaches the components and
hermetically seals the container. If the portion of the claim referring to
the adhesive states:

"...and the components of the container are affixed to each
other with an adhesive that hermetically seals the container..."

the role of the adhesive is stated to both affix and seal the container. This
is an example of means plus function as both the means (the use of an
adhesive) and its function (to affix and hermetically seal) are stated in the
claim. If someone uses an adhesive, for example, to attach the components
in a manner in which it could not seal (e.g., the adhesive does not form
a continuous bead) and uses a different component to hermetically seal
the container, the claim would not be infringed. It would be far better to
simply state that the portions of the container are attached to each and
hermetically sealed.

Finally, you are again reminded that your goal should be to build a patent
portfolio focused on protecting your intellectual property and positioning
your company with a solid patent portfolio that would enable you to

either exclude others from encroaching in your marketplace or enable you to increase your profits by obtaining licensing fees for the use of your patents by others. To accomplish this, you must be cognizant of what other applications you plan to file. Please remember that you can only claim an invention in a single patent. You are not allowed to claim an invention twice, so make sure that you are filing the strongest set of applications that you can.

References

1. L. A. Bejat, M. A. Gist, M. C. Leemhuis, P. J. Mehta, E. C. Stelter, D. S. Schneider, and K. M. Wright, U. S. Patent #9,454,125 (2016).
2. P. M. Barrett, *Glock: The Rise of America's Gun*, Broadway Paperbacks, New York, NY (2013).
3. G. Glock, U. S. Patent #4,539,889 (1985).
4. G. Glock, U. S. Patent #4,825,744 (1989).
5. G. Glock, U. S. Patent #4,893,546 (1990).
6. 550 U.S. 398 (2007).
7. J. R. Thompson, Y. S. Ng, E. Zeise, H-T. Tai, and E. C. Stelter, U. S. Patent #6,538,677 (2003).
8. G. F. Fritz, G. P. Kasper, A. S. Kroll, and M. Mosehauer, U. S. Patent #4,473,029 (1984).
9. E. T. Miskinis and T. A. Jadwin, U. S. Patent #4,546,060 (1985).

9

Conducting Prior Art Searches

Introduction

Thorough prior art searches are extremely important. Such searches are valuable, because, among other reasons, than they educate you regarding how others are addressing similar problems and where the technology is heading. And yet, those who innovate and drive technology forward are often reluctant to conduct prior art searches. There are many reasons for this. Reading legal documents such as patents can be a burdensome task, yet they disclose a lot of very valuable information. Spending time reading such documents may seem counterproductive to advancing technological research and development, but the knowledge gained from prior art searches may actually help to guide these advances. Unfortunately, there is not much that can be done to make this more palatable, other than convincing inventors of its extremely high value.

More pertinent to the present discussion is that inventors often do not know how to conduct searches and where to go for help with conducting searches. And then, when they do search the patent literature, they come out with so many hits that they cannot possibly evaluate them. To add insult to injury, those searches often fail to turn up patents that the inventors know exist, suggesting the searches were not well conducted.

The information obtained through patent searches is in marked contrast with the knowledge that innovators tend to have gleaned from more academically traditional sources, including textbooks, trade shows, benchmarking competitive products, and general scientific literature. And, while all those are, indeed, legitimate sources for information on the prior art, examiners tend to rely heavily, although not exclusively, on the patent literature. Accordingly, it is extremely important to search the patent database when drafting patent applications. The good news is that there is an efficiency of scale. Specifically, when putting together a patent strategy that encompasses an entire project, as opposed to just filing individual applications aimed at obtaining patent coverage for solutions to specific technical problems, the results of the search will often transcend, to a large degree, multiple applications,

It is the purpose of this chapter to facilitate prior art searching.

Types of Prior Art Searches

For the purposes of this discussion, and unless otherwise specified, terms such as "search" and "prior art" will refer exclusively to the patent literature, as library searches of the general technical literature are well understood. There are two distinct types of prior art searches: clearance searches and novelty searches.

Clearance Searches

The goal of a clearance search is to minimize the chance that the technology that you intend to use in your proposed product is actually infringing on patents owned by someone else. Clearance searches focus primarily on the claims of issued patents that are active in the countries of interest such as those in which the product will be produced, marketed, or transported. In addition, they may also include the claims of patent applications that have not yet been allowed. The inclusion of such applications is to inform you of potential infringement issues that may arise in the future. However, your product can only infringe on actual allowed claims in issued patents. Moreover, proposed claims in applications are exactly that. They are proposed and may not be allowed. However, should the application be successfully prosecuted and the proposed claims allowed, you may have to hustle to alter your product to avoid infringing them. That is a risk assessment decision that you will have to make.

The only relevant factor that is considered in clearance searches is whether or not some aspect of your product reads on the claims of one or more patents that are owned by others with whom you do not have cross-licensing agreements.*

Clearance searches, which are discussed in detail in *Patent Engineering* [1], do not involve novelty and, although there are certain aspects that overlap with novelty searches, they are sufficiently different as to warrant their own discussion. However, as this book is about executing a patent strategy and not about avoiding patent infringement lawsuits, they will not be discussed further.

Novelty Searches

In contrast to clearance searches, novelty searches look at all prior art. Whether or not a particular invention is claimed, and whether or not a patent is active or had even been issued, is irrelevant. The only requirement is that your invention has not been disclosed or is not obvious.

More pernicious is the fact that your entire invention does not even have to be explicitly disclosed in a single patent. Rather, if your invention can be pieced together or found to be obvious from the teachings in the prior art, even if the particular prior art is in a different field, an examiner can decide that your invention lacks novelty and is not, therefore, patentable.

The Impact of KSR on Novelty Searches

What prior art can the examiner include in his analysis? In the recent KSR v. Teleflex case [2], the Supreme Court, in its decision authored by Justice Kennedy, issued guidelines for examiners when deciding the patentability of an invention. As these requirements impact the extent of your prior art searches and how you will need to structure your claims and define the

---

* The reader is cautioned that, through the "doctrine of equivalents" your product does not have to exactly read on a patent, as long as it is sufficiently close that your particular aspects would be equivalent. For example, suppose that a patent calls for attaching two components using an adhesive and your product, which is essentially the same, uses an epoxy, which is not an adhesive. It would probably be ruled that your product reads on that patent through the doctrine of equivalents. You are urged to consult your legal counsel for a more detailed explanation.

problem in order to circumvent that art, let us discuss how an examiner would be able to connect patents before and after the KSR decision.

Prior to the KSR decision, the combining of different references, especially in distinct and separate technological areas, was generally not allowed unless there was some motivation, teaching, or suggestion that they could be combined. If there were no mention of combining the references, there was a strong argument that it would not be obvious to do so. Moreover, if the references were from different technological areas, it could be argued that it was especially non-obvious to combine them. In other words, there had to be a strong motivation to combine the teachings of different references, especially those in different fields, before an examiner could claim that a combination of pieces of prior art rendered the present invention obvious. This changed due to the KSR decision.

Specifically, KSR did not negate the motivation test, but found that, by itself, a lack of a taught motivation was not sufficient to warrant patentability. There had to be other factors to make an invention nonobvious over the prior art.

Further, according to the KSR decision, a person of ordinary skill in the art would not be an automaton. Rather, that individual would have imagination and creativity so that, if the prior art fit together like pieces in a puzzle, the new invention should be construed as being obvious in light of the prior art. Moreover, if there are a finite number of recognized solutions proposed in the prior art, one of ordinary skill is assumed to be able to do the testing to see which ones work.

The mere fact that the prior art is in a different field from the present invention is no longer grounds for excluding it. Finally, it is generally assumed that adapting newer technology to older art only requires ordinary skill in the art unless additional significant problems have to first be solved to permit that adaptation.

While expanding the definition of obviousness, KSR also imposed some restrictions on the examiners. For example, the examiner must have some reason for combining references. Thus, if references are directed towards solving different problems, it can be argued that there is no reason to combine them. In addition, that references teach away from being combined† is an effective argument for patentability. Finally, if the combined art would require many possible solutions, of which only a few would work, it

---

† The term "teaches away" is commonly used in patent law when references argue against doing something, thereby making your invention nonobvious.

would be unreasonable to expect one of ordinary skill to test every possible solution.

The discussion of the KSR case is relevant to conducting prior art searches because it guides you, the inventor, into the range of issues that you will have to address with your search results. You cannot assume that you can search only within the field of your invention. You need to be on the lookout for art that, albeit in a distinctly separate area, may still be applicable to you. You must also look for literature that teaches that combining pieces of prior art would either be inappropriate or cannot be done. It also helps you focus on your definition of the problem that you solved. It is not sufficient to simply combine an arbitrary number of earlier patents and come up with a new product, even in a field that relies on technology that was not available at the time of the prior art. You have to focus on the problems encountered and solved to be able to combine the prior art.

With this, it sounds like you might be ready to throw up your hands and quit, afraid that prior art searches may be hopelessly complex and time consuming. That need not be the case. It is the goal of this chapter to supply the tools that allow you to conduct an expedited but productive novelty search.

Methods of Conducting a Search

In past years, conducting a search for prior art was expensive and involved. More often than not, you had to employ a search company that had access to the patent office data bank or a similar source of information. You could either submit terms or key words to be searched to a company to which you invariably paid a hefty fee, or perhaps even sit down with the individual conducting the search so that the search could evolve as it progresses. Once the search was completed and patents had been identified, you had to order copies of those patents and wait until they arrived. At that time you began the painful process of manually going through them, picking out those that were relevant and discarding the rest. More often than not, this process had to be repeated, as results were either inconclusive or you found a few patents that provided leads for further searching. Unfortunately, very often highly relevant material was missed by you and the searcher. However, it was unlikely that the examiner would miss those references, resulting in an obviousness rejection that might have been difficult to circumvent.

With the advent of the internet, searching has become much easier and available to individuals. The first place to search is the United States Patent and Trademark Office (www.uspto.gov). However, there are also commercially available search engines that you may want to consider using as well.

Each type of search engine has its own advantages. However, they also have disadvantages, which will be discussed forthwith. But before we do that, perhaps it would be advantageous to discuss how you can whittle down an incredible amount of prior art to a meaningful and comprehensible quantity. When conducting searches, please keep in mind how the KSR decision both broadened the scope of the literature that an examiner could consider and reduced your ability to argue against an examiner's inclusion or combination of art.

Fortunately, it is not necessary to find every single piece of what can be construed to be prior art, analyze that art, and prepare arguments as to why any combination of that art does not render your invention obvious. It is necessary to locate just the closest related art comprising approximately six pieces.

It is important to remember that there is no way that you can anticipate every piece of so-called[‡] prior art that an examiner may choose to cite. However, unless the prior art discloses your invention in, essentially, its entirety, the examiner will have to combine the pieces of art in some manner as to negate the novelty of your invention. If you can effectively argue that the closest pieces of art do not solve the present problem and give no clue as to being able to solve it, you can often render the citation of other art moot.

In some instances, an examiner can find related art that is close to your particular invention, but was missed or at least not cited by you. Even here, however, if you have included sufficiently close related art, there is a good chance that you may be able to transcend that presently being referenced by the examiner.

Finally, it is important to remember that you are establishing a patent portfolio aimed at owning the problem rather than just specific solutions to a problem. It is unlikely that you will be awarded every patent for which you apply. However, if you design and execute your patent strategy properly, including the prior art searching, you should be able to obtain most

---

‡ The term "so-called" is used here because the related art found by the examiner or may not be related to the actual invention. It is incumbent on the inventor(s) to critically analyze the examiner's findings and argue against the inclusion of proposed art that is not relevant to the invention.

of the patents and those that you do not receive should not significantly adversely affect your ability to protect your intellectual property.

In order to commence a prior art search, you need a starting point that allows you to focus the search. Fortunately, there are, in general, multiple potential starting points, some of which may be more effective than others in a specific instance. In fact, you may wish to employ several starting points to see which ones are most effective for a specific invention.

Key Word Searches

Perhaps the most commonly used, but often least efficient, starting point focuses on key words. Key words are appealing because they hone in on what you consider the novel aspects of your invention. In addition they are relatively easy to search using various on-line tools. Indeed, they can and do turn up much prior art. And that is one of their limitations. Used by themselves, they can turn up so much prior art that it is difficult to separate the proverbial wheat from the chaff. In addition they often miss much because the specific key words or terms that you choose to describe your invention may not be the same as those chosen by others to describe similar technology. This can be true even within your own company, let alone competitors. As an example, consider a patent entitled *Electrographic Reproduction Apparatus* [3]. Kodak, to whom this patent is assigned, typically uses the term "electrophotography" to describe similar technology. Xerox, which offers competitive products, generally uses the term "xerography".

It is clear upon reading this patent that the intended use of this technology is in the area of electrophotographic printers. The term "electrography" was used to broaden the coverage of the patent, which is perfectly legitimate. However, using either key word "electrophotography" or "xerography" would not have turned up this patent.

Moreover, it should also be apparent that, in general, using the key word "xerography" would not find most relevant Kodak patents, just as using the word "electrophotography" would miss many patents assigned to Xerox.§

It is also apparent that using key words can result in too many hits to be processed in a reasonable and timely manner. Even using the term

---

§ Using the key word "xerography" and the assignee name "Kodak" at www.USPTO.gov resulted in 126 hits. Conversely, using the key word "electrophotography" and the assignee name "Kodak" resulted in 913 hits. In contrast, searching on key word "xerography" and assignee name "Xerox" gave 2597 hits, whereas using assignee name "Xerox" and key word "electrophotography" had 2348 hits.

"electrography" resulted in 273 hits for patents assigned to Kodak and 101 assigned to Xerox.

How, then, can someone use key word searches to hone in on relevant prior art? The patent in this example discloses an electrophotographic printer that can produce duplex prints (i.e., documents printed on both sides of the paper) in a single pass of the paper through the printer. In contrast, duplexing is generally accomplished by first printing one side of the document, flipping the paper and sending it back through the printer, and then printing the second duplex side.

The technology described in this patent was innovative, but would probably not be found by searching for the key words for which you might normally search. Neither "electrophotography" nor "xerography" was mentioned in the patent. Searching just the abstract at the U.S. Patent and Trademark Office for the terms "duplex" and "printing" resulted in 358 hits. None of the hits showed the patent of reference 3.

This example was shown because it clearly illustrates some of the problems routinely encountered using key word searches. You can get too many hits to process. Alternatively, you can also miss important and relevant patents. If you increase the number of terms that you use in the key word search, you may reduce the hits to a more manageable level, at the risk of missing important prior art – art that the examiner will find. And, if you use terms that are familiar to you, you can readily miss important disclosures filed by others who happen to use, for whatever purpose, different terminology. It is important to remember that, although a patent is supposed to teach about the novel technology, it is not required to make a heroic effort that encompasses all terms that might be used to describe similar technology.

In summary, important prior art can be found using key word searches, but such searches can be problematic, generating too many results in some instances, too few in others, and often missing important prior art. It is suggested that, if you are using key word searches and know of certain prior art, it is definitely worthwhile to see if your search turns up that prior art. That is one way of performing some sort of test of the efficacy of your key word search. Key word searches can be quite useful if you have no other way of initially finding relevant prior art. However, there are other methods of searching that can be much more effective.

Enhancing Searches

So what alternatives do you have for starting a prior art search? You have knowledge. You probably know about some prior art and may have copies of some relevant patents. You may know individuals, preferably from competitive companies, who have worked in comparable technological areas. You may have some patents already. You may even know of applications that either you or your competitors have filed. All of these provide more opportunities for both refining and broadening your prior art searches. Let us discuss how to apply this information when conducting an effective and efficient prior art search.

We will discuss the tools contained in various search engines in the next section of this chapter. For the remainder of this section, let us focus on how you can use the knowledge of prior art that you already have.

If this is your initial foray into a technological area, you may have to commence your search using key words. These can evolve into a more productive, enhanced search. The good news is that, as you are trying to implement a patent strategy, many of your search results will apply to multiple patent applications and will also help to direct, facilitate, or guide further searches that focus on the specific advantages that each of your applications presents over that previously known.

Effective, efficient, and productive searching can be accomplished once you have at least one patent in hand. If the patent belongs to your company, that is fantastic. However, it is also quite good if the patent belongs to someone else. Either case furnishes you with opportunities to enhance your searches.

It is, perhaps, obvious that key words can be obtained from patents. For example, it is unlikely that one would have searched on the term "electrography" unless one knew specifically of the previously mentioned patent, *Electrographic Reproduction Apparatus* [3]. Patents also give you the names of inventors and assignee companies, both of which can be searched.

Features of some search engines allow you to forward-search patents. That is to say, you can search to see which patents and patent applications have cited a patent, allowing you to search the literature for relevant art subsequent to when a patent was issued or an application filed. This is a powerful tool, as a citation indicates interest in the earlier patent and it is likely to come up during examination.

The names of individuals, especially those in other companies, who are working in comparable areas are also likely sources of relevant patents. Again, once you have found some prior art, finding additional art becomes easier.

Do not neglect to search the published applications of yet unissued patents. Just because a patent has not been issued, and may not, in fact, ever be issued, does not preclude its being treated as prior art. Perhaps more to the point is that, by the time applications are published, they generally constitute prior art that may be, in fact, more timely and relevant to the older art.

One of the most powerful tools available through certain search engines is the ability to do so-called "vernacular searches". This is a highly effective method of generating a few relevant pieces of prior art. Instead of searching for key words, you simply type in your first claim and see what comes up. From the list that is generated, you then input your key words. This reduces the number of citations to perhaps half a dozen of the most relevant patents. It takes a few minutes and reduces a Herculean work load to a reasonable number of patents that must be perused.

Finally, file histories that are made during prosecution of a patent application, whether successful or not, are excellent sources of what the examiner viewed as prior art and how the inventors attempted to circumvent that art. Certainly, you should have ready access to the applications, and their associated office actions that have been generated, filed by your company. Even those filed by others can yield valuable citations that probably should be addressed in your disclosures. Remember that what one examiner considered as prior art and whether or not that examiner accepted a response from the inventors does not guarantee that the same art cited or the same responses would be accepted by another examiner for another patent application. However, being cited once raises the probability that certain art will be raised again for complementary patent applications. Let us now turn our attention to a few examples of commonly used search engines, how they can be used, and their strengths and limitations.

Search Engines

It is should be clear that conducting a search can be enhanced by various means as previously discussed and done without, in general, incurring an inordinate expenditure of time, effort, or money by the inventors. This can be accomplished using various search engines and/or hiring a company that specializes in patent searches. However, the information that you get back from commercial searches is only as good as the information that you input to the search company, and often benefits from your sitting down with the searchers during the actual search. Even so you will still have to sort through the results, which may or may not be relevant. I would urge you to consider conducting your prior art searches yourself or with your teammates.

Conducting prior art searches of the patent literature is more readily accomplished because of the prevalence of internet search engines. Some of these search engines are government run. Some are commercial and require hefty licensing fees to access them. Some are nominally free. However, there is a cautionary note. Many of the free commercial search engines make money by data mining. While these engines are often quite good and user-friendly, it may be advisable not to use them from your company's computers. It may be even more preferable to avoid accessing them from even your own computer and rely on public internet access such as in a library. After all, you may not want your competition to learn that you are searching their patents relating to a specific technology.

As a disclaimer, the author is not endorsing any particular search engines and, in fact, is making no pretense of evaluating them. There are just too many to allow for a just analysis of the strengths and weaknesses of each and, in fact, specific features change so often that focusing on these topics would cause this book to rapidly become outdated. Rather, features of several search engines that were found to be particularly useful will be discussed, as well as some perceived shortcomings with these engines. Let us start by discussing the United States Patent and Trademark Office (USPTO) website and search engine and, subsequently, explore the features of several other search engines.

The U.S. Patent and Trademark Office

The USPTO (www.uspto.gov) is, without a doubt, a tremendous resource and is free to use. This website offers a discourse on patents and trademarks, the patenting and trademark processes, and fees associated with each. Of more immediate pertinence, this website also allows the searching of both patents and published abstracts, as well as file histories.

To commence a patent search from the USPTO website, click on the tab at the upper left marked "Patents". U.S. patents are then accessed by clicking on the tab denoted PatFT. Once there, you decide whether you want to search from the default period of 1976 to the present or if you want to go back to 1790. You can limit your search to specific fields such as the inventor, assignee, patent number, or who has referenced the patent, as well as much other information. Alternatively, you can conduct your search through the default "all fields". You can enter two terms and fields in this operation. However, you also can delve into more detail. This is accomplished by clicking on the tab marked "Advanced" at the top center of the page. You can also search by patent number.

When using the advanced search option, it is necessary to use the correct Boolean format. For example, if you wanted to search for specific terms that might be found in the abstract, you would enter ABST followed by a backslash, or ABST/. Then you would enter the terms to be searched, with the appropriate conjunctions "AND", "OR", or "NAND" and whatever parentheses are necessary to connect the terms.

When you locate a patent that is of interest to you, you just click on the highlighted number and a text document of the patent appears. If you want to see figures, you will have to then click on "images", which will give you the first page of the patent. Clicking on "Full Document" on the left will present a PDF of the actual patent, complete with figures.

You can also search on the published applications by clicking on AppFT, and using the same methods and options as is the case when searching patents.

A major benefit of the USPTO website is the ability of individuals to conduct limited file history searches. Specifically, there is a tab for the Patent Application Information Retrieval (PAIR) page that, by inputting a patent number, patent application number, or publication number, you can see what transpired during the prosecution of the patent application, including the office actions by the examiner and the responses to those actions by the applicant.

There are two PAIR sites. The access to one is limited to registered patent attorneys and patent agents. The other one, designated as "Public PAIR" is accessible to anyone. This is an exceedingly useful site as it allows you to read the examiner's correspondence with the inventors of the application of interest, including the prior art cited by the examiner and the reasons for citing that art. It also allows you access to the response of the inventors to the examiner's arguments and how the examiner responded to those arguments. This is very useful information when writing your patent application, as it can possibly allow you to avoid the pitfalls that others have encountered when attempting to patent technology that is close to what you are proposing.

An annoying limitation of the USPTO search engine is that it is not very user-friendly and can be confusing, as they seem to use software from around 1990. For example, when conducting even a simple search using an inventor's name, say John Smith, you would have to input his name as Smith; John.

European Patent Office

The European patent office has its own website (https://worldwide. espacenet.com/) corresponding to that of the USPTO. This search engine, unlike that of the USPTO, is menu driven and fairly intuitive. It also allows access for searching in the patent offices of various European countries, along with the present status of a patent (is it active and have the maintenance fees' been paid?). This engine also allows computer-generated translations of patents, which can facilitate incorporating such prior art into your disclosures. An important feature of this search engine is that it readily allows forward searching as well as the searching for cited art in a patent.

World Intellectual Property Organization (WIPO)

Another useful search engine is presented by the World Intellectual Property Organization (WIPO), whose website is https://patentscope. wipo.int/search/en/result.jsf. This patent search engine also has translation and international link capabilities, but does not seem to be much more user-friendly than that of the USPTO.

Google Patents/Google Scholar

Google Patents (https://patents.google.com/) is a very user-friendly website that offers the ability to do vernacular searching. It can also link to Google Scholar (https://scholar.google.com/), which gives references to articles, in addition to patents. Google Patents also lists patent applications, thereby giving you access to that related art in one step. The capabilities of Google Patents is expanded by use of their advanced search (https://www.google.com/advanced_patent_search), which allows you to search by a variety of parameters including but not limited to phrases, key words, dates, inventors, and assignees.

Google Patents includes both United States and foreign patents. Overall, it is a very thorough search engine.

Innography

One of the most powerful and user-friendly search engines is that of Innography (https://app.innography.com/). This search engine allows vernacular and key word searching, allows search results to be saved, and has tools that rank the strength of a patents according to the search criteria.

¶ Many countries, including the United States and most European nations, require maintenance fees to be paid every few years. If these fees, which increase with time, are not paid, the patent becomes public domain and the holder of that patent ceases to have any legal protection from it, other than establishing prior art in the event that someone else seeks to patent the same or a similar invention.

Good, focused search results can often be obtained within minutes. The unfortunate limitation of this search engine is that it requires hefty licensing fees to use.

Concluding Remarks

As previously stated, the role of this discussion is merely to introduce the reader to some of the various available search engines. There are many others and comprehensive listings are available on the internet. A detailed evaluation of the strengths and limitations of each one is well beyond the scope of this book. Moreover, as is the case in most products ranging from automobiles to tools to sporting goods, much of the choice rests in what works best for you. You will need to spend some time exploring. In addition, you may want to use different search engines, depending on the specific data that you are seeking. Try out different search engines and decide what works best for you.

References

1. D. S. Rimai, *Patent Engineering*, Scrivener Publishing, Beverly, MA (2016).
2. KSR International Co. v. Teleflex, Inc., 550 U.S. 398 (2007).
3. D. K. Ahern, W. Y. Fowlkes, and D. S. Rimai, U. S. Patent #4,714,939 (1987).

10

The Mindsets of Innovators and Attorneys and other Cautionary Notes

Communications

Mankind possesses the gift of being able to communicate both verbally and in writing. However, there are occasions when one must wonder how encompassing that gift is. This is certainly true when there are interactions between inventors, attorneys, and, along the way, patent examiners.*

During his career, the author has had many opportunities to work with members of both the technical and legal communities. The people in both were world class and dedicated to achieving excellent results. The scientists, engineers, and technicians were very creative, knowledgeable in their fields,

---

* A patent examiner is not usually an attorney. Rather, an examiner is generally an individual who possesses a technical background and has been trained to determine whether or not a patent application fulfills the requirements of patentability. The examiner generally reports to a primary examiner, who must also sign off on all office actions.

and dedicated employees. Similarly, the members of the legal staff were thoroughly knowledgeable, willing to share their expertise with anyone interested, and intent on obtaining good patents. Both groups comprised individuals who wanted to protect the intellectual property they were creating. However, interactions between the members of these two groups often led to frustration.

The author has heard statements from technical people referring to attorneys such as:

"I gave them everything they wanted and they still got it wrong."
"I don't understand what they wrote."
"The application has no resemblance to my invention."
"Why do they want me to do all those things? I don't have the time for that."

Conversely, comments from the attorneys were often:

"They don't provide the information or data that I need."
"They are nonresponsive."
"They don't understand that what they have is not an invention."

And the list can go on ad infinitum. It boils down to the members of the technical and legal teams, despite all being very intelligent and knowledgeable, simply were not communicating well. This may have more to do with the mindset instilled in their training than it does with any inability to understand a common language.

Of Differing Mindsets

There is a quote often attributed to George Bernard Shaw that "Britain and America are two nations divided by a common language" [1]. A similar situation often applies to members of the technical community and the legal experts with whom they work to obtain patents.

Both groups want to obtain solid patents that accurately describe and protect their intellectual property. However, their interactions often lead to confusion and frustration among members of both groups, with each one not understanding what the other is saying or doing. It is important that you, as an innovator, understand what your legal counsel and the patent examiners are saying and why it is being said in a certain manner. Throughout this process, it is also important to recognize that there are legal consequences for saying something incorrectly. A patent is a legal document and not a scientific treatise.

Before you, a technically educated and innovative individual, throw up your hands in frustration, let us consider the source of this confusion and miscommunication. The confusion originates from the training that leads to a mindset within each group.

To illustrate this, let us consider what Newton's law of motion $F=ma$, with F representing an applied force, m the mass of an object that has been subjected to that force, and a the acceleration of that object under that force, means to members of each of these groups. To a scientist or engineer who has taken courses in mechanics and elementary physics and whom the attorney would classify as one of extraordinary skill in the art, this law means that to change the velocity of an object requires that a force be applied. However, to someone with this technical background, Newton's law also means what can be inferred. In other words, upon integrating the force over a distance encompassing a field that is conservative, that is, involves no dissipative forces, one can define a quantity W called the work done. Moreover, another quantity E is defined as the energy so that the change in energy is the inverse of the work done. If you raise a ball that is on a floor and place it on a table, you have performed work by imparting a potential energy to the ball due to its now elevated position. Moreover, if the path traversed by the object results in the object being back where it started, there is a symmetry which, according to Noether's theorem [2, 3], leads to a conserved quantity. In the present instance, this implies conservation of energy. In other words, if, after you carefully placed the ball on the table and it rolls back off, its state of energy is the same and no work has been performed. Conversely, if the path chosen requires the continuous application of a force, it would imply to you the presence of a nonconservative force field such as might be caused by friction or fluid drag.

Why is this discussion important? It is important because it defines what the term "means" means to you as a member of the technical community. We are taught to infer what a statement implies and to infer what we can. After reading a chapter in our textbook on mechanics, did we not have to solve problems that tested and strengthened our understanding of the material just presented? We were becoming, in legal parlance, individuals who had extraordinary skill in the art.

A technical person may then infer a generalization of Newton's law to the case where, during the acceleration, the mass is changing. This would occur, for example, with a rocket that is expending its fuel to provide the thrust. Such an individual would reformulate Newton's law in a more general form, namely, the force is equal to the time rate of change of the momentum P, which, in turn, is defined as the product of the mass times the velocity of the object, or

$$F = \frac{dP}{dt}.$$

A technical person would further infer that, as the rocket requires that work be done to launch the rocket, there must be an opposing force (i.e., gravity) that has to be overcome.

The legal expert would not infer any of the above analysis, as Newton's law, as first stated, simply relates the force to the acceleration, with the mass being the proportionality constant. Generalizing Newton's law to include a variable mass would be novel information that would not be obvious. Similarly, a legal expert would not infer the existence of gravity.

Going further, an individual of ordinary skill in the art would recognize that a force needs to be applied to the rocket in order to launch it. That individual would realize that, should the applied force cease, the rocket would fall back down. An individual of ordinary skill in the art would recognize that it would take more force to launch a more massive rocket, but would not realize that the necessary applied force would be different if the rocket is being launched from the moon, which is smaller than the earth, or from Jupiter, which is much larger.

In other words what would $F = ma$ mean to an attorney? It would mean exactly what it states. There would be no inferred concept of work or conservation of energy. Moreover, what would one of ordinary skill in the art be expected to know? Think back to life before you took your first physics course. You simply thought that you would have to apply a force to lift that ball off the floor. Now, suppose that the ball weighed 100 kg and you had to place it on the table. Perhaps you are strong enough to lift it, but perhaps not. As one of ordinary skill in the art, you realized that you can roll the ball up an inclined ramp, perhaps enlist the help of several friends to lift the ball, or perhaps use a block and tackle to elevate the ball.

As illustrated, you have several options that you could employ in order to elevate the heavy ball to the top of the table. These constitute a finite number of options that you can test. And, as specified by the KSR decision [4] discussed in Chapter 9, the reader of prior art is not an automaton and can be expected to conduct such tests. As one of ordinary skill in the art, it would be reasonable to expect you to know these options, but not necessarily which one would be the most suitable to accomplish this task. Perhaps the block and tackle presents the challenge of being able to be affixed to the ball. Perhaps having friends help lift it presents a challenge of positioning the people and establishing their grips on the spherical surface.

It would not be expected that, for example, if the ball were of immense size that precluded the practicality of the aforementioned known art, that you, as one of ordinary skill in the art, would be able to apply Archimedes' principle by building a container around the ball in proximity to the table and fill the container with a liquid of sufficient density to allow the ball to float up to the height of the table.

This analogy should be carried with you when reading patents as you are conducting prior art searches. The attorney who wrote the patent means exactly what is stated. It is not left as an exercise for the reader to infer other meanings or extensions. Such inferences or extensions may be opportunities for additional patent coverage that you may choose to seek. You must divorce yourself from the role of an expert or one of extraordinary skill in the art and just read precisely what the patent says. Do not add or subtract anything from the patent.

It is also important that you do not try to argue that the patent is wrong or what it teaches will not work. It is possible that such is the case, but that would have to be left to a court to decide during an assertion and is pretty much irrelevant as you prepare your application. Moreover, whether or not the prior art patent is correct (e.g., is valid) does not negate its constituting prior art that you will have to circumvent.

Let us consider some hypothetical examples. In the first example, let us consider a case where you are part of an artillery battery responsible for shelling enemy fortifications with heavy cannon-balls. Unfortunately, at this particularly late time in the battle, you are the only member of your battery who is not a casualty and you now have to load the balls into the cannon without assistance. You decide to roll the balls up an inclined plane into the muzzle of the cannon because the balls are too heavy for you to lift by yourself. You quickly invent a ramp that is supported just outside the muzzle of the cannon and proceed to file a patent application. The examiner rejects your application, stating in the office action, that a patent issued to a farmer who has built a ramp to load cylindrical bales of hay into the upper level of a barn, the ramp being supported by the opening of the barn door. The examiner states that it would be obvious in the present situation to mount the ramp immediately outside the muzzle of the cannon, so your stated invention lacks novelty.

It does not matter that the problem the farmer was solving differs from your situation. In either case, a heavy object with cylindrical symmetry[†] is being elevated to a given height using a ramp. That in one instance the ramp is supported by the structure into which the object is being loaded and in the other it is being supported by a member immediately outside

---

† An object having spherical symmetry inherently has cylindrical symmetry.

the opening would be considered as obvious in light of the specific geometry encountered in the intended application.

Now let us suppose that the cannon-balls, being as heavy as they are, had a tendency to roll uncontrollably back down the ramp as you repositioned your hands. To solve this problem you devised stops that would retract into the ramp as the cannon ball was pushed up the ramp, but, once the cannon-ball passed, they would extend by action of a counterweight, thereby creating a stop that prevents the ball from rolling back more than a preset distance.

The examiner now cites a combination of two patents. The first one is, once more, the farmer with his ramp to load cylindrical bales of hay. But that does not teach about the use of the stops. The examiner then cites devices in the parking lots of rental car agencies that retract so that a driver can drive a car into the lot, but, when not subjected to the pressure tires from incoming cars, is elevated so that, once in the lot, the car cannot back or drive forward out of the lot without damaging the tires. The examiner states that the farm ramp, in light of the parking lot stops, makes your invention obvious.

However, it would certainly appear that there is no reason to simply combine the teachings of these two patents. The parking lot is presumably level and the function of the device is to prevent someone from willfully exiting the lot without authorization. It is not to prevent a car from rolling back down an incline. There should be some reason for combining the teachings of multiple patents to create an argument that an invention is obvious, and that seems to be lacking here.

If the stops were incorporated for other purposes such as for supplying footholds that would allow a farmer to scale the ramp while pushing the bales of hay upward, arguing against an obviousness rejection might be more problematic. However, if the problem that you solved involves incorporating the retractable stops into the ramp and, to prevent the cannon balls from rolling off the side of the ramp by making the ramp concave, you might have a patentable invention.

The lesson to be gleaned is that you need to carefully define your invention in terms of the prior art that you find. There should be some reason for an examiner to combine the teachings of prior art, especially in unrelated fields. However, just because a field is unrelated to the one in which you are working does not mean that the prior art can, a priori, be ignored. KSR has made this fairly clear.

Also, as a technically trained individual (again, in legal parlance, one of extraordinary skill in the art) you should not infer meaning into prior art that is not stated. KSR allows you to adjust the length and materials of the ramp that you are using, compared to those used by the farmer.

Such adjustments (or experiments) to optimize such properties of a ramp to suit requirements of its specific application are considered by KSR to be within the grasp of one of ordinary skill in the art. It would not be expected that one of ordinary skill in the art would be able to curve the ramp or otherwise adjust its shape to facilitate using specific muscle groups as the object is slid up the ramp. In other words, you, as an individual of extraordinary skill in the art, recognized the role of potential energy and addressed that issue by making the ramp concave and utilizing the retractable stops when designing your ramp, whereas the farmer did not seem to do so, at least from the teachings in his patent.

Deciding what constitutes obviousness is often more of an art than a science. This is, unfortunately, often difficult for highly skilled technical people to grasp, as they are trained to infer what is meant by a disclosure, rather than what is meant by what the disclosure says. One distinguished attorney with whom the author has had the pleasure of working would always ask "what is the hook?" [5] He was looking for the feature that would not appear obvious to an examiner. Perhaps you, as well, should consider looking for such features or "hooks".

The lesson here is that technical and legal professionals are trained to think differently. As patents are legal documents, you must suspend the way that you normally think and begin to think in legal terms. This is not easy to do. However, it will go far in traversing the gap in communications that often exists in this area.

Cautionary Notes

The generation, prosecution, and assertion of patents are legal, rather than technical, endeavors. As such, they come with conditions and rules that differ from those familiar to members of the technical community. However, you need to play by these rules when working in this area.

Detailed discussion of the rules and constraints is best left for discussions with an attorney. However, it is worthwhile, in relation to this book, to discuss some common errors made by technical people. Let us discuss a few of these that are readily avoided.

Be Careful About What You Write

At some point you may find yourself in court as a witness in an assertion or infringement case and whatever you have previously written can come back to haunt you. This is especially true if your employer or you (if you are an entrepreneur or independent innovator) are asserting your patents against an alleged infringer. You are called to the witness stand as the expert witness, being an inventor named on at least one of the patents being asserted. The defendant in the case is trying to have your patents declared invalid. You find yourself in the uncomfortable position of having to explain why your written comments (given to colleagues within your company or to others) stating that you do not believe you have an invention are, in fact, incorrect.

How is it that you have to testify regarding comments that were confidential within your company? At the commencement of a lawsuit, there is a court ordered process called "discovery" in which all relevant documentation, including written documents, notes and annotations, computer records, and oral recordings, have to be turned over to the opposition's attorneys. Your comments are about to be discovered!

Comments such as "we did not invent anything", "there is nothing novel in what we did", or annotations on patents belonging to another company stating words to the effect "this would invalidate our patent" etc. should be avoided at all costs. Should you come across a patent that poses concerns to you, notes to your attorney and the other members of your team to the effect that "we should discuss this patent" are a lot more innocuous than would be the previously mentioned comments.

Validity of a Patent is a Legal Question

As a technical expert it is not presumed that you are a legal expert. Your attorney should decide your company's position regarding the validity of a patent. Even here, it should be recognized that such a finding is only one attorney's opinion and, absent a court ruling, does not invalidate a patent. You certainly can present evidence to your attorney that supports your concerns about the validity of a patent, but do not render a judgement yourself.

Attorney-Client Privilege

In general, communications between an attorney and the client are confidential, i.e., not subject to discovery. However, this does have limitations, especially if fraud is suspected. In other words, appending a written note to your attorney indicating that you do not think a solution to a technical problem, as proposed by a coworker, constitutes an invention would, in general, not be subject to discovery, unless fraud were suspected.[‡] However, the same note sent to a coworker other than your attorney would, in general, be discoverable and can be used by a defendant to argue that your patent is not valid.

In addition, bear in mind who the client is. Sure, you are working with the attorney that was hired or employed by your employer. That makes your employer the client – not you. You are the client to the extent that you are conducting business, as directed by your employer, with that attorney. Superfluous interactions between you and the attorney may not fall into that realm. Along this note, patent agents, although legally permitted to file and prosecute patent applications, are not attorneys and interactions with them may not be subject to attorney-client privilege.[§]

Patents are Very Specific

As discussed in detail earlier in this chapter, the thought processes of technically and legally trained individuals are often quite different. This frequently leads technical people, used to reading scientific and technical books and journal articles, to overarching or incorrect interpretations as to what a patent actually says. If you have a question regarding the interpretation or extent of a patent, seek legal guidance.

In addition to the difference in training, an attorney can also search the file history of a patent. This can shed additional light on both what is meant and what is the extent of coverage by the patent.

Solving a Different Problem from that Described in the Prior Art

As discussed earlier in this chapter, the field of the prior art is often not relevant. The question that the examiner will and you should ask is whether the teachings in the prior art can be combined with other art to anticipate your invention. A secondary question is whether or not there is sufficient

---

‡ If you appended a note, for example, to your attorney indicating that the proposed solution was not an invention because it had been previously disclosed, but it was decided to file on that solution anyway without disclosing the prior art with a fraudulent intent to obtain a patent, such a note would probably be discoverable.

§ To circumvent this difficulty, patent agents are often directed to work under the auspices of an attorney, thereby extending attorney-client privilege to the patent agent. However, if the agent is working independently, there may be no such legal confidentiality.

reason to combine the teachings in a patent that has solved a problem in an unrelated field with patents within your field of endeavor.

It can be especially valuable if you find prior art that teaches not to combine pieces of prior art or, in legal vernacular, teaches away from your invention. Anything that can steer an examiner towards accepting the non-obviousness and novelty of your invention will increase the probability of successfully prosecuting your application.

Consider Using a Patent Engineer

A patent engineer possesses technical expertise in your area, as well as a working legal knowledge of patents and patent law [6]. As such, a patent engineer can be a valuable asset to you when formulating and implementing a patent strategy. The contributions from such an individual include formulating a coherent and comprehensive strategy to protect your intellectual property, proposing claims, writing drafts of the patent applications, and conducting prior art searches. Perhaps most important, a patent engineer can free up your time to advance the technology while generating a valuable patent portfolio.

Concluding Remarks: Scientific Papers vs. Patents

Despite the fact that patents describe solutions to technical problems in sufficient detail as to allow those solutions to be practiced by someone possessing ordinary skill in the art, patents differ greatly from the literature with which most scientists and engineers are familiar. Specifically, scientific literature describes in sufficient detail the results of a study so that the reader, who is presumed to have some level of expertise in the field, can reproduce the study and obtain the reported results. The reader must also be able to ascertain that the reported conclusions are supported by the data, although agreement with those conclusions is not required.

As such, a scientific paper will omit details that are considered to be understood by the reader, while concentrating on the more critical points. In contrast, patent claims must report every aspect that is necessary to practice the invention and the disclosure must contain all the information necessary to support the claims. This was discussed to some extent in Chapter 8 and will be further explored in Chapter 12. However, for the moment, let us consider a simple, hypothetical example to illustrate this point.

Suppose you, as an inventor, want to write a scientific paper reporting your discovery of the process to hard boil an egg. For the sake of brevity, you would report bringing a quantity of water to the temperature at which the water boils, immersing the egg into boiling water, and allowing the egg to remain in the boiling water for a period of between five and ten minutes. It would be assumed that many technical details, including the quantity of water, the size of the container that holds the water and the fact that it is heat resistant, how the temperature of the water is elevated to its boiling point, how the container is supported while the water is being heated and the egg boiled, and how the egg is immersed into and removed from the water are all items that are assumed to be understood by the reader. Moreover, you, the inventor, might speculate in your paper on the coagulation of the protein that comprises the egg under the effects of the heat giving rise to the solidification of the egg.

While this style is one with which, presumably, most readers are familiar, it would be incorrect for use in a patent application. Every detail that is considered apparent to the reader of the technical paper (i.e. one of extraordinary skill in the art) and thus not discussed in the paper is important to describe this invention and should therefore be included in a patent application. How big a pot should be used and how much water is necessary? Can someone use a pot that holds half a cup of water or does that individual need a pot that holds over a gallon or something in between? Are there preferred size limitations? Perhaps one could use a gallon pot, but it would waste a lot of energy and take a lot of time to heat that much water. Could a Styrofoam container be used? How is the pot supported while heating? Do you hold it in your hands or is there a mechanical support that holds the pot over the source of the heat? Do you need such a source of heat or could you use an immersion heater or solar reflector or convex lens? And, of course, how do you introduce and remove the egg from the water? Do you toss it in or lower it gently?

Reading and writing patent applications is vastly different from the texts and journal articles with which we are familiar and requires a very different mindset to successfully accomplish. However, it is absolutely necessary for you to do this if you are going to properly protect your intellectual property. Writing applications will be discussed in more detail in Chapter 12.

References

1. http://quoteinvestigator.com/2016/04/03/common
2. E. Noether, Invariante Variationsprobleme, Nachr. Ges. Gottingen, pp. 235–257 (1918).

3. R. Courant and D. Hilbert, *Methods of Mathematical Physics*, vol. 1, Interscience Publishers, New York City, NY (1953), pp. 262–266.

4. KSR International v. Teleflex Inc. 550 U.S. 398 (2007).

5. R. Schindler, private communication.

6. D. S. Rimai, *Patent Engineering*, Scrivener Publishing, Beverly, MA (2016).

11

Reviewing Your Proposed Patent Applications

Look Before You Leap

You defined your invention, proposed at least one independent claim and, hopefully, a set of dependent claims that describe your invention. You conducted a prior art search and found several relevant patents or other documents that, perhaps, appear close to your invention. Perhaps you found articles or patents that, although not in your field, can be potentially argued to anticipate your invention.

Your invention is part of the technology that you and your teammates are developing for your new product. Similarly, the patent application on which you are presently working is part of the portfolio that you and your coworkers are developing to protect your valuable intellectual property. As previously stated in this book, when you develop and implement such a patent strategy correctly, you will have established a proprietary position that allows you to exclude others from your market, enables you to access technology belonging to your competitors through cross-licensing agreements, and produces profits for you or your company by charging licensing fees to those who need access to your patents. However, when done incorrectly, a patent portfolio may be a costly endeavor that provides little protection and just teaches others how to solve problems. In the worst case scenario, you may not even have your proposed patents allowed. You may even find that you cannot get your applications approved because of premature disclosure or contradictory statements made in your other applications.

It is at this time, before you submit your patent applications to the patent office, that it is vital for you and your teammates to assess what and when you intend to file. As the goal is to build a patent portfolio that allows you to own the problem, rather than just obtaining patents that propose specific solutions to specific problems, it is important that all your patent activities be coordinated. Let us discuss how you do that.

Is There other Relevant Art?

Presumably, other inventors on your team have also conducted prior art searches. While it would be anticipated that much of the uncovered art would be the same as that which you found, it is likely that other pieces have been discovered. Some of this may be due to the specific problems found with each invention. However, some of these findings might be due to the different search criteria employed. In either event, it is often worthwhile for team members to share their search results and, where appropriate, for you to include these references even if not directly related to your specific invention. This is especially true if you are trying to write a common disclosure that will encompass many or all of the patent applications and may even be useable for future applications.

It should be remembered that it is not just the claims in the prior art that are relevant. Rather, if the prior art discloses your invention anywhere, you will not be able to obtain a patent on that invention. Moreover, you should carefully examine the prior art to see if the separate pieces in combination can give your invention. An examiner can and will combine any number of references if the combination teaches that which you believe is novel, thereby negating the presumed novelty.

With that being said, you should read the art closely and determine whether or not there are any gaps that would prevent them from simply being combined. In other words, do you have to do something that is not taught or solve an unspecified problem in order to combine the separate pieces of art? If so, that can be used to argue against its being obvious to combine the art. Alternatively, the problems that you have to solve can give rise to separate claims, perhaps dependent claims.

In any event, you should discuss the prior art in the background of the invention section and explain why that art cannot just be combined. Again, please read the art carefully and do not infer what is not stated. Rather, discuss this art in the background section and describe the gaps that prevent that art from being combined.

Redefining the Invention

During your prior art search, you may have found related art that, either by itself or in combination with other prior art, renders your invention obvious. What do you do now? You have several alternatives. Let us discuss these possible situations and illustrate them with several hypothetical and actual examples.

Let us consider, as a hypothetical example, a problem whereby a prospector wants to separate water from sediment by passing the water containing sediment through a mesh filter. The mesh comprises a series of fine interwoven wires that serve to block particles in excess of 1 mm while allowing water to pass through. To provide sufficient rigidity, the wire mesh is attached at its perimeter to a frame. Moreover, the prospector also found that it is beneficial to make the frame circular to fit over the top of a five gallon bucket that is commonly sold in hardware stores.

During the prior art search, the prospector found that someone had invented a window screen that comprises interwoven wires to form a mesh. The mesh is attached to a frame that can be inserted into a window frame to keep out bugs.

Does this prior art preclude the prospector from patenting the sediment filter? The answer is most likely, "yes". Despite the fact that the window screen is blocking the entrance of insects while allowing the flow of air, the examiner would most likely conclude that it would be obvious to use a similar mesh for the purpose of filtration. That most windows are rectangular, whereas the preferred embodiment of the present invention would be circular would also, most likely, be deemed obvious as the frame would be designed to fit the shape of the opening.

The prospector now decides that the wire would corrode when subjected to the flow of water and decides that a mesh of comparable spacing made of a tough fabric such as nylon or polyester would be preferred. Would the fabric filter be patentable? Prior art search finds that polymers such as polyester or nylon are both woven into fabrics as cloth. The examiner would probably conclude that, even though the prior art does not specify the use of the polymer as a filter, it would be obvious to combine the wire mesh window screen with the ability to weave polymers such as nylon or polyester into a filter.

The prospector has several options in order to obtain a patent on the mesh filter. It is clear that, absent some very innovative change that would have to be made to enable the wire window screen to serve as a filter, that aspect would not be patentable.

The prospector could, then, focus on the use of the polymer mesh. Does the literature teach the use of polymer fibers of the thickness and spacing required for use as a filter? Better yet, does the literature teach why such a thickness and spacing would be problematic? For example, does the literature suggest that thick fibers would break under repeated bending or abrasion? These conditions would certainly be anticipated in the desired application as a filter. Or, do the fibers have to be attached in some manner, perhaps with an adhesive, to keep them separated so that unduly large openings are not created when making a mesh having the aforementioned spacing?

Alternatively, the prospector may find that it is advantageous to mount the mesh at an oblique angle so that the sediment can be washed off the screen into a capture vessel while still separating the sediment from the bulk of the water. This would prevent the mesh from becoming clogged and requiring a manual intervention to clear. Moreover, this would not be encountered with the window screen, whereby bugs would just fly off the screen.

In either case, the prospector has redefined both the problem solved and the solution to that problem (i.e., the invention) to circumvent the prior art. Again, it should be emphasized that the problem has to be carefully defined in the background section of the patent application, clearly stating why the prior art does not solve the problem, and the claims must clearly state every component necessary to practice the stated invention. Avoiding multiple responses to office actions that create a long file history is important and can generally be achieved by carefully defining the invention and discussing the limitations of the prior art in solving the problem that is the subject of the invention.

As an actual example, let us consider two patents [1, 2] in the area of electrophotography. Specifically, let us consider two patents relating to overcoats applied to the photoreceptor. These patents are U.S. Patent # 5,728,496(1998) hereafter referred to as Patent 1 and U.S. Patent # 5,807,651(1998) hereafter referred to as Patent 2.

In many modern electrophotographic printers, the photoreceptive element is organic, as opposed to harder inorganic photoconductors such as selenium. Organic photoreceptors have become more prevalent because of the higher quality of the printed images that are obtained with such materials. However, they are much more susceptible to being damaged, from either particulate contaminants that could perforate or abrade the photoreceptor or from ions generated by the required charging degrading the organic materials.

One way to address these issues is to overcoat the photoreceptor with a hard ceramic such as silicon carbide, a sol-gel, or an amorphous form of carbon having diamond-like carbon-carbon bonds and known as "diamond-like carbon" or "DLC".

There was a fair amount of research done at Kodak regarding such overcoats. However, there was also a lot of prior art [3–6]. The existence of that art precluded the ability to obtain patent coverage for overcoating an organic photoreceptor with a ceramic in order to minimize damage.

Patents 1 and 2 were obtained by redefining the problem solved by the use of the ceramic overcoats. Specifically, it was found that using a photoreceptor comprising a ceramic overcoat improved transfer efficiency when electrostatically transferring toner images from the photoreceptor to a compliant transfer intermediate [7].

But wait! Is this not just combining two known technologies, namely the ceramic overcoated photoreceptor and the compliant transfer intermediate, with each one doing exactly what it is supposed to do? The answer is no. As demonstrated by the examples cited in the patent, there was an unanticipated improvement in the transfer efficiency when both elements were used in combination with each other. This improvement was demonstrated in Patents 1 and 2 with examples that showed the improved transfer efficiency obtained when practicing the combination described in these inventions over and above that obtained when using either element separately.

Moreover, the improvement obtained was explicitly stated so that the examiner would have no problem understanding exactly what the inventions were and how the benefit had not been anticipated by any such combination described in the prior art. The fact that an unanticipated improvement had been obtained made this combination patentable.

Finally, the two patents were issued with regard to this combination. Patent 2 claimed the apparatus, whereas Patent 1 claimed the method of using the apparatus described in Patent 2. As discussed previously in this book, these embodiments are generally, at the present time, considered to be two distinct inventions, thereby mandating two separate patents.

There are some cautions that should be stated. It is generally desirable to broaden the independent claims as much as possible to afford the most encompassing protection and have the patent achieve the greatest value. However, because of disclosures in the prior art, it may not be possible to obtain broad coverage. Generally, more narrow coverage can be obtained by combining one or more dependent claims with the originally proposed independent claim, resulting in a more restricted patent. Alternatively, you might be able to find an unanticipated improvement that allows you to circumscribe the prior art. This was obviously done to obtain Patents 1 and 2. Whether or not such patents are of sufficient value is a business decision and has to balance the costs and the amount of information disclosed with the degree of protection that might ultimately be obtained.

If you decide to combine claims or redefine the problem solved, you should, once again, conduct a prior art search to ensure that you really do have a novel and patentable invention. Otherwise, you may be wasting a lot of money and disclosing information needlessly.

Are the Proposed Patent Applications Claiming Distinct Inventions?

It is far easier to try to claim the same invention in more than one application than might be initially apparent. Certainly, you and your teammates are solving distinct and distinguishable problems, so it should be easy to claim distinct and distinguishable inventions. However, let us suppose, for example, that both of you are working on a subsystem in which the electrical resistivity is important. For your problem, you have to specify a resistivity that would preclude ionization as two charged members having a high difference of potential are brought into contact.[*] You have found that, in order to do so while still allowing the full potential to be reached within a given process time, you need to have a resistivity of between 10^6 and 10^8 $\Omega\cdot$m. Your coworker, whose responsibilities includes product safety, finds that, in order to keep someone from being electrocuted, the same subsystem requires a resistivity between 10^7 and 10^9 $\Omega\cdot$m. There is an overlap in the claimed resistivity ranges. As far as an examiner is concerned, this would constitute claiming the same invention twice.

---

[*] This is often referred to as Paschen discharge. The electric field at which Paschen discharge occurs decreases monotonically with increasing air gap or distance between the biased components. Thus, if it is desirable to keep Paschen discharge from occurring as two members are brought into close proximity over a period of time, it is necessary to limit the current flow to the members by inserting a component of a controlled resistivity.

You can also run into this problem if your range of factors overlaps those in the prior art. If your range includes a previously claimed range, the examiner will determine that your patent application is not novel. This can occur even if your range abuts or is sufficiently close to that claimed in an earlier patent.

How do you work around these problems? If the problem arises because of overlap between the claims of two patents originating from your team, you can use a common disclosure and discuss both problems and their respective solutions. Then, when writing the claims, the claimed ranges would have to be limited so that they can abut, but not overlap, each other.

If the problem arose because another patent discloses, but not necessarily claims, a range where the values of the factors overlap, you will have to narrow your range. You can claim a subset of the previously reported values, especially if you can demonstrate an unexpectedly beneficial result with that subset. However, the difference between the subset that you are trying to claim has to differ substantially from that previously disclosed and you cannot be solving the same problem.

You can also try to bracket the previously disclosed range, again citing an unanticipated benefit, especially if you are solving a distinct problem.

The good news here is that, as you are generating a patent portfolio and, as such, filing either at the same time or in a period of less than one year apart, the other filings cannot be considered to be prior art, so they cannot be combined in a manner that the examiner deems makes your invention obvious. However, unless your applications are being filed on the same day, a disclosure of a solution to a technical problem in an application that claims a different invention will still count as a prior disclosure. This will be discussed in more detail later in this chapter.

Do the Proposed Patent Applications Encompass Your Technology?

By this time you should have a detailed plan laid out regarding the applications that you are planning to file. These should include both those applications that will be filed concurrently and in short order and those applications that will have to be filed at a future date.

Now is the time for you to review the technological problems that you have solved or have yet to solve. Do the applications that you are proposing to file encompass those problems? Are there alternative solutions that can be readily implemented, especially if the underlying assumptions are changed, that would allow a foothold by a competitor into your technology? If so, applications protecting that intellectual property should also be drafted. It should be remembered that you can only protect your marketplace and build a patent portfolio that is valuable if there is no easy way to circumvent your intellectual property.

Will Your Competitors Need Your Patents?

Patents are only of value if someone else needs access to your protected technology. This obviously includes competitors, but can also include companies in complementary or even totally separate businesses. When writing claims and drafting patent applications, it is important to be cognizant of the needs of others. After all, you do that with your products. You should consider your patents as part of your product stream, generating income and giving you access, through cross-licensing agreements, to technology owned by others.

Broadening the scope of your patents can be accomplished in one of several ways. Perhaps the most efficient way is to write your independent claims in such a manner so as to encompass the needs of others. In addition to this, and sometimes as an alternative, it may be possible to add dependent claims that focus on solving the problems that force limitations on the products of others. Finally, it may be necessary to file additional patent applications that address the needs of others.

With this being said, do not be short-sighted. Patents have a life of up to twenty years and technology rapidly evolves. Just because a competitor is not doing something today does not mean that your patents will not be needed in the near future.

Do You Need Patents Belonging to Others?

Perhaps a better way of stating this question is, do you need access to the technology that is protected by patents that are owned by others? If you do, you have several options. These include:

a. **Redesign your product so that it does not read on those patents.** This may be simple if the blocking patents are not part of a comprehensive portfolio and you have alternative designs that are reasonable to implement.

b. **Cancel your product's introduction.** Obviously, this is a costly and painful decision, but it might be necessary under extreme circumstances.

c. **Buy a license to use that technology.** This will most likely be the situation if the patents are owned by not-for-profit organizations such as universities, patent trolls, or financial or other institutions that use patents to generate a revenue stream, but who do not manufacture products themselves.

d. **Seek cross-licensing agreements.** This is most readily accomplished if the company in question needs access to your patents. The strongest position that you can be in would require that the company is practicing technology, without first obtaining a license from your company for patents that your company already owns. That requires a detailed analysis of the claims, conducted by an attorney done in conjunction with a technical analysis of the allegedly infringing products.

e. **Have an attorney conduct a legal analysis regarding the validity of the patents.** This is sometimes the appropriate course of action, especially if you have sound reasons for questioning a patent's validity. However, until a court rules that a patent is invalid, there are risks associated with taking that approach. Remember that, absent an actual and specific ruling regarding a patent's validity, your attorney's opinion is just his expert opinion and may or may not be consistent with a court's determination.

There is, of course, a sixth option. You can always decide to knowingly infringe upon patents owned by others. However, that could readily prove to be a very costly mistake, especially as willful infringement can incur substantially higher damages than inadvertently and in good faith infringing a patent. Even the costs of a lawsuit that vindicates your company can be extremely expensive.

Will Your Present Disclosures Compromise Future Applications?

In some ways this may be the most difficult question to answer because it requires determining the future. However, as the goal is to develop a patent portfolio that encompasses your intellectual property rather than just filing disconnected individual patents on specific inventions, you must keep this question in mind as you proceed.

You know what problems your team has solved. You also know what problems are presently being addressed. You may or may not know what problems you will have to face in the future or how you will solve them. Yet you will have to assess and balance your positions regarding these issues.

It is perhaps easiest to just postpone filing your applications until all the problems are solved and your product is ready for market. Unfortunately, that is often not a viable path. Patents are awarded to the first to file, not necessarily the first to invent. Procrastination may lead to your not being able to practice the very technology that you have invented. Moreover, as time goes on, it is more and more likely that certain aspects of your advancements may unwittingly or inadvertently be disclosed. This can happen through customer tours of your plant, trade shows, advertisements, or just inadvertently throwing out the trash in a non-secure manner. It can happen if a visitor sees confidential material left on a coworker's desk or from an unfortunate comment. Even if those gaining access to view your upcoming product sign a confidentiality agreement, an accidental disclosure can still occur.

Whatever the cause, these all constitute disclosures. Once disclosed, a one-year clock by which all filings must be completed starts ticking. And, if a competitor learns about your technology, they may be able to invent enough to impede your business.

You have to be careful. You do not want to disclose more than is absolutely necessary in your patent applications, as too much information, especially speculative comments, can prevent you from obtaining coverage on future developments. This is especially risky as the future developments will be building on what you presently have and can very readily result in disclosing enough that you have lost novelty for those yet to be determined technologies.

Presumably, it has taken time to put together the applications that you are proposing to file at this time. Your technology has likely advanced during that period. Before you file, you and your teammates should lay out what you have done and what has yet to be done and make sure that anything related to the future developments is scrubbed from the applications. It is all too easy to say too much, especially when writing a common disclosure that encompasses a plurality of patent applications. In the worst case scenario, it may be necessary to postpone filing your applications until some future problems are solved. However, that approach should be the exception rather than the rule.

Concluding Remarks

It has been emphasized throughout this book that your goal should be to develop an all-encompassing patent portfolio that allows you to own the entire problem or technology rather than just specific solutions to individual problems. To achieve this goal you must maintain a holistic view of your entire project, its challenges, and your accomplishments, and incorporate those factors as you develop and implement your patent strategy.

References

1. D. S. Rimai, P. M. Borsenberger, S. Leone, M. B. O'Regan, and T. N. Tombs, U. S. Patent #5,728,496 (1998).
2. D. S. Rimai, P. M. Borsenberger, S. Leone, M. B. O'Regan, and T. N. Tombs, U. S. Patent #5,807,651 (1998).
3. T. Takei, K. Saito, T. Aoike, and Y. Fujioka, U. S. Patent #4,845,001 (1989).
4. N. Kojima, H. Nagame, M. Seto, S. Yamazaki, S. Hayashi, N. Ishida, N. Hirosi, M. Sasaki, and J. Takeyama, U. S. Patent #5,059,502A (1991).
5. T. Mitani, H. Nakaue, and H. Kurokawa, U. S. Patent #5,168,023 (1992).
6. K. Kato, E. Shiozawa, and Y. Kishimoto, U. S. Patent #5,215,852 (1993).
7. D. S. Rimai, C. D. Baxter, M. C. Zaretsky, and L. H. Judkins, U. S. Patent #5,084,735 (1992).

12

Writing Your Patent Applications

Your Intended Audience

It is vital for you and your coworkers to always keep in mind that the goal of establishing your patent portfolio is to create something of value that protects the technological foundation on which your market(s) and product(s) are based. A portfolio that fails to achieve this goal is, at best, weak, leaving inroads that allow your competition to encroach into what you were hoping to be your space. At worst, you taught others how to solve the problems that you encountered. Thus, your goal is to craft a series of patent applications that will establish and protect your intellectual property and your place in the market. How do you go about accomplishing this?

It is imperative to realize that patent applications are presentations which, be they written or oral, have to first identify and incorporate two key components to be successful. The first is to identify the intended audience. It is vital that the presenter fully understand why the members of the intended audience should be spending their valuable time on the presentation. Moreover, the presenter must clearly identify the technical expertise of the audience. It is equally important that the material in the presentation be properly aimed for the intended audience.

The second key component of a successful presentation requires the author to decide what information has to be transmitted to the members of the audience and to make sure that those members are not distracted by irrelevant side issues, no matter how fascinating the author may find them.

Before discussing the intended audience of patents and patent applications, let us illustrate the concept of intended audiences that you, as a member of a technical community, commonly consider when making presentations. Such presentations often comprise three distinct audiences.

Papers that are to be presented to members of scientific communities, wherein the intended audience comprises individuals with expertise and interest in a particular discipline generally delve in depth into the scientific findings that are being reported, while omitting business details and speculative interpretations of the results. Alternatively, presentations made to technical coworkers having expertise in a variety of disciplines that may very likely differ from yours would not go into the same depth as presentations aimed at audiences with similar backgrounds to yours. Rather, they would discuss, relatively briefly, the findings. More time would be devoted, however, to discussing how coworkers could implement the findings into the project. Finally, presentations made to managers would focus on how the findings would impact product development.

The list of potential audiences is quite long. An article submitted for publication in *Physical Review B** would be written at a much more technical level than an article discussing similar material but being published in a journal aimed at the educated lay public, such as in *Scientific American*. In addition, it is important to present the information using the vernacular to which the audience is comfortable. For example, readers of *Physical Review B* are familiar with information presented using advanced mathematics. In fact, members of that audience would be uncomfortable if the material were presented without using mathematical formalism even if the information content was precisely the same. Conversely, readers of *Scientific*

---

* A research journal published by the American Physical Society (APS) consisting of peer-reviewed articles in condensed matter physics that are aimed at researchers.

American, in general, would not be conversant with the level of math commonly used in *Physical Review B*.

An all too common mistake made by researchers is to assume that those to whom a presentation is pitched all have the same expertise and interest in the topic in which the presenter is conducting research. While this may be the case when the presentation is being made to individuals working in the same field, such as those reading a *Physical Review B* article or attending a presentation at a scientific meeting, it is seldom accurate outside of those venues.

In summary, anyone presenting information to an audience, be it in written or oral format, must first address why the audience would want or needs that information, present it in a manner that is comprehensible to the members of that audience, and decide and focus on what information the presenter needs to present to that audience, omitting everything that is extraneous.

A patent application is a written presentation aimed at a specific audience with the intent of conveying specific information. The only complicating factor is that a single patent application should be part of a larger strategy and care must be taken to coordinate all aspects of that goal. Let us first discuss the makeup of the intended audience.

In the ideal world patents are granted in order to encourage technological advances. They are designed to teach discoveries to the public and, in exchange for teaching how to implement and use those discoveries, patents grant the inventors or their assignees the exclusive rights to practice those discoveries for a legal proscribed period of time (presently twenty years from the date of filing the patent application).

However, you live in a real and competitive world. If you were interested in teaching others all the technical aspects of your inventions, you would write a book or teach a course on the subject. From your vantage point, your goal is to protect your intellectual property rather than to teach the world all about its finer aspects. In short, your audience is not necessarily all those other people who are also trying to make a profit by offering novel products that would compete with yours or, worse yet, render your products obsolete. So exactly who comprises your intended audience?

The intended audience for your patent includes four distinct groups of people. These are the patent examiners, perspective jury members (along with legal counsel and judges) who would hear any assertion cases, and business people who might be interested in licensing your technology. A fourth group, made more important by the Leahy-Smith America Invents Act of 2011 [1–5] are the legal professionals and your patent applications must address this audience, as well. Let us consider the background and information that each of these groups would require.

First let us consider the patent examiners. These are the first individuals to whom your presentation (i.e., the patent application), must be pitched. After all, if you do not convince the examiners that you have an invention that is properly discussed and claimed in your application, you will not be awarded a patent. No one will negotiate with you for the rights to use a patent that was never issued. Worse, you will have disclosed your intellectual property to the world without gaining any proprietary rights to that property. And, as patents should be considered part of your value-adding product stream, neither you nor your company will be able to realize any revenues from licensing or access to competitors' technologies through cross-licensing agreements that having a patent could have enabled. Sure, there will probably be some individuals or organizations that want to emulate your advances. However, that does not benefit you. Your primary goal is to obtain patent coverage and, thus, examiners are the first and foremost members of your audience.

A patent examiner generally has some technical expertise in the area in which he or she is employed. That expertise can be an engineering or science degree, possibly augmented with some industrial experience. An examiner, although not a lawyer, does have legal training relevant to the prosecution of patent applications. In fact, after about 5 years of practice, an examiner can become licensed as a patent agent without taking the bar exam required for others seeking that certification.

An examiner is supervised by a primary examiner and both sign off on all office actions. This provides, in general, a measure of redundancy to ensure that the arguments presented to the applicant are reasonably cogent. Naturally, when correspondence is strictly written, there is still a strong possibility of a misunderstanding occurring. The course of action that can be taken in that case is presented in a later chapter that discusses the prosecution of patent applications.

An examiner will be looking for the following information:

1. Do the claims describe an invention; that is, is the solution to the described problem novel and non-obvious to one of ordinary skill in the art?
2. Do the claims describe the purported invention accurately and completely?
3. Are the claims supported by the information presented in the disclosure?

The examiner is not looking for a theoretical description of the solution or the problem beyond what is necessary to be convinced that the solution is not obvious. The examiner is not looking for assertions of how important the invention is or how disruptive† it will be to previous products.

The examiner is also not looking for a discourse on how long it took you to come up with the invention, although a discussion on what did not work may help convince the examiner that your solution is, indeed, not obvious.

The examiner is not interested in what you perceive the market value of the invention is or how it will help the economy of the United States.

The examiner is also not interested in the breadth of the claims aside from the fact that the broader the claim, the broader the related art that can be searched.

You are, in effect, asking the examiner to grant you a monopolistic right to practice your technology. The examiner must be satisfied that, in order to grant you that right, you have a novel solution to a technical problem that, was not only not described in the literature, but could not be cobbled together by an arbitrary number of patents, patent applications, or any other disclosures. The examiner will use his or her skills and considerable access to search engines to try to come up with what is termed by the patent office as related art. It is your job to convince the examiner that what you are describing is truly novel. As discussed in Chapter 10, the distinguished attorney Roland Schindler, with whom I have had the pleasure of working would always ask "what is the hook?" [6] by which he meant what would unambiguously convince the examiner that the application under consideration described an invention. This will be referred to as the "Schindler hook".

Jury members, who must render decisions in infringement lawsuits arising from your asserting your patents, are a second group that comprise your intended audience. These people will, in general, have neither legal nor technical expertise. However, they must be able to understand your inventions(s) and why the target of your assertion was, in fact, infringing upon your patent(s). Jury members tend to be intelligent individuals who are dedicated to delivering a just decision.

In fact, jury members will be subjected to a barrage of information coming from attorneys and technical experts on both sides of an assertion that attempt to explain to or convince the jury what a patent claims, what the claims mean, whether or not the defendant has actually infringed

---

† The term "disruptive" is often used to describe a new technology that renders previous products or methods obsolete. Examples include inexpensive, high quality digital cameras making silver halide photography essentially obsolete and the advent of inexpensive handheld calculators rendering slide rules obsolete.

upon the patent (legal jargon: the device reads upon the claims), and whether or not the claimed invention is obvious, thereby rendering the patent invalid.

On a personal level, you, as an inventor, would likely be called as an expert witness to describe your invention, probably developed many years earlier, to the jury. You would be questioned by attorneys representing your company and cross-examined by attorneys representing the defendant. You will have to explain your work in a way that the jury can understand while fending off the antagonistic questions of the opposing legal counsel. Would you prefer to testify about a well-written, comprehensible patent or one that requires you to explain many subtleties to the jury members? A well-written patent can go far in allowing jurors to understand the patent without having it explained in painstaking (and biased) detail.

What information do the jury members need? First, they need to understand the claims in a patent. Second, they need the information that would allow them to clearly and unambiguously determine whether or not the product sold by the defendant is infringing on your patent. After all, their first responsibility is to decide whether a defendant's product is reading on those claims.

In addition to being able to determine whether or not infringement has occurred, the jury may have to decide if your patent is valid. It is likely that the opposing counsel will argue that your patent is not valid for reasons of obviousness or because of a lack of novelty. Your patent has to present enough information that the jurors can see through those arguments and conclude that your patent does represent a valid invention and that the defendant has, in fact, infringed upon it.

It is further likely that the jury will have to assess damages, which is to say, how much money you lost because of the infringement. While an economic analysis does not belong in a patent application, a discussion of the importance of the invention to the enablement of the technology is important. In other words, does the invention represent a minor component that can be easily omitted with little loss or is the invention required to make the product work?

The third group of your perspective audience comprises managers or other decision makers who may be considering whether or not to license your patent(s). These individuals need to understand your claims. They also need a short summary or introduction that allows them to quickly ascertain whether or not your patent(s) are of interest to them. Their decisions are based on whether or not they need access to your patents in order to market their products.

The fourth group within your intended audience to whom you have to tailor the information presented in your patent are the legal professionals who will be involved in your assertions. Attorneys and judges will play pivotal roles in assertions ranging from trying to convince jurors what a patent does and does not cover to whether or not a patent is valid to validating the size of jury damages awards. And, while this has been the case for a long time, the roles of these professionals have become more important with the creation of the Patent Trial and Appeals Board, or PTAB.

The PTAB was created by the Leahy-Smith America Invents Act of 2011 with the intent of strengthening the patent system and avoiding expensive patent lawsuits by giving patent owners a relatively fast and inexpensive method of resolving assertions as an alternative of going to court. Whether or not the PTAB has achieved those goals has been the subject of an ongoing debate [5]. Moreover, as reported by Love and Ambwani in the University of Chicago Law Review [7], a very high percentage of claims challenged in the PTAB were found to be either totally or partially invalid. Whether this represents a shift in how legal authorities are going to view the validity of patents in general or just represents the results of those challenged at the PTAB remains to be seen. Suffice-it to say, this Board exists because of U.S. law and until, and if, Congress changes that law, it is an organization with which inventors and assignees will have to interact. Accordingly, patent applications have to be written with the possibility that the judges on the PTAB will be reviewing the resulting patents and, therefore, these individuals become an important fourth group in your target audience.

The legal professionals comprising this board, as well as those representing both the plaintiffs and the defendants, are interested primarily in whether or not the issued patent is valid. They will be looking at the claims and whether or not the broadness of those claims exceeds what the details in the specification supports, as well as whether or not the invention is obvious or lacks novelty. As such, they will be assessing the description of the problem that you solved, as well as why the prior art, either as individual pieces or as a combination, does not predict your invention. It should be remembered that, according to the Supreme Court in their KSR v. Teleflex decision [8], one of ordinary skill in the art is not an automaton and can reasonably be expected to try a reasonable combination of the teachings in the prior art to produce what you have patented. If that can be accomplished, it is likely that your patent will be found to be invalid. The Schindler hook [6] is at least as important when dealing with the PTAB as it is for initially obtaining the patent.

When Writing Your Patent Applications

While focusing your patent application on the members of the intended audience, it is vital not to forget that you and your team mates are putting together a patent portfolio. You do not want to teach more than is necessary in any specific patent application, remembering that what you presently disclose may constitute prior art in subsequent patent applications. Moreover, you do not want to unnecessarily discuss limitations of those patents that you previously obtained. Although such discussions may enhance your ability to successfully prosecute your present applications, disclosing limitations to your earlier patents may impede your ability to successfully assert them and may decrease their value for licensing. You want to optimize your output while not compromising previously issued patents that you own by limiting what those patents teach or claim and, at the same time, you do not want to prematurely disclose information that will form the basis of future filings. Finally, you need to remember that you can only claim an invention in a single patent and you must exercise due diligence to make sure that multiple patent applications do not attempt to make the same claims. The reader is reminded to compare and contrast the claims being proposed in all the applications in order to avoid redundant filings.

As you put forth your proposed patent application portfolio, you will have to prioritize your patents, as discussed in Chapter 7. It is absolutely essential that you avoid prematurely disclosing material on which you may wish to file applications at a later date. The best case scenario resulting from a premature disclosure is that you have one year before your present applications will be viewed as relevant prior art, whereby they may be combined with other art to render your invention obvious to the examiner. In the worst case situation, your applications may totally disclose the invention on which you intend to file, thereby precluding your ability to obtain patent protection.

Can the proposed applications be written using a common disclosure? If a single disclosure can be used to support the claims of multiple patent applications, you will save a lot of time and legal expenses. You would, of course, have to vary the disclosures somewhat to define the problem that was solved in the specific patent application and explain how the invention solved that problem, but a lot of material that must be contained within each patent application does not necessarily have to be uniquely written. The reader should note, however, that each patent application must be totally self-contained so that an examiner can understand the problem and its solution that you are claiming.

In order to address the issue of premature disclosure, now would be the time to decide whether the applications related to this project, or other similar projects, will require the disclosure of material relevant to claims in the other patent applications. If so, the applications will have to be filed on the same day so that one does not constitute a prior disclosure used against another. Let us now discuss the order and details involved in writing the various sections of patent applications.

Claims

The writing of claims is discussed in detail in Chapter 8. Accordingly, we will only present, as a review, some key features in this chapter.

As previously discussed, patents are legal documents, designed to establish a proprietary and monopolistic right to practice and commercialize your intellectual property. The technology to which you establish those rights are described in the claims. As such, claims are the preeminent portion of the patent, with all other information presented in the patent designed to support the claims.

Claims are broadly classified as either independent or dependent. The independent claims should be an explicit description of everything that one would have to do in order to practice your invention. As discussed with regard to Glock's patents in Chapter 8, not everything in the claim has to be novel. However, each phrase that is required for someone to practice the invention must be included. The claims in Glock's patents contained mostly known art, with the novel advancement called out at the end of the independent claims. However, as the known art was required in order to practice the invention, it had to be included. Had Glock failed to do so, the patent applications might have been rejected as being too broad or, even if they were allowed, might be ruled invalid during an assertion. Remember, you are writing initially to the examiner who has to see an explicit recipe of how to practice the invention.

Conversely, if material is not absolutely essential in order to practice the invention, it generally should not be included in the independent claims. Rather, if such material would be an important factor in the preferred mode of practicing an invention, it should be incorporated in one or more dependent claims that relate back to an independent claim.

As an example, let us, once again, consider the independent claim of U.S. Patent #6,538,677 also discussed in Chapter 8. This claim reads:

> "*A method for generating variable density halftone images with electrography comprising the steps of: grouping sets of adjacent pixels into a set of adjacent cells where each cell corresponds to a halftone dot of an*

image; selectively setting exposure levels for a gray scale writer to grow halftone dots from zero size to a desired size equal to or less than a maximum size by increasing exposure of one pixel in the cell one exposure level at a time until the pixel reaches a first total level of exposure and selectively repeating this step for the rest of the pixels until the cell is at its desired size and at an initial density; selectively adjusting exposure of the initial density of cells at the maximum size by sequentially increasing the level of exposure of each pixel in the maximum size cell by one exposure level at a time for each pixel until all pixels are at the same next level of exposure and then repeating this step to further increase the density of the cell to desired density; discharging areas of a charged image member in accordance with the selected levels of exposure of the prior steps to form a latent image of variable density halftone dots on the image member; enclosing a cylindrical magnetic roller in a concentric sleeve; rotating the magnetic roller in a first direction; disposing the magnetic roller and the sleeve in a container holding a two-component toner comprising hard magnetic carrier particles and toner particles; rotating the concentric sleeve in a direction opposite to the direction of the magnetic roller and in a direction co-current with an imaging member; contacting the sleeve and the latent image on the image member; transferring toner particles from the sleeve to the latent image to develop the latent image; transferring the developed image to a copy sheet; fixing the developed image on the copy sheet."

This claim, describing a half-tone imaging algorithm, incorporates into the independent claim the requirements of 1) *"a cylindrical magnetic roller in a concentric sleeve"*; 2) *"a two-component toner"*; 3) *"hard magnetic carrier particles"*; 4) *"rotating the concentric sleeve in a direction opposite to the direction of the magnetic roller"*; and 5) *"and in a direction co-current with an imaging member... "*

The above claim, as previously discussed, is for a mathematical algorithm that is useful for generating an electrostatic latent image on a photoreceptor, commonly used in electrophotographic printers. However, the claim is restricted, presumably unnecessarily, by imposing multiple conditions such as those enumerated above in items 1 through 5, as well as the additional requirements that we have not enumerated. None of these is necessary to practice the writing algorithm. Assuming that the inventors really did want to restrict their invention to an electrophotographic printer (as opposed to any other sort of electrographic printer, as suggested in the first sentence of this claim), they restricted it to a system using a cylindrical roller with a concentric sleeve. Not all electrophotographic systems even use that configuration.

The inventors further restricted their invention by requiring the use of a "two-component toner". It is presumed that they really meant "two-component developer" comprising magnetic carrier particles and toner or marking particles. "Two-component toners" do not exist and its inclusion would illustrate the point that the attorneys, being legal rather than technical experts, totally missed this important point and the inventors apparently did not read the application with sufficient care. The point here is that this requirement restricts the patent to a non-existent device, thereby rendering the patent worthless to the owner and merely teaches competitors about this writing system while providing no protection. This error may have been avoided if the inventors, rather than the attorneys, had written the draft of the claim. Making certain that the claims correctly describe the creations of the inventors is the responsibility of the inventors. The attorneys are there to ensure that all legal requirements are met.

It would have been far better to build a claim tree that includes both the independent claim for the writing algorithm and then tying the preferred methods of practicing the invention (e.g., in an electrophotographic printer) to dependent claims that relate back to either the independent claim or earlier dependent ones. Specifically, it would have been a more powerful patent to just discuss the writing algorithm in the independent claim. Dependent claims could have then been written that relate directly back to the independent claim, thereby providing further protection for the preferred mode of practicing the invention when using an electrophotographic printer comprising a "two-component developer". An additional dependent claim that refers back to the first dependent claim could have then claimed its use with a cylindrical magnetic core within a sleeve, omitting the requirement that the core and shell be concentric. This would have broadened the coverage of the patent. Moreover, the dependent claims could still be held as valid during an assertion even if the court rules that the original independent claim is invalid. This type of strategy would enhance the value of and protection afforded by the above patent.

Requirements that the toned image be transferred and fixed have absolutely no relevance to this invention and unnecessarily further restrict the value of this patent, and should have been omitted from the claims in total.

It should be noted that dependent claims can serve a valuable function when writing patent applications. They refine and claim the preferred mode of practicing the invention. As the dependent claims unfold, they restrict the invention. This can help during the prosecution of an application, should the examiner find that your initially proposed independent claim is too broad and reads on other literature. In that case, combining one or more dependent claims may result in your successfully obtaining a patent that maintains most of its value, although more limited in scope.

The limitation in scope may not be all that critical if this application is part of a broader portfolio aimed at owning as much of the problem as possible.

In summary, independent claims must completely state whatever is required to practice the invention in its most basic form. Refinements on ways in which the invention could be practiced should be included in dependent claims, which ultimately relate back to the independent claims, but may immediately relate back to other dependent claims. If something is not required to practice the invention, it should not be part of the claims, as this would unnecessarily restrict the patent, thereby limiting its value while teaching others how to solve the problem.

The claims are the foremost component of any patent and it is vital to get them right. When writing claims, you should ask yourself how you would explain your invention (that is, the claims) to members of a jury. It is recognized that subject material can make some inventions easier to explain than others. Glock's patents, with appropriate figures and props, could be readily explained by an expert witness to a jury. The imaging algorithm patent, notwithstanding the additional complications caused by unnecessary additions to the claims that would also have to be explained, would be much harder to present in a comprehensible manner. Again, assume that you, as the inventor, will be the expert witness explaining your invention in court.

There are two features that sometimes appear in claims that should, if at all possible, be avoided. The first is the so-called "form plus function". In this instance both a specific embodiment as well as its purpose or function are stated in the claim. As an example, consider a hypothetical claim for a device comprising a material mounted to a substrate and contained within a container with said container hermetically sealed to the substrate by use of an epoxy. This claim shows form – the use of the epoxy, but also shows function – to hermetically seal. If someone else used an O-ring to seal the container to the substrate and then used epoxy containing gaps to attach the container to the substrate, the patent would not be infringed as the epoxy could not serve as a hermetic seal.

The second feature to be avoided is claims that would require more than a single entity to infringe a patent. For example consider a patent for a method to attach two boards to each other by driving nails into boards. The claim, in this hypothetical example, reads: a method of attaching two board using nails by:

1. Making nails sufficiently long to penetrate the first board and enter the second;
2. Driving nails into the boards in such a fashion that the nail protrudes through the first board and enters the second.

The problem with this claim is that a manufacturer of nails may never use them to attach boards. Conversely, a carpenter would probably just buy the nails and not make them. As someone must practice every word of a claim in order to infringe on a patent, no one entity would be infringing this patent unless it both made and used the nails as described.

In addition to being able to explain each claim (or, alternatively, your invention), you should also ask yourself how you could unambiguously show that someone is infringing on your patent. It will be up you to enforce your patents.

Background of the Invention

This is the section in which you must "bait" the Schindler hook. You need to at least get the interest of the examiner and perhaps, ultimately, members of the PTAB. You need to clearly define the problem that you solved. And, at least of equal importance, you must be able to convince the examiner and the PTAB that the solution that you found is not obvious, based on the prior art. It is in this section that you must carefully define the problem so that its solution is not anticipated by any combination of the prior art. And, like the other sections of a patent application, other than the claims, once submitted to the patent office, this section cannot be revised. You need to get it right the first time.

You should discuss the limitations of the prior art in detail, delving into why they do not solve the present problem. In addition you should discuss why the prior art cannot be combined. However, you are cautioned to be very circumspect about discussing prior art that you own. You do not want to provide a paper trail that limits the applicability of your own prior art in case you decide to assert or license those patents. Patents owned by other companies are fair game for critical analysis by you.

Broaden Your Thinking

When defining the problem that your invention solves, broaden your thinking beyond the scope of your present goals. Can your technology be used to solve problems in seemingly unrelated fields? An example of that involved several engineers who approached me, in my role of an intellectual property manager, with a novel apparatus and method of fusing toner in an electrophotographic printer. (The reader is, again, referred to Appendix 1 for a more in-depth description of the technology used in electrophotography.)

In typical electrophotographic printers, the toner image is permanently fixed to a paper receiver after having been transferred from the photoreceptor by the application of heat and pressure over a short but finite period of time (typically 100 ms). In order to apply heat for the time required to soften and fix the individual toner particles into a coherent mass and onto the paper, a heated roller comprising a metallic core that is overcoated with an elastomer is used. A typical fuser operates at temperatures around 150 °C, which is high enough to soften the toner but low enough not to destroy either the paper or the elastomer.

The engineers approached me with a novel fuser that eliminated the need for the elastomer, stating that the proposed fuser should be able to heat to 150 °C without a problem. I asked if there was any reason that it could not be used at 1,000 °C, to which they responded that the paper would burn. I then asked them "who said anything about paper?" The key here is that they were thinking about a fuser for a high speed printer, whereas I broadened its potential to a sintering device for ceramics that could enable a printer-like device to be used for structural printing. Yes, this would subject the proposed invention to additional searching, but would not the much greater range of applicability and potential value be worth the effort?

Refocus Your Invention by Redefining the Problem

In some instances it may be necessary to refocus your invention. One such instance involved a study of using diamond-like carbon (DLC), a ceramic, to overcoat organic photoreceptors to make them more robust in an electrophotographic engine. Because there were many examples in the patent literature of ceramics being used for this application, the ability to obtain a patent on the use of this material was pretty much precluded.

During electrophotographic testing of the DLC-overcoated photoreceptors [9, 10] that transfer a toner image from a compliant intermediate transfer member‡ to paper, unexpected results were obtained, thus providing the bait for the Schindler hook. However, just combining the DLC overcoated photoreceptor with a compliant intermediate without some unanticipated benefit would not be sufficient to enable patentability. Specifically, it is necessary to define the problem that your invention solved so that the combination of components results in an unanticipated benefit over and above any that would be known from the separate benefits of each. In this

‡ Compliant transfer intermediates are discussed in Appendix 1.

particular case, the known benefits obtained using a compliant transfer intermediate included simplified paper handling and improved transfer to paper using small toner particles. The advantage to using a ceramic over-coated organic photoreceptor included a more robust photoreceptor that would require less service.

The problem encountered was that using a compliant transfer intermediate requires additional transfers of the toner image, as the image (or images in the event of printing color separations to produce a color print) have to be first transferred to the intermediate and then from the intermediate to the paper. The transfer efficiency is less than 100% for each transfer, resulting in image degradation, thereby compromising the ability to combine these features. Moreover, using a ceramic coated intermediate was found to decrease transfer efficiency when practiced by directly transferring from an organic photoreceptor to paper, compared to doing a similar transfer without the use of the ceramic.

However, when combining the compliant transfer intermediate with the ceramic overcoated organic photoreceptor, the transfer efficiency was unexpectedly improved [9, 10]. The problem is now defined as the necessity of improving transfer when using a compliant transfer intermediate. The solution is presented in the section of the patent application entitled "Detailed Description of the Invention". Refocusing the invention and the presentation of the unanticipated benefit obtained by combining these features set the Schindler hook.

Would it have been better to have obtained a broader patent that covered just the use of a ceramic overcoated organic photoreceptor? The answer is obviously "yes", but, in light of the prior art, this was not going to happen and it would have been a waste of time and money to pursue that endeavor. Are the patents obtained valuable? To the extent that both compliant transfer intermediates and ceramic overcoated photoreceptors are both commercially used, yes. It should be noted that whomever owns a patent has the full rights to that patent. In other words, a competitor could not use that combination of technology even to solve a different electrophotographic problem, even if the competitor were not interested in improving transfer efficiency.

Another example of properly defining the problem solved by an invention involved the thermal assisted transfer process used to transfer electrophotographically produced images. This process, described in more detail in Appendix 1, involves heating a thermoplastic coated receiver to a temperature sufficient to soften both the thermoplastic and the toner while pressing the receiver against the toner image-bearing photoreceptor. Upon separation the toner image has transferred to the thermoplastic, which, upon heating, acts as a hot melt adhesive to hold the toner to the receiver. Upon separating the thermoplastic-bearing receiver from the photoreceptor, the toner image is transferred to the receiver.

The problem encountered is that the thermoplastic not only bonds to the toner, but it also bonds the receiver to the photoreceptor, thereby preventing transfer from occurring and, in fact, damaging both the photoreceptor and the receiver, to say nothing of totally ruining the printed image.

The solution to this would be to introduce a release agent that facilitates separation. The obvious choice would be to coat the photoreceptor with that release agent, as that would facilitate both release and transfer. Indeed, such an application does work. However, the problems encountered were 1) any release agent applied to the photoreceptor would have to be frequently renewed, presumably in-situ. This would complicate the printer as a suitable replenishment station would have to be included in the machine; and 2) the presence of a release agent on the photoreceptor adversely affects the deposition of the toner onto the photoreceptor during the toning of the electrostatic latent image.

If we merely stated in the application that the problem solved was the bonding of the receiver to the photoreceptor and that the problem was solved by introducing a release agent, no patent would have been awarded, as the use of the release agents for the purpose of preventing bonding was well known.

So exactly what was the problem the invention solved? We had to redefine it. It was not just incorporating a release agent into the transfer process. It was incorporating a release agent into the transfer process in a manner that was automatically renewable and without degrading the toning of the electrostatic latent image.

The Schindler hook was baited by describing the entire problem, along with the limitations of known prior art in the Background of the Invention section. The definition of the problem includes 1) the need to use a release agent; 2) the need to replenish the release agent in-situ; and 3) the avoidance of degradation of the toning of the electrostatic latent image.

In fact the examiner initially missed much of the definition of the problem, focusing instead of just the use of the release agent. However, our attorney replied to the office action, stating "no one in his right mind would try to improve transfer by putting the release agent onto the component that is supposed to accept the toner". The Schindler hook was set. The examiner acknowledged that incorporating the release agent in this manner was not known and yielded unanticipated results. The patent was allowed [11].

The proper and complete definition of the problem solved is crucial if your patents are to be allowed. As was hopefully made clear in the examples cited, this often involves going beyond the description of the immediate problem (for example, releasing the receiver from the photoreceptor) and delving into the reasons that implementing the obvious solution is not feasible. If you do not do this, you will likely not be able to traverse the prior art.

You should list all the limitations of the prior art and the benefits obtained by your invention in the Background of the Invention section. You do not know on what the examiner will focus and describing the many limitations that you have overcome may help convince the examiner (or members of the PTAB) that the prior art could not solve those problems. If writing a common disclosure to protect multiple but related inventions, it may be desirable to define all the problems solved by the inventions, although it may be necessary to modify this section to focus in on the problems solved by the specific invention that will be claimed in each individual patent application. Again, the goal is to ensure that the examiner understands the problem or problems that a particular invention solves.

Once you have stated the problem, clearly enunciate why the prior art, either as individual pieces or in combination, does not solve the problem.

As previously discussed, an examiner can include prior art that lies outside the technological area in question. However, according to KSR v. Teleflex [12], there must be some reason to consider combining prior art from other fields with the art in the present field of the invention.

It is absolutely vital that you properly define the problem or problems solved in this section. If your advancement solves more than one problem, describe all of them and how it solved them. Be explicit.

This is the one chance that you will have to bait the Schindler hook and catch the attention of the examiner and, perhaps later on, the members of the PTAB. It is absolutely vital that this be given a lot of thought and analysis before submitting your patent application.

Detailed Description of the Invention – The Intended Audience

The next section of a patent application to be written is the Detailed Description of the Invention. This section may include several subsections in addition to what is often termed, by itself, the Detailed Description of the Invention. These include the Figures, Description of the Figures, and the Parts List. Alternatively, each of these subsections can be treated as separate sections, but probably should be written concurrently with your description.

It is vitally important that the inventors remember their targeted audiences and what information they must convey to the members of those audiences when writing this section of the application.

There are three target audiences. The first is, naturally, the patent examiners, namely the examiner and the primary examiner, both of whom will be deciding whether or not your advancement meets the legal definition of an invention. As previously stated, convincing the examiner that you have an invention, as opposed to a novel combination of known technologies, is absolutely vital. Failure to obtain a patent in the first place will pretty much eliminate its value to you, other than, perhaps, keeping someone else from patenting the same invention at a later time.

Examiners will be looking for several items in the Detailed Description of the Invention section. First, they will be looking to see if every claim is supported in this section. In other words, the details of every claim must be explicitly stated in this section. Unlike a college textbook, there can be no "left as an exercise for the reader". Each claim must explicitly and totally describe what is necessary for someone to practice the invention. The Detailed Description section must explicitly state the same material, in the exact and same detail, that is in the claims. Failure to do so will result in your patent application being rejected.

The examiner will also be looking for enough information to determine that the proposed invention is, indeed, novel and nonobvious. This is the section wherein the Schindler hook is set. In particular, the examiner must be convinced that your inventions cannot be cobbled together by any combination of related art, with the related art being determined by the examiner.

The examiner will be looking for correct legal format, including correct formatting, especially of figures, and proper patent office defined grammar. These are items with which your legal counsel can help.

Finally, the examiner will determine whether or not the filings and responses were done in a timely fashion, according to statute.

The second group of people in the target audience for your patent comprises members of a jury who will be trying to understand the details of your invention and whether or not a defendant is actually infringing on that invention. The jury members may also be tasked with determining the damages that you suffered – how much money you lost, as a result of an infringement. When writing this section, picture yourself as an expert on a witness stand explaining your invention to a jury of laymen.

The third group of people comprising your audience is the jurists – the legal experts of the PTAB and the attorneys arguing before them. These people will be looking at the same factors as did the examiners, but perhaps more critically, as the plaintiff's and defense attorneys try to convince the members of this board what the patent means and does not mean and why the patent is valid or invalid, depending on their perspective.

The one group of people to whom this section, or, for that matter, any section of a patent should *not* be aimed consists of your peers, which is the "wrong audience" as far as patent applications are concerned. These are generally considered to be people of extraordinary skill in the art and may include coworkers of comparable education or experience, as well as individuals who occupy comparable positions at competitive companies or who are members of the same professional societies as you, etc. And yet, all-too-often, inventors write descriptions of how they solved a problem in a manner that is more suitable for their peers than the audience to whom this section is intended. This is a serious mistake and can compromise both the issuance of patents and your ability to assert them.

When drafting disclosures, inventors should consider the following guidelines to avoid making some common errors:

a. Do not use local vernacular or terms that are not well understood. Every company develops its own phraseology to describe its technology and uses terms that someone outside that particular company would probably not unambiguously understand. Alternatively, terms may be used in a more limited or different sense than is common. Yes, you can be your own lexicographer, but you must define your terms. Unless otherwise defined, all terms assume their common meanings, which may not be what you mean.

b. Do not speculate beyond the present invention or inventions. This does nothing more than compromise your ability to file subsequent patent applications by prematurely disclosing information. This can be the case even if that information is not fully developed and further research or development is required. Yes, speculation is fine when discussing your invention with colleagues within your company. It is not good beyond that.

c. Do not assume that you must understand or explain how your invention works in order to obtain a patent. Explaining how your invention works can be either a pro or a con, depending on the technology being presented and whether or not the explanation can help convince the examiner that your invention is not obvious. It is necessary just to explain what to do in order to practice your invention. However,

an explanation can be used against you in the future, arguing that subsequent inventions are obvious in light of your
explanation. Again, your colleagues within your company
would probably appreciate understanding your invention,
along with all its implications.

d. Be explicit in describing your invention. In his book on
blacksmithing [13], McRaven relates how a blacksmith told
him how to forge weld. According to the instructions, "get
the iron hottern' (*sic*) hell and beat the devil out of it…" That
description may or may not be adequate for an artisan skilled
in the art of blacksmithing (i.e. one of extraordinary skill in
the art), but would certainly not be adequate to describe how
to practice forge welding. How hot is hell and how hard and
with what weight hammer and how many blows does it take
to drive the devil out?

At all times, bear in mind that in the Description of the Invention you
must describe your invention, its operation, and the evidence that it actually solves the intended problem to the appropriate audience. The intended
audience, which does not consist of those of extraordinary skill in the art
(although the examiner would most likely not be categorized as one of
ordinary skill in the art), must be able to follow your teachings and practice
your invention. Although, according to KSR v. Teleflex [12], one should
not assume that ordinary skill in the art equates to being an automaton and
some reasonable amount of testing is permitted, the patent must be fairly
specific. As opposed to the widely used statement in college textbooks, it
cannot be left as an exercise for the reader.

The Detailed Description of the Invention

It is hopefully clear by this time that specific information regarding the
invention is required in this section of a patent application. Before discussing what information should be included in a patent application, it is
worthwhile to repeat a cautionary note. Specifically, it is very important
that patent applications relating to distinct inventions that are discussed in
a single application be filed on the same day to prevent one from being used
as prior art against the other. Perhaps the simplest example of this would
be two inventions, the first being a piece of equipment that accomplishes
a certain task (an apparatus invention) and the second being a method of
accomplishing a task using that equipment. It should be evident that the
filing of one discloses, out of necessity, both inventions. Of course, when

putting together a patent strategy, the chances of releasing information prematurely increases and due care must be taken. In case of a question about disclosing information, consult your attorney.

With that being said, let us now explore what needs to be stated in this section. Everything that is required to practice the invention must be explicitly described in detail here. There should be no details left for anyone to fill in or complete. There can be nothing left as an exercise for the reader, nor should anything be treated as being intuitively obvious. All information that is required to practice the invention must be included in the claims, irrespective of whether or not it is a novel feature. Moreover, if something is stated in any claim, it must also be disclosed in this section.

Any preferred methods of practicing the invention, sometimes referred to as the "best mode of practice" should also be included in this section, again in explicit detail. And, if something is a preferred method of practicing the invention, it should, in general, be included as one or more dependent claims.

Details that may be instrumental in your ability to practice the invention should be included. For example, in US Patent # 4,968,578 [11], which discloses the use of a release aid incorporated into the thermoplastic, there is a description of how the thermoplastic can be coated onto the paper. As stated in the patent, this includes "solvent coating, extruding, and spreading from a water latex". It was also stated that extruding is preferred because it does not require the use of solvents.

Suitable thermoplastics, including their glass transition temperatures[§], coating thickness, and surface energies, are disclosed because they are relevant to being able to practice this invention and are included in the claims.

In that reference, the first dependent claim states that the substrate is paper. Why is this a dependent claim? The reason is that other substrates could be used, but paper is preferred.

There is discussion as to how to incorporate the release agent into the thermoplastic coating because this is pertinent to someone being able to produce the receiver and practice the invention.

These details are mentioned here because they are examples of factors that technical people may often assume are understood by the reader and, therefore, do not state them. However, that would be aiming the disclosure

---

§ The glass transition temperature, commonly denoted as T_g, of a glassy thermoplastic polymer is the temperature at which the stiffness of the polymer, more properly referred to as its Young's modulus, decreases sharply from about 3 GPa to about 3 MPa within a small temperature range.

to the wrong audience and failure to include that information may prevent you from obtaining a patent.

It is also important to include examples that demonstrate the advantages obtained when someone practices the invention, as well as the limitations observed when the invention is not practiced (i.e., counterexamples).

Counterexamples serve several purposes. By highlighting the limitations of existing technology, counterexamples serve to illustrate the improvements obtained when practicing the invention. However, they also help establish the novelty of the invention, as going beyond the factors claimed by the invention have demonstrable negative consequences. In other words, you are trying to establish novelty by showing that you have an unanticipated result. A clear improvement that is not obtained when someone does not practice the specifics of the invention certainly helps establish novelty.

The inclusion of counterexamples also helps establish non-obviousness. Specifically, it is hard for an examiner to assert that your invention is obvious in light of related art that includes values of factors[¶] demonstrably outside your claimed invention. This is especially clear if you actually demonstrate, using counterexamples wherein the values of the factors are outside your claimed values and show that one does not achieve the claimed benefits using those factor values.

Examples and counterexamples should clearly demonstrate the importance of the claimed values of factors in an invention to avoid the possibility of an examiner citing, as prior art, a patent that describes a similar invention, but whose factor values lie just outside of the values you claim. For example, if you have a process that requires the application of between 100 and 150 volts, an examiner may cite that your invention is obvious in light of someone using 90 volts. However, if you demonstrate that 95 volts does not allow you to obtain the benefit of your invention, that reference falls aside.

Although it is important, as already discussed, not to include material that is not related to your claims, it is also important to recognize that the claims you initially propose may not be allowed. You should have enough disclosure to support rewriting your claims to establish patentability. Clearly, you will have sufficient disclosure to support the dependent claims and those claims can often be combined with the original independent

---

¶ The term "value of factors" is commonly used in statistically designed experiments to designate the size of a variable or "factor" that may be under consideration.

claims to establish an invention of more limited scope. However, you may have to totally rewrite your independent claims and you will need a sufficient description to support that rewrite. Anticipating possible examiner rejections and allowing enough disclosure to support new claims without unduly compromising your ability to file future applications is a fine art and should be discussed with your teammates as well as your legal counsel.

Figures

Figures, while not always required, are frequently necessary to properly and completely describe the invention, how it is used, and/or the prior art. Suitable subjects for figures include, but are not limited to, schematics showing the structure and components of the apparatus and the inventions incorporated therein, chemical structures, process flow charts, graphs depicting results obtained when either using or not using the invention, and pictures of the results obtained when and when not practicing the invention. Figures are often part of the Detailed Description of the Invention section. However, they may also be presented as a separate section. This is especially true when figures are used to illustrate both the background and actual invention.

When deciding on what figures to include in your patent application, think about your intended audiences. Obviously, examiners will want figures that clearly show the invention. However, you should also think in terms of your being on the witness stand, explaining your invention to the lay jury members. They do not, very often, understand the technological area in which you are working, let alone the problem you solved or how you solved it. Under these circumstances, what charts or slides would you want to be able to show the jurors? You should also remember that, while it may be possible to correct figures that are not in proper legal format, you will not, in general, be able to change, add, or remove figures once you have submitted your patent application.

There are legal formatting requirements for the figures and, if you are not cognizant of them, your attorney may help guide you. Alternatively, you can enlist the aid of a draftsman who routinely does this type of work. In any event, clear and detailed sketches or drawings will certainly facilitate getting a set of figures into the final, required format. Let us now examine an actual figure from U.S. Patent #8,780,147 [14].

This patent relates to a modified ink-jet process, but the specific field or details of this particular invention are not relevant to the present

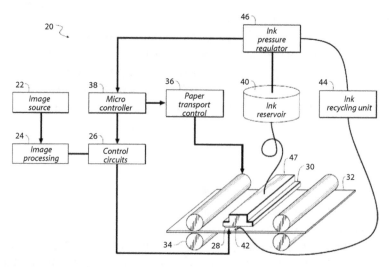

Figure 12.1 An actual example of a figure from U.S. Patent # 7,870,147 (2014).

discussion. Rather, let us focus on the details of the figure, shown in Figure 12.1.

This figure is a schematic of a continuous inkjet printer [15], designed to continuously emit a stream of ink that is either deposited onto a receiver such as paper or deflected into a catch basin.[**]

The figure, itself, is numbered (in this case as "Figure 1" in the patent) and it is called out, as such, in the patent application. If a figure presents existing technology and is used to set the stage for discussing the invention, it can be called out in the Background of the Invention section of the application instead of in the Detailed Description of the Invention. If components of the figure highlight the invention or parts thereof, it should be discussed in the Detailed Description section. Also, if information contained in a figure is pertinent to describing the invention, it is worthwhile to further discuss that figure in the Detailed Description section even if it was discussed in the Background section. The explanation of your invention should be completely contained in the Detailed Description section even if it means being somewhat redundant. This section should be self-contained.

[**] An alternative inkjet technology relies on a so-called "drop on demand" process, whereby ink droplets are produced only when they are needed to form an actual pixel on a receiver. This technology is often more suitable for low volume inkjet printers.

Every component in a figure should be given a number and that number explicitly called out when discussing the particular component in this section. Such a numbering scheme is seen in Figure 12.1. In fact, the entire printer engine is given a number 20 in the upper left corner. The numbering system chosen is arbitrary, but it is highly recommended that you choose a system that would facilitate comprehension. For example, if a printer contains separate heads that are similar in function but jet different colors, it may be worthwhile to designate them with the same numerical value followed by a different letter.

All numbered components should be listed in a table referred to as a **Parts List**. The purpose of this is to allow members of your intended audience to quickly and easily understand the function of each component. Again, think of the members of the jury as you explain your invention. As you show multiple figures, would it not facilitate comprehension of the jurors could just look at a slide showing what each component was?

The example figure used here also lists each component by a title such as "Paper Transport Control" for part number 36 in the figure and "Ink Reservoir" for part number 40. This is not necessary but can help to keep the description clear.

In addition to the parts list, patents generally contain a section entitled **Brief Description of the Drawings**. While this can be included in the Detailed Description section, it usually precedes that section. The information contained for each figure in this section is similar to the caption beneath Figure 12.1. The goal, once again, is to facilitate comprehensibility of the patent.

There should be an additional topic discussed in the Detailed Description of the Invention section namely how you would conclusively know that someone's product is reading on your claims. It will be up to you to enforce your patents and, to do so, you must be able to demonstrate that your patents are being infringed.

It is recommended that you discuss the measurements, tests, or alternative methods that would conclusively demonstrate the infringement. However, as differing methods of measurement or tests can yield different results, it is suggested that you disclose a single method of testing, if possible. If it is not possible to specify a single method of demonstrating the infringement because varying operating conditions may mandate that different methods be used under different circumstances, it should be specified what method should be used under specific conditions.

Let us demonstrate this issue with a specific albeit hypothetical example. There is no shortage of skillets being sold today alleging to have better non-stick surfaces.[††] Many are advertised by showing fried eggs or burnt food being readily removed. However, how would you know if a surface of a skillet were truly less adhesive or more abhesive[‡‡] than another skillet's surface? Mittal has tabulated several hundred adhesion tests [16], each of which was designed for a specific purpose. To say the least, varying tests routinely give contradictory results. Let us illustrate the issue of determining how strongly food such as a fried egg will stick to a skillet using a standard "peel test", such as discussed by Mittal, whereby an adhesive material such as a tape is applied to a surface and then the force needed to peel the tape is measured. This begs a number of questions. What is the adhesive material? 3M, for example, markets a variety of tapes ranging from those with very strong adhesion to Post-It Notes that readily peel. The age of the tape is a factor as the adhesive material on tape changes with time. We are probably all familiar with objects taped years ago wherein the tape has fallen off and we are probably equally aware of items whereupon we wanted to remove applied tape, but found it too hard to do because of the time. 3M even markets a series of masking tapes for painting with varying durations for being able to remove the tape.

In addition to the above, tape can be removed by peeling at 90°, or normal to the surface. Alternatively, one can fold the tape back on itself and peel it at an angle of 180°. One can even try to shear the tape by pulling it at 0°. Each generates a different value of the adhesive force.

Moreover, how much pressure was applied to the tape and for how long can also affect adhesion. Most of us have probably gently pressed masking tape against a surface when we wanted to ensure that we would be able to remove it. Similarly, I am sure that most of us have had the experience of items falling off that we taped to a surface. Our response was to press harder on the tape for a longer period or to apply more tape to cover a greater area.

And, of course, we have all probably had to remove price tags from items that we bought and found that, upon application of heat, the tag became much less adhesive.

Mittal's suggestion was to use an adhesion test that most closely simulates the conditions under which the item will be used. That is good advice, but it still does not unambiguously address how a skillet's abhesive nature is to be determined so that there is no question of whether or not someone else is infringing on the patent on the abhesive coating on the skillet. The cautionary note here is that being able to specify in a patent how

---

[††] The technical term for a surface to be non-adhesive is "abhesive".

infringement would be detected can go far in convincing a jury that your patent has been violated.

Other Sections of a Patent and Their Intended Audiences

Congratulations! By this time you have almost finished your patent application and, if done correctly, you have given the background and perhaps even defined the problems and solutions for the other patent applications that you intend to file concurrently. There are just a few more short sections that you need to write.

Every patent has a **Title**. The title may or may not be descriptive, but should have a maximum length of 7 words. The title does not have an intended audience, but may help to point someone to a solution to their problem and may generate interest in licensing technology to solve a problem.

The **Field of the Invention** section relates to the department in the USPTO that will receive and examine your application.

The **Brief Description of the Invention** and **Abstract** sections are generally little more than restatements of the first claim, which, after all, defines the invention. These sections are often sufficient to attract the attention of others to whom you may wish to license your technology or with whom you wish to enter into cross-licensing agreements.

Finally, a list of **Cited References** should be included. The list should aim for about half a dozen closely related pieces of prior art; however more or fewer are acceptable if that is most appropriate. Please remember that you will have to supply the patent office with copies of the cited art. Please also remember that you are citing art because it helps you define the problem and make the case as to why your advancement is legally an invention; that is to say, why it is novel and non-obvious.

Other Information that You Will Have to Provide

As the submitter of a patent application, you should be prepared to provide a **List of Inventors**. Inventors, as discussed in Chapter 2, are individuals who have made an inventionable contribution to at least one claim in the patent application. Just being a teammate or coworker is not sufficient. Also, explaining how an invention works does not make one an inventor. And certainly someone acting as a skilled pair of hands under the direction of an inventor is not an inventor unless that individual came up with some-thing that constitutes an inventionable contribution to a claim. The reader is cautioned that inventorship often becomes an emotional issue for individuals who may have made important contributions towards advancing the technology, but who may not meet the legal criteria of inventorship. In case this situation arises, or if there are any other questions regarding who is named as an inventor on a specific patent application, the individuals should be prepared to present their contributions to your attorney, who will decide the issue. Having the correct inventors is extremely important as a failure to do so may result in a patent being found to be invalid.

With that being said, as a patent application goes through prosecution, claims change. As such, individuals who are initially listed as inventors may not be inventors when the patent is finally awarded. Alternatively, someone not initially listed as an inventor may become one as claims are added or changed. Since inventorship is a legal issue, in case of difficulty deciding whether or not someone is an inventor, discuss that person's contributions to the advancement with legal counsel.

You will also have to provide several legal documents. These include an assignment of the invention (who will own the rights to the patent) if appropriate. The inventors will also have to sign documents, under penalty of law, attesting to the fact that what they stated is true to the best of their knowledge and that they have read and understood the patent.

And now, if you have not previously done so, is the time to sit down with your attorney or patent agent and prepare the application for submission to the patent office, as will be discussed in the next chapter.

References

1. http://bitlaw.com/source/America-Invents-Act/index.html
2. https://en.wikipedia.org/wiki/Leahy-Smith_America_Invents_Act
3. https://www.gpo.gov/fdsys/pkg/PLAW-112publ29/content-detail.html
4. https://www.uspto.gov/aia_implementation/bills-112hr1249enr.pdf
5. P. J. Pitts, Wall Street Journal pg. A 13 (June 11, 2015).
6. Roland Schindler, Esq. Private communication.
7. B. J. Love and S. Ambwani, University of Chicago Law Review https://lawreview.uchicago.edu/page/inter-partes-review-early-look-numbers.
8. https://www.supremecourt.gov/opinions/06pdf/04-1350.pdf (2006).
9. D. S. Rimai, P. M. Borsenberger, S. Leone, M. B. O'Regan, and T. N. Tombs, U. S. Patent #5,728,496 (1998).
10. D. S. Rimai, P. M. Borsenberger, S. Leone, M. B. O'Regan, and T. N. Tombs, U. S. Patent #5,807,651 (1998).

11. W. A. Light, D. S. Rimai, and L. J. Sorriero, U. S. Patent #4,968,578 (1990).

12. https://www.supremecourt.gov/opinions/06pdf/04-1350.pdf

13. C. McRaven, *Country Blacksmithing*, Harper and Row, New York, NY (1981), pg. 87.

14. T. N. Tombs and D. S. Rimai, U. S. Patent #8,780,147 (2014).

15. S. F. Pond, *Inkjet Technology and Product Development Strategies*, Torrey Pines Research, Carlsbad, CA (2000).

16. K. L. Mittal, private communication.

13

The Next Step: Prosecution of Your Patent Application

Introduction

You and your team have advanced technology by coming up with novel and nonobvious solutions to a series of technical problems related to an envisioned product that has unique capabilities that should take the market by storm, making all other products obsolete. You want to recoup your R&D investments as well as the costs of tooling and distribution. In other words, you want to build a wall of protection around your intellectual property that will keep competitors from encroaching on your market. To do this you recognize that you will have to build a patent portfolio.

You have conducted a thorough prior art search. In part this search was accomplished because of your knowledge of the marketplace. You know what your competitors' products and their capabilities and features are. You also know the limitations of those products. That is how you recognized your opportunities and, by solving problems that encumbered your competition with the limitations of their products, you have designed and developed your technology.

You have exercised due diligence in conducting your prior art search. You have inputted into this search your knowledge of your competitors' products, as well as information gleaned at scientific conferences and publications and trade shows. You have also used the modern on-line patent search engines to find existing patents and published patent applications.

You have discussed holistically the technology advances made by you and your colleagues and, based on both these findings and the results of your prior art searches, you have developed a patent strategy that aims to both protect your intellectual property and, in addition, would be strongly desired or required by your competitors.

You have carefully defined the problems that you have solved in a way that, hopefully, circumvents obviousness or lack of novelty objections that an examiner may envision. You have proposed sets of claims that should cover those inventions upon which you and your teammates are ready to file concurrently and have written disclosures that support those claims without compromising your ability to file additional applications representing further advances in the future. You are sure that the proposed applications do not attempt to claim the same invention more than once.

Your disclosures may be common to multiple applications or you may have found it preferable to write separate disclosures. In either event, the disclosures also support the dependent claims and give you latitude should you have to revise your proposed claims based on the resulting office actions.

And you have peered into the future and have envisioned how your strategy will proceed with additional filings as your technology continues to advance.

You have worked hard and accomplished much by getting your applications into their current state. However, you recognize that patents are legal documents and, as such, need someone with legal expertise to weigh in and advise you. It is time to meet with legal counsel.

Meeting with Your Legal Advisors

Hopefully, you have had the opportunity to discuss your proposed patent applications and your patent strategy with your legal advisors prior to the present time. This is often the case with larger corporations that have their own staff of patent attorneys and agents, but is often not the case for smaller companies, individual inventors, or entrepreneurs. It may not even be true for all proposed patent applications with larger companies, as even large corporations with powerful legal staffs sometimes have to supplement their legal departments by using outside counsel.

If your company has and you are able to avail yourself of your corporate patent attorneys, you may be very fortunate. These attorneys can often spend more time with you because they are not concerned with billable hours. More important, they generally develop a level of expertise in your company's technology that allow them to critically assess your proposed patent applications and can offer valuable suggestions regarding necessary details that you should include, avoiding obviousness rejections, formulating and implementing a strategy around your technology, etc. In-house patent attorneys often have the technical skills that allow them to help define the Schindler hook [1]. This will facilitate writing the patent applications so that the examiner recognizes the novelty and nonobviousness of your advancement and allows your patent. This is extremely valuable, as they will be approaching the application from the legal background required when filing patent applications instead of a technical background.

Perhaps most important is that your legal advisors can help you draft your claims so that you do not have to correct your claims and your discussion of them in the Detailed Description of the Invention section. This can become very involved when a specific application is part of a broader proposed portfolio and a change in one application can necessitate corresponding changes in the others. Moreover, such changes can be exceeding problematical when there is still material that may require further development but would likely be the subject of future filings.

While the use of outside counsel generally puts more burden on the inventors to get the information in patent applications correct, they still provide extremely valuable services. They will be the ones looking at your claims to make sure they are legally correct and properly describe the invention. They should also be ensuring that your disclosures properly support the claims.

At least as important as ensuring that all legal requirements for the patent applications have been met is ensuring that your legal experts have developed an understanding of both the inventions and your patent strategy. Examiners will respond to your applications in what is termed "office actions", in which they will be citing both legal and technical reasons for their decisions. It will be up to your attorney to help you understand the legalities and to help craft the responses to these office actions. It is up to you, the inventor, to be sure your attorney understands the technical aspects of your proposed inventions, including how they solved technical problems and why the related art failed to solve those problems.

Improper responses can cost you additional money, delay or prevent you from obtaining necessary patent coverage, unnecessarily limit the scope of your patents, and can endanger future filings. Most attorneys are conscientious and seek to properly represent their clients. If you believe there is a communication issue between you and your attorney and that you have not been able to resolve despite repeated efforts, you may want to seek another attorney. However, there is a caveat to this. Please make sure that you are not changing attorneys just because you are getting a message that you do not want to hear. Your attorney may understand your inventions and may be raising concerns based on his or her legal expertise. It is incumbent upon inventors to understand what their attorneys are saying as much as it is necessary for their attorneys to understand the inventions. Communication is a two-way street.

It is also likely that legal counsel will prepare the additional documents, mentioned in Chapter 12, that you must also submit at the time of filing your patent applications. These include the notice of assignee and the oath that you are the inventor and that you have read and understood the patent application, under penalty of law.

It is also worthwhile to note that your legal counsel represents whomever engaged that particular law firm or attorney. If you are an entrepreneur or a creative individual, working on your own and hiring your own attorney, you are probably the client. However, if you are an employee of a corporation or company and that corporation or company engaged that attorney, you are not the client. Rather, your employer is. Attorney-client privilege is a long-standing tradition in the legal field, but it is important for you to remember that confidentiality with you is limited to the extent that your actions are consistent with those of your employer.

Likewise, care should be exercised when engaging a patent agent rather than an attorney. Patent agents, although legally empowered to handle most aspects of obtaining patents,* are not attorneys. Under some circumstances, such as when the agent is an employee of a law firm that has been engaged to pursue patent-related activities, attorney-client privilege would generally extend to cover interactions between the agent and the client. However, if the agent is acting as an independent practitioner, there may not be such privilege. This can become significant during an assertion, because, in the absence of attorney-client privilege, records of discussions may be subject to the discovery process. Suffice-it to say, make sure that

---

* Patent agents are not authorized to represent clients before the Patent Court.

your interactions with legal representation is covered by attorney-client confidentiality.

Submission of Your Patent Application

The patent application has been completed and you and the other inventors are satisfied with it. Alternatively, if the application is part of a larger portfolio, it has been reviewed by the inventors and other team members, as appropriate, and everyone is satisfied that the disclosed invention is properly described by the claims.

Again, please remember that before filing your application(s) you, the inventor, may be the one called as an expert to the witness stand in the event of an assertion to explain to lay jurors the problem that you solved and how you solved it, i.e. your invention. It will also be your task to convince them that the solution was not an obvious combination of information specified in the prior art, as the defendant's attorneys will probably allege. And, it may fall upon your shoulders to explain how the defendant's product reads on your claims. This is your last chance to make sure that you understand all the information that you are submitting and to which you have sworn that you have read and understood.

You are now ready to submit the application(s) to the patent office. The actual process of submitting your patent applications to the patent office is fairly straightforward, but rather involved. It also has to be done correctly, in accordance with government requirements. And, like most things in which the government is involved, there are forms to be filled out and fees to be paid in addition to the applications being submitted, accompanied by copies of the art cited in the applications. It typically takes an experienced paralegal several hours to organize and submit a patent application. While it is possible for you to try to reduce your costs by handling the submissions yourself, it is probably not a good use of your time and would be difficult for you to do. It is definitely recommended that your application submissions be handled by your legal representative.

You have two options on the method you choose to submit your patent application. You could send in paper copies of the written application or you could submit it electronically. There are two principal reasons for submitting it electronically:

1. It would give you an earlier priority date, namely the day that it is submitted. Sending in paper copies would generally take at least a day to arrive. Remember, we live in a competitive

world and a patent is awarded, under present law, to the first to file rather than the older standard of the first to invent.

2. The patent office appears not to want to handle paper any more than do most modern businesses. In order to encourage electronic and discourage paper submissions, the patent office charges an additional fee for paper submissions. Presently, the fee for an electronic submission is $280, with an additional fee of $280 (total fee of $560) for paper submissions.

As mentioned in Chapter 8 a patent typically contains between one and three independent claims and up to twenty total claims. The reason for this is economic, as each independent claim in excess of three incurs an additional fee of $420 and each claim in excess of twenty requires an additional payment of $80. It is important that you map out your patent strategy so that you focus on those claims that will add value to your patents and do not just add claims because you can.

Fees associated with patent applications and patents can change and the reader is referred to https://www.uspto.gov/learning-and-resources/fees-and-payment/uspto-fee-schedule#PCT%20Intl%20Stage%20Fee for an up-to-date fee schedule.

Once the application is submitted, the waiting period begins. While the time between the submission of an application and its final disposition varies greatly, periods between two and three years are not uncommon and much longer times can transpire, especially if the prosecution is complicated by numerous rejections. Be patient.

And be aware that eighteen (18) months after having submitted your application, it will be published and accessible for everyone to see at the USPTO Patent Application Information Retrieval (PAIR) website [2]. Unless you are licensed to practice before the Patent Office, you will only have access to "Public Pair". Everything that you have disclosed is now public information.

Prosecution of Your Patent Applications

As previously mentioned, the process of guiding your application through the patent office is referred to as prosecution.

When your application arrives at the patent office, the date of submission (the priority date) is recorded, a patent application number is assigned and, based on what you have stated to be the field of the invention, it is sent to the appropriate department. There, it is assigned to an examiner, who will ultimately decide whether your application properly describes an invention.

The examiner will respond to your application at least once and, during the course of prosecution, probably on multiple occasions. The responses are termed "office actions".

Initial Screening by the Examiner

The examiner will first determine if the claims in the patent are searchable. If, for example, they do not appear to present a solution to a technical problem, e.g. if you have submitted a proposed perpetual motion machine, your application will be rejected outright. However, other factors will also affect search ability. For example, incorrect usage of the antecedents[†] "*a*" and "*the*" will make the claims unsearchable. Let me illustrate this point and the reason for it in a simple hypothetical example.

Let us suppose that a claim requires that you insert a ¼-20[‡] machine screw through a ¼ inch diameter hole in a piece of metal and fasten it to the metal with a nut. The claim would read as such:

> "Position *a* metal member comprising *a* thickness, *an* abutting surface, *a* surface that is opposite to *the* abutting surface, and *a* hole that penetrates through *the* thickness of *the* metal member;
> Insert *a* machine screw comprising *a* shaft with *a* nominal diameter of ¼ inch, *a* length that exceeds *the* thickness of *the* metal member by at least 1/5 inch, and *a* head, a portion of which exceeds *the* diameter of *the* hole in *the* metal member and *a* thread pitch on *the* shaft of 20 threads per inch through *the* hole in *the* metal member;
> Affix *a* nut having *a* thread size commensurate with *the* shaft on the side of *the* metal member that is opposite to *the* surface abutting *the* head of *the* machine screw;
> Tighten *the* nut to draw *the* head up against *the* surface opposite to *the* abutting surface of *the* metal member."

---

† The term "antecedent" is used here instead of the more commonly used term "articles" because "antecedent" is used in patent law.

‡ ¼-20 describes the diameter of the machine screw (just under ¼ inch so that it can fit through a ¼ inch clearance hole and the number of threads per inch, in this instance is twenty (20).

Why is all this painstaking detail necessary? Remember, you are writing claims so that the lay public can understand how to practice your invention. You are not writing them for your coworkers. The examiner will be looking for that detail in order to decide whether or not there is sufficient detail to allow someone to read your patent and practice your invention. Now let us discuss why this detail is necessary. Let us first examine the use of the antecedents "a" and "the".

The first time an item is mentioned, it is prefaced by the antecedent "a" because it does not refer to any particular item. Indeed, initially you were merely selecting a piece of metal that has a hole in it from, perhaps, a scrap heap and a screw of the proper size from a bin. However, once the piece of metal, the screw, and the nut have been selected, the claim discusses the use of those specific items. You do not want someone to insert the screw and then attach a nut to a random screw still in the bin.

Why include the discussion about the screw having a head of a certain size? You do not want the screw to pass all the way through the hole, as would happen if you chose a set-screw that does not have a head that is larger than the hole.

Why include the discussion about positioning the metal? Again, there must be sufficient detail to allow someone to practice the invention. It is conceivable that the metal could be resting on the ground so that the screw could not extend through the metal.

What is missing is any detail of how to tighten the nut. In their ruling on the KSR v. Teleflex [3, 4] case, the Supreme Court stated that a certain amount of experimentation was permissible and that someone attempting to practice the invention was not an automaton. In other word, the patent specifies that the nut is to be tightened, but leaves it to the reader to determine the best way for that individual to accomplish that task using known technology.

Now put yourself into the proverbial shoes of the lay juror who knows nothing about your invention. You must provide sufficient detail so that members of that jury could practice your invention while precluding some wise guy from setting up scenarios such as leaving the metal on the floor so that the screw could not pass through it, or choosing a screw without a head so that it would fall through, or affixing the nut to a different screw that did not go through the hole.

As discussed in Chapter 12, the members of the intended audiences who must be addressed in the patent are not likely to have the background or knowledge your coworkers possess. An examiner will be looking to see if you are claiming a novel and nonobvious solution to a technical problem and that your proposed claims are appropriately supported in your disclosure. Jurors, who generally lack a technical background in your area of expertise, are trying to understand your invention. Legal scholars may be trying to explain to the jurors what your patent means and does not mean. You will, in general, be aiding yourself if the jurors can understand your invention with minimal help from the legal professionals.

It is worthwhile to briefly examine the term "head" as applied to the machine screw. Absent any information within the disclosure to the contrary, words assume their common meaning. Thus, without further elaboration, the head of the machine screw would be rightfully assumed to exist in a common form such as a hex or torx head, or a head that could be turned by a flat blade or Phillips screwdriver. However, it would appear that, as used in the hypothetical claim, the term "head" may include a head with an overhanging ear on either side or a pin such as a roll pin that goes through a hole in the shaft. Alternatively, a head can constitute a removable member such as a nut or a fixed component made of a different material that is mechanically fixed or adhesively attached to the shaft. Such head configurations could be claimed in the dependent claims. However, the term would have to be defined in the specification. As previously discussed, you can be your own lexicographer, provided you define the terms. Should you choose to include such manifestations of heads in the dependent claims, the examiner will also look for supporting disclosure of such in the Detailed Description of the Invention section.

Once the examiner is satisfied that your claims properly describe an invention, attention will be turned to the technical disclosure. First and foremost, the examiner will be checking to make sure that whatever you have described in the claims is explicitly supported in the Detailed Description of the Invention. Other aspects will also be checked, such as the proper format of the figures.

If there are deficiencies that are not substantive, the examiner may notify you of them and give you the opportunity to rectify them. If the deficiencies are substantive, your application will probably be rejected.

The next step taken by the examiner is to decide whether the claims that you presented constitute a single or multiple inventions. For example, while in the past it was possible for a patent to contain both method and apparatus claims, today it is more likely that an examiner will conclude that these claims can be practiced independently of each other, thereby constituting distinct and separate inventions and requiring that each be claimed in its own patent.

If an examiner, in fact, decides that the submitted patent application claims multiple inventions, the application will be rejected and the inventors will be notified, in the accompanying office action, that they must elect which claims to prosecute first. This is referred to as a "divisional" because the patent application must be divided into separate applications for each set of claims. The good news here is that the disclosure, if properly written, already covers all the inventions, so that little additional work is required on the part of the inventors.

Conducting a Prior Art Search

If the examiner is satisfied that all the preliminary requirements for patentability are met by the application, he or she will commence a search. And, no matter how thoroughly you have conducted your prior art search, examiners will do their own. And, of course, there is a fee[§] for the search. In 2018, at the time of writing this book, this fee is $600 [5].

It is likely that examiners will find and allege that you either missed or did not consider some prior art. This is especially true when art from nonanalogous fields is introduced. It is very hard to predict what examiners will find, but a thorough search and analysis by you, as discussed in your Background of the Invention section of your application, will often go far in enabling you to traverse[¶] the examiner's objections. While examiners have some expertise in your field, they are not experts and often their assertions are not correct, as we will discuss in the next section of this chapter.

Although examiners tend to predominately search the patent literature, they do not restrict their searches to those data bases. Rather, they will also search, and include in their results, reference and text books, journal articles, and whatever else can be considered to be prior art.

Prior to the KSR v. Teleflex [3, 4] ruling, patent examiners were somewhat restricted to using art from nonanalogous fields. Specifically, there had to be some explicit reason to combine the nonanalogous art with closer art in order to conclude that an invention was obvious. This has changed as a result of that ruling. Today, it is still possible to argue that a piece of art is from a nonanalogous field. However, stronger arguments are necessary for patentability. Accordingly, it is increasingly more likely that examiners will cite prior art from unrelated fields and you will need to respond to the examiners' assertions.

---

§ Patent offices worldwide are sources of revenue for their respective governments.
¶ The term "traverse" is used here rather than the more commonly used term "overcome" because "traverse" is used by legal practitioners.

There are several possible office actions that may result from an examiner's search. Three are discussed here.

1. The examiner cannot find art that, either by itself or by fitting the pieces together like the pieces of a jigsaw puzzle, leads someone to your solution. In this case you will receive a notice of allowance.
2. The search may turn up a piece of art that you missed that pretty much states your proposed invention. Remember, the art does not have to claim your invention or even propose a solutions to the problem on which you were working. It merely has to disclose what you were doing. In this case you will receive a rejection.
3. Finally, the examiner may find multiple pieces of prior art and asserts that the combination of those pieces, no matter how complicated or long the chain or combination is, arrives at the solution to your problem. Should this occur, your application will also be rejected.

Let us explore this last point in more detail. On more than one occasion, I have seen teams of researchers and engineers develop innovative products that were different from and more innovative than anything against which those products would be competing. In essence, before those individuals developed that product, no one had conceived of it. However, the product came about by using known technology in a new way, with each component of that technology functioning in exactly its known manner. The individuals working on that would understand that they were using known technology, but would ask if they could get a "combination patent" because no one thought of using that technology in quite that manner.

The answer is "no". If the components performed in the manner that was expected, there is no novelty. Glock did not patent the distinctive and original polymer frame for his pistols, presumably because the polymer functioned as it would inherently function. Glock was simply substituting another known material that functioned as expected, polymer for steel, to be used in the frame. Even though other manufacturers and professional services that are extremely familiar with firearms, such as police and military forces, were extremely skeptical about the ability of Glock's pistol to function reliably, the polymer frame did function reliably. Yet, no patent was obtained for Glock's polymer frame, despite the facts that the polymer frame is the most distinctive feature of Glock pistols and that using a molded polymer instead of machined steel decreased both the weight and the machining costs of the pistol. The skepticism of professionals who routinely handle firearms to the use of polymer instead of steel was also not sufficient to provide nonobviousness or novelty.

There are two options for obtaining patents where the combination of known technologies may ordinarily result in a rejection. Such a rejection could perhaps be avoidable or successfully challenged if the proper supportive information was originally included in the patent application before submission. In the first, if it is unexpectedly found that the combination of known technology yields an unanticipated advantage that would not be expected from the simple combination of the components, you may have a patentable invention. Is the whole greater than the sum of the parts? If that is so, this unexpected advantage should have been enunciated in the Background of the Invention section of the patent application before submission. That advantage, based on the prior art, would likely be deemed nonobvious. Remember, you can change the claims during prosecution, but not the disclosure itself.

The second option is to explore why the distinct technologies described in the prior art were not combined previously to build the present product. Specifically, were there technical hurdles that had to be overcome to allow the pieces of the prior art to be combined? If you were solving problems that had to be solved to allow this combination, then you may have patentable inventions and the solutions to these problems should be the subject of your patent applications. Again, it is absolutely crucial that within your application you properly define the problems that you solved in the Background of the Invention section, explaining the significance of these problems. In the Detailed Description of the Invention section, you must disclose how you solved these problems. You might want to consider including figures that illustrate the difficulty of combining the pieces of the prior art and how you overcame these challenges. Remember that each solution constitutes a separate invention, requiring a separate patent application, although it might be possible to piggyback the inventions into a common disclosure.

As a final note, examiners will sometimes indicate, while rejecting your patent application, that they will allow a patent for some of the claims if you eliminate the others. Alternatively, they might indicate that they would allow your patent if you restricted your claims by combining the independent claims with one or more dependent ones. We will discuss how you go about responding to office actions in the next section.

Responding to an Office Action

Responses to office actions will require close cooperation between you and your legal representative. That is because examiners use legal reasons for rejecting your patent application which is, after all, disclosing a solution to a technical problem. In other words, the rejection often, but not always, involves a legal discussion of technical issues.

Your ultimate goal is to obtain a patent that protects your innovation as part of a broader portfolio that builds protective barriers around your technology. It is a great feeling when you receive a notice of allowance. The office action will discuss the legal reasons why the examiner is allowing your patent, including a discussion of its relationship to the prior art and where the prior art falls short in teaching your invention. Aside from paying the issuance fee (in 2018 at the time of writing this book it is $960 [5]), you should just sit back and wait for the patent office to issue your patent, which will most likely occur in a number of months. It is especially exciting when the notice of allowance is in the first office action. However, as will be discussed in the next chapter, when this occurs, you might want to reexamine your claims to determine whether or not they were too restrictive and if there is an opportunity to enhance your patent portfolio. This will be discussed in Chapter 14.

It is more likely that examiners find so-called related art. They will then allege that the art they cite results in your proposed invention lacking novelty and, therefore, does not meet the requirements of being patentable. In other words the examiner is saying that your proposed invention is not an invention. This can occur especially if an examiner finds a single piece of art that pretty much shows your proposed invention. It is possible that you may have missed that piece of prior art during your own search.

Should this occur, examine the cited art closely and, if it, indeed, does disclose your purported invention, you have two options. The first is to abandon prosecution of your patent application. By not responding to an office action, your application will die after a period of time. The second option is to draft new claims, thereby establishing a new and different invention, provided you have sufficient disclosure and if a resulting patent would still have sufficient value to you.

It should be noted that sometimes, despite the best efforts of everyone involved, both the inventors and the examiners miss an earlier patent or other piece of prior art that completely discloses the present invention and allows a patent to be issued. It is incumbent on inventors to disclose that information to the patent office, should the inventors become cognizant of it prior to the issuance of the patent. In any event, if there is an attempt to assert that patent, it is likely that the defendant's attorneys will find that art and effectively use it to have your patent nullified.

It is more likely that examiners will find several pieces of art that they piece together and then conclude that your invention is obvious and, accordingly, not patentable. At this time the resulting office action will indicate that your claims have been rejected.

You now have several possible courses of action should your claims be rejected. You could decide not to respond to the office action, resulting in your patent application being rejected. This would most commonly occur if you decided that the examiner was correct and that any further discussion may create a file history that damages other potions of your patent portfolio or that modifying the claims to circumvent the cited art would substantially degrade the value of the present patent application.

However, you could decide to respond to the office action. If you choose this path you have two options on how to proceed. These options include challenging the examiner's reasoning and rewriting the claims.

In the first option, you could challenge the examiner's reasoning. This is done by arguing that the examiner's assertions that the separate patents could be strung together to teach your invention is incorrect. It should be noted that arguing that the cited work is in a nonanalogous technological field or that the problem that you solved is different from those in the cited art will not circumvent the assertions of the examiner. You must be able to show that the teachings in the cited art would not allow someone of ordinary skill in the art to follow those teachings and implement your solution. Let us illustrate these points using an actual example [6].

In some high volume electrophotographic copiers and printers, the photoreceptor is cleaned to remove residual toner after transferring the bulk of the toned image to paper. In some machines this is accomplished using a cleaning roller comprising a hard, inner, cylindrical core to which is attached a brush or "rug" made of synthetic fibers. The cleaning roller is rapidly rotated against the photoreceptor, thereby removing the residual toner. The toner is then removed from the roller using a vacuum. The cleaning roller is then referred to as a "vacuum fur brush cleaning roller", which, in this section, will be shortened simply to "cleaning roller".

It should be noted that the fibers used in the cleaning roller were manufactured by one company, predominantly used in the production of carpets, and the quantity of fiber sold for cleaning rollers was fairly miniscule. The rug would then be woven, using these fibers, by a second company and the rug wrapped around and attached to the cylindrical core by a third company, each company specializing in its own products.

The problem encountered was that, when a new cleaning roller was used in conjunction with a previously unused photoreceptor, a scum quickly formed on the photoreceptor. As the scum absorbed the incident light, thereby attenuating its intensity, it altered the discharge characteristics of the photoreceptor, thereby creating artifacts in the electrostatic latent image, which then became visible defects in the visible toned print. Needless to say, this often resulted in an expensive service call and down time for the printer.

Upon investigation, it was found that the cause of the scum formation was the deposition of finishing agents, used in the production of the fibers, onto the photoreceptor. These finishing agents functioned as a glue, adhering contacting particles such as the calcium carbonate used as a filler in paper. It was also found that, by subjecting the new cleaning roller to a specific cleaning process designed to remove the finishing agents prior to installing the cleaning roller into the printer, the scum formation could be eliminated. We applied for a patent on the roller and the method of removing the finishing agent from the fibers contained therein.**

The patent application was initially rejected. In her office action, the examiner correctly cited a patent showing a vacuum fur brush cleaning roller. She also cited a patent describing the use of a painting roller to apply paint to a surface and asserted that, even though the painting roller patent did not teach the cleaning of the paint roller, the painter must have cleaned it after painting. Then, because of the existence of the vacuum fur brush patent, in light of the painting roller patent, the patent examiner concluded our invention was obvious and, therefore, not patentable.

In order for us to obtain a patent, it would be necessary for us to break the chain of prior art. The use of a vacuum fur brush cleaning roller in an electrophotographic printer was known. However, the rejection hinged on tying together the teachings of that patent with the paint roller patent. If the connection could be broken by our response, we should be able to obtain the desired patent.

It would not have gotten us anywhere to argue that the paint roller was nonanalogous art. It was also irrelevant that the painter was solving a totally different problem using the paint roller. If the teaching of one patent can be combined with the teaching of another, your invention becomes obvious, irrespective of their fields of invention. It also would not matter

** At the time of applying for this patent (1996), we were able to combine the roller and the method of removing the finishing agent into one application. It is likely that today these would be considered as distinct inventions and require that two patent applications be filed.

that the examiner was inferring information that was not in a patent if that particular operation were inherent to the use of the disclosed technology.

Our response was two-fold. First, if the painter cleaned the roller, it would have been cleaned *after* it was used to apply paint. It would not have been cleaned *prior* to its initial usage, as was required in our case in order to solve the scum formation problem. Second, it was not inherent to the use of a painting roller that it be cleaned after use, as it is often not cost effective and is time consuming to do so. Rather, it is common to discard the roller after it has been used to apply paint to a surface.

Based on this response, the patent was allowed and ultimately issued. The key element here was to convince the examiner that the combination of the art cited by the examiner would not solve the problem, as specified, in the patent application.

The second option when responding to an examiner's rejection is for you to rewrite the claims so as to circumvent the cited art. That can often be done by narrowing the claims somewhat so as to focus more sharply on the specifics of the problem that is of interest to you. Upon occasion, an examiner will indicate that, whereas your independent claim is rejected in light of some cited pieces of prior art, if you restrict your application by eliminating the independent claim and rewriting one or more dependent claims to change them into independent claims, the patent may be allowable. More frequently, the examiner will simply reject all your claims in light of alleged prior art, leaving it up to you and your legal counsel to formulate a response. Let us illustrate this point and what has to be included in your Detailed Description of the Invention to allow you to respond to the examiner and patent your invention.

Let us assume that a hypothetical left-handed widget has remarkable non-stick properties while maintaining a high coefficient of friction so that items placed on it do not slide off, but can be readily removed by peeling. The left-handed widget was awarded a patent 30 years ago. It was subsequently found that, if the left-handed widget is electrically biased to a potential of between 800 and 1,200 volts, it is extremely effective at destroying odors. This benefit was patented 2 years ago.

Recently, you found that if the left-handed widget was electrically biased between 500 and 1,000 volts, it emitted very soothing tones that induced sleep, thereby curing insomnia. Moreover, you also found that the left-handed widget was particularly effective at curing insomnia when a bias of between 500 and 800 volts was applied and spectacularly effective when a bias of between 500 and 600 volts was applied. You apply for a patent, claiming the benefit of curing sleep insomnia by biasing the left-handed widget between 500 and 1,000 volts.

You write your patent application with the first (independent) claim stating:

"A device for curing insomnia, that device comprising a left-handed widget."

You then include three dependent claims, each of which claims the widget with the applied voltages being 500 to 1,000 V, 500 to 800 V, and 500 to 600 V.

You receive an office action rejecting your application in light of the 30-year old patent disclosing the left-handed widget. You respond by rewriting the independent claim to now read:

"A device for curing insomnia, that device comprising a left-handed widget that is electrically biased between 500 and 1,000 V."

and revise the now two dependent claims to refer to the revised independent claim.

You receive a notice that your application is rejected and the rejection is made final. What this means and how you address it will be handled in the next section of this chapter. Suffice-it to say, the word "final", as used in this context does not mean "final" as most of us understand the word. Rather, the word has a specific meaning that can be addressed. Specifically, you must file a "Request for Continued Examination" (RCE) and pay the appropriate fee ($1,200 for a first request).

You file the RCE and submit your patent application with the revised claims. You receive an office action rejecting your application, in light of the 2-year old patent that destroys odors by electrically biasing the left-handed widget to a potential of between 800 and 1,200 volts. Why is this? There is an overlap of the range of applied voltages, specifically at 800 V to 1,000 V. Your invention now reads on the earlier patent. It does not matter that you found a solution to a totally different, previously undisclosed, problem. The ability of the left-handed widget to solve your problem is inherent to the left-handed widget. You would have had to do something to the widget to differentiate it from what was taught in the earlier patents.

So, you try again. This time you restrict the independent claim to a voltage range of between 500 V and 750 V to avoid the 800 V to 1,200 V range specified in the two-year old patent. The patent is, again, given a final rejection. You file an RCE and pay the required fee (now $1,700 for second and subsequent RCEs). After some time your application is again rejected. This time it is because the range that you are now claiming is not explicitly supported in the disclosure. You had specified 500 V to 600 V and 500 V to 800 V, but nowhere did you explicitly state that you would have an advantage if the applied voltage were between 500 V and 750 V. Yes, you did cite a range of applied voltages between 500 V and 800 V and, having studied graphical interpolation, could have easily compared the results obtained at the stated upper ranges of 600 V and 800 V and decided that 750 V gave a significant benefit. But, members of your intended audience cannot rightly perform that interpolation. Moreover, there is no indication that an interpolated result would show the proposed benefit. You must claim only what you have explicitly disclosed, in this case the range 500 V to 600 V.

There is a delicate balance between what you disclose in a patent application in support of your proposed claims and what you include, should your initial claims be rejected and you have to fall back to more restrictive claims. What does this mean for the present example? You clearly found that the left-handed widget could cure insomnia when biased between 500 V and 1,000V. However, as written, you could only claim the narrow range of 500 V to 600 V. The usable range of voltages between 800 V and 1,000 V is protected by the two year old patent that belongs to someone else. Whether or not that would restrict someone offering the product with a bias within that range would be up to the owner of that patent. You can restrict its usage in the most beneficial range of between 500 V and 600 V, but, had you done your prior art search more thoroughly, it is likely that you would have been able to obtain broader coverage. As it now stands, you have taught the world about how to use your discovery, leaving the range between somewhat above 600 V and somewhat below 800 V unprotected.[††]

Rejections, Final Rejections, and RCEs

The concepts of rejections and final rejections, along with the use of requests for continued examination (RCEs) were introduced in the previous section of this chapter. Let us explore these items in more detail.

[††] I have deliberately not specified 601 V to 799 V because of the "doctrine of equivalents". That legal doctrine can be used to decide that someone is infringing a patent, even if the infringer is not practicing exactly what the patent claims, if the practice reads sufficiently close to the claim to be determined to be equivalent to the claim.

When examiners reject a patent application, they will generally give the applicant a chance to review and respond to the reasons for the rejection. Should your response require conducting a new prior art search, as would often be the case if you revise your claims, the resulting office action will probably be a rejection with the annotation that the rejection is made final. Similarly, should you decide that the examiner's analysis is incorrect and respond accordingly, and the examiner does not agree with your arguments, your application will again be rejected and the rejection most likely made final.

However, the term "final" used in the present context does not mean final as most of us know the word to mean. Rather, it means that the examiner does not have to consider the application any further. However, upon receipt of a request for further examination and the payment of the required fees, it is likely that your application will be reviewed once more, together with any new searches that may be required on the part of the examiner. In essence, your application is treated as new. Speculating on why the system works this way is not worthwhile. Suffice-it to say, these are the rules by which we must play the game.

Interviewing the Examiner and Filing Appeals

There are times that, no matter how much correspondence occurs between you and the examiner, there appears to be a gap in the understanding that cannot be closed through written correspondence. And, as previously stated, all correspondence becomes part of the file history that can be searched by a defendant's attorneys in the event that you decide to assert your patents. At this time different steps can be taken.

The first step is to arrange to talk with the examiner, either in person or, more commonly, by telephone. This is referred to as "interviewing the examiner".

Interviewing the examiner tends to be a fruitful way of resolving differences that have prevented your receiving a notice of allowance. The differences can be either technical or legal and it is strongly recommended that your legal counsel take the lead in both setting up and conducting the interview, with you being present to clarify specific technical issues. You should discuss the interview in advance with your attorney and should limit your comments to the specific matter under consideration. Please also remember that, as in the case of all correspondence, the interview becomes part of the file history. And, as you, presumably, are seeking broad patent coverage on multiple inventions, be doubly careful not to say or disclose anything that could compromise other filings – either present or future.

Appealing a Decision and Abandoning an Application

After exhausting all reasonable paths forward with an examiner, and remembering that the supervisor or primary examiner must concur with the office actions put forth by the examiner, and failing to obtain meaningful patent coverage, you face the decision of what to do next. You have two options: 1) you can decide to abandon the case; or 2) you can file a notice of appeal.

Abandoning an application has some advantages, especially if the particular patent application is but one of a number in a portfolio. Specifically, the increased file history that would be generated as you go through the appealing process, the more you can endanger the value of the other patents that you might own or subsequently obtain. In addition, there will be more expense incurred each time you request continued examinations.

It would be unrealistic to expect every application for which you apply to be allowed. If you and your attorney have drafted claims that are not overly broad, but that do properly reflect the invention and you have done a thorough job researching the prior art and have defined the problems solved so as to circumvent that art, it would be reasonable to expect a 70% to 90% success rate in your prosecutions. A higher rate might suggest that you are drafting your claims too narrowly or that you are filing applications in so-called "white spaces" i.e., those areas that have little technological value or interest. It is, of course, possible that you are the first in an upcoming area and have simply beaten everyone else to the patent office. However, as technological developments are generally built on prior advances, this is relatively rare. At some point you may have to realistically decide that the potential damage to your portfolio and the ever increasing expenses of prosecuting an application simply more than offset the value of possibly obtaining a specific patent. This is the time to abandon that application.

On the other hand, if you believe that obtaining this particular patent is of immense importance and that you and your attorney are thoroughly convinced that, legally speaking, the examiner and the primary examiner are wrong, you can file a notice of appeal. There are times that an examiner will, upon receiving the notice of appeal, revisit an application and award you some coverage. After all, if an examiner is overruled by the appeals board, it does not look good. However, be aware that, absent that reversal, an appeal is an expensive and, at best, an uncertain proposition, with the known outcome of increasing the file history. Appealing is an option that should be exercised judiciously.

Final Comments

The prosecution of patent applications is an involved, legal process that generally takes several years to conclude. Because it is a legal process, your attorney should take the lead, with your lending technical support, as required. It is, however, of great importance that your attorney understand, not only the particular invention under consideration, but the technological advances for which you are attempting to build a patent portfolio. And, of course, this includes, in addition to those applications being prosecuted 0are still being developed and for which there will be ongoing patent applications.

References

1. R. Schindler, private communication.
2. https://www.uspto.gov/patents-application-process/checking-application -status/check-filing-status-your-patent-application.
3. https://www.supremecourt.gov/opinions/06pdf/04-1350.pdf
4. https://www.law.cornell.edu/supct/html/04-1350.ZO.html
5. https://www.uspto.gov/learning-and-resources/fees-and-payment/ uspto-fee-schedule#Patent%20Search%20Fee
6. D. S. Rimai, T. H. Morse, J. R. Locke, R. C. Bowen, and J. C. Maher, U. S. Patent #5,772,779 (1998).

14

What Next?

Introduction

You've done a lot. You and your teammates have made significant advances in your technology and you have decided to protect your intellectual property by filing patent applications. You have recognized that the value of individual patents that just protect a single solution to a specific problem is limited. You have also recognized that having teammates filing disconnected patent applications for their separate inventions also has limited value. What is worse is that type of approach can be costly to implement, can undermine your being able to obtain valuable patent coverage, and, because of statements made in either the applications themselves or during prosecution, you will have established a file history or a paper trail that may impede your being able to obtain future patents or even successfully assert the ones that you have.

You have prioritized both your inventions and potential patent applications and determined a course of action that should allow you to obtain those patents necessary to protect your intellectual property. During that process, you sought to own the problem [1] rather than just seeking patents on particular technical solutions to specific problems.* You have coordinated your patent activities to best facilitate obtaining broad coverage without prematurely disclosing information that may limit your ability to obtain future patents.

You have proposed claims that completely describe each of your inventions and ensured that no two applications are claiming the same invention. You took deliberate care to ensure that you have claimed one invention per application. You conducted a thorough prior art search and, perhaps, revised both the claims and the description of the problems that you solved so as to circumvent the teachings of the prior art. You then wrote disclosures that supported your claims, including a description of the preferred mode of practicing your inventions.

You reviewed your entire folder of proposed patent applications to ensure that you were, indeed, on a path to owning the problem. During the review process, you have recognized what technology will need further development, making it suitable material for future patents and carefully avoided disclosing that information in your present applications. After all, you do not want your own developments to become prior art used to reject your future applications.

And, during this entire process, you always remembered who constitutes the intended audience for your patent applications. You included descriptions of how you would unambiguously establish infringement of your patents and envisioned yourself explaining your inventions to members of a jury.

You met with legal counsel, probably on multiple occasions and educated them about your inventions. With their guidance, you revised the claims and the disclosures, and perhaps even the descriptions of the problem solved for your applications, as you prepared to file your patent applications, some concurrently and some sequentially, depending on the specific material disclosed in each. Yes, you have done a lot of work to get this far.

And you have done even more. The big day arrived and you filed your applications, which are now being prosecuted. Perhaps some were allowed.

---

* As a reminder, all-too-often inventors file applications for novel solutions to specific technical problems that they have solved, losing sight of trying to broadly protect their intellectual property. "Owning the problem" refers to generating a patent portfolio that impedes others from practicing your technology and invading your market space without obtaining a license from you. In order to own the problem, you seek to obtain patent coverage on alternative approaches to your envisioned products, including the enabling technology and you focus heavily on those patents that your competitors would need to enhance their products.

Perhaps some even received first office action allowances. Others may have been rejected. Some of the rejections required you to elect which claims you wanted to prosecute, thereby requiring divisionals. With others you have attempted to refute the examiner's assertions that combinations of the prior art made these inventions obvious. And, with still others, you had to rewrite or limit your claims.

With several of your patent applications, after responding to the examiner without success and concluding that there was a misunderstanding somewhere, you and your attorney have opted to interview the examiner. Overall, you have been and continue to be busy with these patent applications. But, at least it is winding down. Or, is it?

Yes, you have done a lot of work. However, there are still further opportunities, accompanied by risks that should be considered. This chapter discusses those opportunities and risks and describes how to incorporate them into your patent strategy.

Divisionals, Continuations, and Continuations-in-Part

Divisionals, continuations, and continuations-in-part [2–6] all have certain similarities, as each is strongly connected to the original patent application. Moreover, each has the ability to strengthen the patent protection related to your invention. However, there are significant differences. Let us discuss each one, starting with divisionals.

As briefly discussed in Chapter 13, if an examiner finds that the proposed claims cover more than a single invention, it is likely that you will be asked to choose which claims you wish to first prosecute. You will be afforded the opportunity to prosecute the remaining claims at a later time. The advantage of having a divisional[†] (dividing the claims into several applications) is that the subsequent applications will be given the original priority date, thereby establishing the earlier date for the purpose of patenting. The disadvantage is that the earlier priority date also means that your patent will expire that much earlier.

Another disadvantage encountered with prosecuting divisional applications is that of increasing the file history. Specifically, divisional applications

---

† The term "divisional" refers to dividing a patent application into two or more applications, electing which claims to prosecute in each application, without changing the disclosure. The term is also often used to refer to one or more of the applications resulting from the divisional.

have to be prosecuted as separate patent applications. Accordingly, an allowance of the elected claims for initial prosecution does not guarantee, or even enhance, the chance of the latter claims being allowed. However, the examiners will conduct separate searches and issue office actions on the subsequent applications to which you will have to respond. And, although the inventions are distinct, the discussions centered on the latter applications are subject to discovery in the event that you choose to assert the claims prosecuted earlier.

Let us illustrate divisionals with a hypothetical example. Assume that you are developing a novel automobile tire whose tread and rubber composition result in faster water shedding for use on wet roads, accompanied by improved traction.

In your patent application you have described how your tread pattern improves traction by allowing water to be channeled away from between the tire and the road surface more quickly. You have also described how the novel rubber composition increased friction. And, you have also described how combining the tread pattern and the rubber composition significantly improved the handling of the car.

You proposed two independent claims – one for the tread pattern and one for the rubber composition – in the patent application. You also included proposed dependent claims based on the two independent claims. You did not claim the combination of the tread pattern and the rubber composition.

The examiner rightfully rejects your patent application because, as the tread pattern and the rubber composition could be practiced independently of each other, the claims would constitute two separate inventions. You were asked to choose which set you wished to prosecute at this time and, in accordance with this request, you chose to prosecute the claims for the tread pattern and removed from the application both the independent and dependent claims that relate to the rubber composition. In effect you have divided your application into two patent applications. This is a divisional. In this example the original patent will now address just the tread pattern and the divisional will address the rubber composition.

It should be noted that a divisional is not necessarily restricted to dividing a patent application into two cases. Rather, you may be asked to divide the application into as many applications as the examiner believes constitute independent inventions. Of course, you can try to respond, if you have good reason, that the inventions cannot be practiced independently of each other and, therefore, constitute a single invention. However, it is generally more advantageous to accept the examiner's assertions and divide the patent application accordingly. You will, of course, be able to prosecute the separate claims subsequently.

Continuations differ from divisionals in that, whereas divisionals occur when an examiner believes that the proposed claims constitute distinct and separable inventions, continuations occur when the patent application already discloses a single invention and the inventor desires to enhance the value of the patent by adding claims. As an example, let us continue discussing the hypothetical tire patent application discussed above. Moreover, let us assume that both the original and divisional applications were allowed.

You can now seek to expand the range of protection around your intellectual property, provided that all claimed material has been properly disclosed in the original patent application, by filing a continuation. As is the case for divisionals, a continuation has both the advantage and disadvantage of the original priority date. It also subjects the owner of the patent to generating another file history that can be searched in the event of an assertion.

However, if successfully prosecuted, a continuation can strengthen your portfolio. This is important for two reasons. First, if the original patent or a claim contained therein is ultimately ruled by a court to be invalid, you can still fall back upon the continuation. Second, the more claims that can be asserted, the higher the likely damages awarded to you should the defendant be found to have infringed your patent.

Let us illustrate this with the aforementioned tire patent. Let us assume, as before, that patents have been allowed for both the tire tread pattern and the rubber compound and that your continuation is to obtain claims for the combination of the two. Within the description of the invention contained in the original application, the benefits obtained by combining these technologies have been disclosed and you are seeking to just obtain additional claims on that subject matter. Upon successful prosecution of this patent application, someone who combined the original technologies would now be infringing on this third patent, the first two constituting the original and divisional patents. This increases the potential for licensing fees or damages to you. Moreover, should a court rule that, say, the tread pattern was an obvious extension of that known in the art and, therefore, invalid, the combination of the tread pattern and the rubber formulation may still be valid.

Continuations-in-part are, in some ways, similar to continuations in that they heavily rely on the same disclosures to support the claimed invention. However, continuations-in-part differ from continuations in that the continuations-in-part also rely on the introduction of new subject matter. Thus, they are often ideal vehicles for obtaining patent protection for developments in your technology that are closely related to the original patent applications, but which have occurred subsequent to those filings.

Determining priority dates for continuations-in-part is more complicated than for either continuations or for divisionals. Whereas the same priority date for the original patent application is assigned to continuations and divisionals, the priority date for continuations-in-part is more complicated and depends on whether a specific claim depends heavily on the newly introduced material or if the supporting information was in the earlier application.

As with continuations and divisionals, there are both advantages and disadvantages to filing continuations-in-part. They can certainly strengthen your patent portfolio. However, since they are related to the original applications, their prosecution lengthens the file history that can be searched during the pretrial discovery process. Balancing the benefits and risks for pursuing divisionals, continuations, or continuations-in-part, applications must be done for each case under consultation with your legal counsel.

Maintenance Fees

As stated in Article I, Section 8, Clause 8 of the United States Constitution, Congress is granted the power "To promote the progress of science and useful arts, by securing for limited times to authors and inventors the exclusive right to their respective writings and discoveries."

It is clear that the intent of the Founding Fathers was to encourage technological and scientific innovation. Unfortunately, governments often view patent offices as revenue enhancing agencies, which results in additional costs incurred by inventors that can discourage the very activity that was written into the Constitution to encourage. That being said, the USPTO requires the payment of maintenance fees, sometimes referred to as "renewals", on three separate occasions. Failure to pay a maintenance fee will result in your patent entering into the public domain.

The first payment of a maintenance fees are due at between 3 and 3½ years. The second is due between 7 and 7½ years, and the third between 11 and 11½ years after the date of issue. There is a grace period (accompanied by a surcharge) of ½ year for each payment due.

The required payment for the first, second, and third maintenance fees are $1,600, $3,600, and $7,400, respectively.‡ Multiply these fees by the

---

‡ There are smaller fees required for so-called "small entities" and "micro entities". Consult your legal counsel to see if you qualify for one of these lesser amounts.

number of patents that are in your portfolio and you have a major expense. It is very important to make sure that your money is well-spent. This is especially true for independent innovators and entrepreneurs, both of whom are trying to use their creativity to make a profit. However, maintenance fees also affect scientists and engineers working for both large and small companies.

Aside from decisions about whether or not to pay certain bills, which in corporations is generally a management decision, why should an inventor be concerned about maintenance fees? The answer is to ensure that you or your employer is getting value for the expenditure. You are, after all, the technical expert who knows where the technology and the marketplace are heading since you first filed your patent applications. You should know what products your competitors are offering and, perhaps, presently developing. You also should be cognizant of what your customers like about both your and your competitors' products. In other words, you are in the best position to recognize the ongoing value of your patent portfolio.

Innovative people tend to take pride and develop a feeling of ownership in the scientific and technological advances that they have created. This is, in general, good as it enables those individuals to overcome the inherent challenges and drive those advances forward. However, the process for deciding whether or not to pay the maintenance fees is not the place for such attachments and pride as that can result in excessive and unnecessary expenses. Rather, deciding on whether or not to pay the maintenance fees requires an analysis on where the technology has gone over the years since the patent applications were first filed, which patents are maintaining value, and which can be allowed to lapse into the public domain. There are considerations that can help with those decisions. These include:

1. Is this the first renewal? It is often difficult to assess the market value of a particular patent or group of patents within the short time allowed before the first maintenance fee payment is due. Fortunately, this is the lowest of the maintenance fees and, absent concrete information indicating that the patents will not be worthwhile, it is generally advisable to pay the fees. Three and a half years is a very short time to determine where technology is going.
2. At the other extreme is the third renewal. It is likely that, by the 11th year, you should be able to determine which patents are valuable and which ones are unlikely to enhance your

portfolio. This is also the most expensive of the maintenance fees. It should also be noted that, by the time this payment is due, more than half the life of a patent has expired. Based on the information that you have, you will have to determine whether there is sufficient value in maintaining the portfolio, either in part or in its entirety.

3. The second renewal is often the most complicated to decide. The patent has been in existence for 7 to 7½ years, which is often, but not always, sufficient to determine whether or not it will be valuable.

The reader is reminded that how fundamental an invention is does not necessarily translate to how valuable patents protecting that invention are. As a reminder, let us review the history of Polaroid's patent infringement lawsuit against Kodak.

As is well known, Edwin Land developed the technology that allowed consumers to take a photograph and hold a finished print with minutes. This gave rise to the Polaroid Corporation. The technology was based on rather innovative photographic chemistry coupled with a number of enabling technologies that allowed the photograph to be developed, after exposure, by pulling a packet comprising the photographic paper and a pod of developing chemicals through a pair of rollers that broke the pod and spread the chemicals over the surface of the photographic paper. However, Land was not able to actually manufacture his packets and contracted with Eastman Kodak to produce them.

After some time, members of Kodak's management decided that Kodak should also enter the instant photography business and compete against Polaroid. They authorized the development of their own instant photographic chemical process that was distinct from Polaroid's and patented that technology. They also sought legal opinions as to whether or not they would be infringing on Polaroid's patents, which covered both its own chemistry and its enabling technology, such as the use of the rollers to spread the developer chemicals.

Polaroid responded by filing a patent infringement lawsuit in which they were ultimately awarded over $900,000,000 in damages and which forced Kodak to abandon the instant photography market and buy back all the cameras that it sold to consumers. This was, obviously, quite costly for Kodak and quite beneficial for Polaroid. It is important to note that, in their lawsuit, Polaroid asserted nine patents that protected its enabling technology and no patents covering its fundamental chemistry inventions, which were distinct from those used by Kodak. Of the nine patents, two were found to be invalid and Kodak was found to have infringed the other seven.[§]

The important message is that it is often impossible to ascertain a priori which patents are valuable and which are not. Fundamental does not necessarily equate with valuable, nor does simple or enabling equate with worthless. You are advised to exercise due caution when deciding whether or not a given patent is worth the expenditure of the maintenance fees. Remember that the required payment of a maintenance fee is not an assessment of your technological innovation. Your decision of whether or not to pay a maintenance fee is simply a measurement of how much value you perceive the market places on your patent.

With that in mind, let us now turn our attention to factors that can affect whether or not you choose to pay a maintenance fee. These factors include:

1. Is the patent presently being licensed or included in a cross-licensing agreement? If this is the case, another company finds your patent(s) of value.
2. Is the patent presently being asserted? Aside from the obvious situation that you are claiming damages against another company for allegedly infringing on your patent, there might be adverse legal consequences for you should you choose to not pay the fees and allow the patent to enter into the public domain.
3. Is the patent being cited by other companies? This would suggest that the patented technology is of interest to those companies.
4. Is the patent part of a broader portfolio? As discussed previously, broad portfolios are generally more valuable than a single patent because of the breadth and depth of the extent of the technology that is covered. However, there may be some patents within a portfolio that do not warrant the expense of maintaining. You will need to look carefully at

---

§ Prior to the introduction of its instant photography products, Kodak did seek a legal opinion as to whether or not the enabling patents were valid. Based on that advice, Kodak erroneously concluded that those patents were obvious and should be, therefore, invalid. It is important to note that Polaroid sought triple damages for willful infringement because Kodak knew of their existence but infringed upon them anyway. However, because Kodak had obtained legal opinion regarding their invalidity, it was found that, although Kodak did, indeed, infringe upon them, the infringement was not willful.

the actual intellectual property being protected by the specific patent under consideration.

5. Is your company either producing or about to produce products based on the protected intellectual property? If your products are successful, it is likely that other companies may try to infiltrate your market space.

6. How readily can a competitor circumvent your technology? This question basically is asking how solidly you built the fence around your intellectual property. Do you own the entire problem or just specific solutions to specific problems encountered during your development?

7. How broad are the claims within a patent and, alternatively, even if the claims are not broad, would it be difficult for a competitor to develop work-arounds? If alternatives to claimed inventions can be readily implemented with little cost or ease of use disadvantages, the value of a patent may be minimal. Alternatively, if the claims present significant barriers to another company's being able to market a competitive product, the patent(s) can be very valuable.

8. Are recent advances driving the technology away from your innovations? Floppy discs gave way to zip discs. These gave way to thumb drives, CDs, and DVDs. Your technical expertise should be able to address this issue.

As discussed in this chapter, it may be too soon to address these questions in the case of a first renewal. By the time a third renewal is due, there should be some demonstrable interest by outside companies in a patent to, in general, warrant its being worth the cost of maintaining. Second renewals are often the most tricky. You will need to exercise good technological judgement, accompanied by a good dose of intuition to arrive at a decision. If you have a solid patent portfolio, a mistake made by not renewing an individual patent might be offset by the coverage offered by the others.

Negotiating Cross-Licensing Agreements and Licensing Fees

As discussed in this book, patents are of value only if someone else needs to practice the claimed inventions. It does not matter whether those inventions are fundamental technological advances or if they are for enabling technology that allows the more fundamental advances to actually work in products. As such, it is important to remember that if a competitor has patented the enabling technology that you need in order to commercialize your fundamental advances, you may be prevented from entering the market-place, as illustrated by Polaroid being able to prevent Kodak from marketing its instant photography products that utilized Kodak's fundamental chemistry.

The ultimate goal of establishing a patent portfolio is to own the problem so that no one else can access your marketplace without your granting a license to do so. However, in our competitive world, this is unlikely to occur and would be expensive to implement even if you could. What you need to do is to have patents that your competition needs so that you can exchange rights to use each other's technology without incurring the expenses and time delays of lawsuits. In other words, you need to be able to enter into cross-licensing agreements whereby your company extends the rights to another company to practice your technology in exchange for the right to practice your competitor's technology to the extent defined by the cross-licensing agreement. But, is this not a business and legal issue that is best left to the management and attorneys to arrange? In part, yes, but in part no. Let us consider several aspects in which inventor input is vital to successfully negotiating a cross-licensing agreement.

First of all, if you are an entrepreneur or independent inventor, you probably will be the ultimate manager who decides on the terms of any cross-licensing agreement. However, there are many technical aspects that also have to be considered into which inventors can have very valuable input. Specifically, your knowledge of your technology, as well as that of other companies extends beyond the specific company with whom you are negotiating a cross-licensing agreement. That knowledge is very important if the resulting agreement is to give you access to the technology that you need, while not just enabling your competitor to access your technology with little benefit to you.

Let us first remember that a patent does not give anyone the right to practice an invention. Rather, it gives the owner of that patent the right to exclude others from using the claimed invention. Accordingly, gaining the right to use a patent does not automatically give you the right to practice that technology if there are other patents that would prevent you from doing so. Those patents can be owned by a third company that is not part of the cross-licensing agreement or by the company with whom you are presently negotiating if that company has excluded those patents from the proposed agreement. Moreover, that company may, itself, rely on other cross-licensing agreements with still other companies in order to commercialize its products. They may or may not be able to transfer those rights, depending on the specific details of that agreement. This is a legal issue that should be left to your attorney to clarify.

What is within your purview as a technical expert is the knowledge of what rights are being proposed to be granted to both companies with this agreement and what is the necessity for each company to obtain those rights. In other words, in your expert judgement, 1) does your company need access to the patents owned by your competitor in order for you to sell your products based on the technology that you have been developing; and 2) if your company obtained those rights, might the patents owned by yet another company still prevent you from practicing the licensed inventions?

Within these considerations lies the question of how much of the problem is owned by your competitor. Can you simply implement work-arounds that readily circumvent those patents? How valuable are the patent rights that you own and that you would be granting your competitor?

These are technical issues. Deciding whether or not your proposed technology reads on the claims of someone else's patent is a legal issue that should be left to your attorney. Deciding on whether or not you need a particular invention in order to produce your products is a technical issue that you are in an ideal position to address.

Now let us consider the case in which you have analyzed the patents owned by your competitor and have decided that your competitor needs your patent rights far more than you need those of your competitor. This is a very likely scenario, especially if you were properly developing a holistic patent strategy to own the problem, as discussed in the earlier chapters of this book, and your competitor was just narrowly patenting particular solutions to specific problems. You should remember that your patent portfolio is part of your product stream and, if properly designed and implemented, can be an important source of revenue for your company. In such an instance it may be more beneficial for your company to offer to license your technology to your competitor in exchange for appropriate fees instead of or in addition to entering into cross-licensing agreements.

Your input in assessing the importance (thus value) of a set of patents can be very important in arriving at an appropriate course of action. Specifically, you are in an ideal position to evaluate the necessity of using your intellectual property in order to produce competitive products. Again, do not confuse "fundamental" with "necessary". The seven enabling Polaroid patents were required for Kodak to practice instant photography. The fundamental patents that protected Land's chemistry were not.

Similarly, your input in evaluating the patents for cross-licensing and licensing should be objective, much like what was discussed earlier in this chapter when deciding to pay maintenance fees on a patent, as it is not the place for an inventor to have an emotional tie to the invention. Rather, it calls for a critical analysis of the monetary value of a patent. It does not reflect the importance of an invention to your company. It reflects the necessity for another company to have access to your technology.

Demonstrating Infringements in Advance of An Assertion

If all else fails, your company may decide to assert its patents against another company whose products appear to read on your patents. You, as an inventor of one or more patents that are being asserted, may find yourself, again, on the firing line. Earlier in this book, we discussed how you may find yourself on a witness stand explaining your invention to a jury if your patent is being asserted. It is now time to consider the second part of this assertion, namely to convince a jury, after you have explained your invention to the jurors, that the defendant's products read on one or more of your claims in your patent. And, as is likely, you may have to show how the defendant's products read upon the claims of several of your patents. After all, there is strength in numbers and asserting several patents makes a stronger infringement case.¶

You find yourself in this situation for two reasons. The first, as previously discussed, is that you are the inventor and understand your patent better than anyone else. The second is that you know the technology and understand both your products and those of your competitor that are allegedly infringing on your patents. So you now find yourself in the position of having to demonstrate that your competitor is practicing your claimed technology. How do you do that?

Demonstrating infringement starts with identifying those products whose technology reads on your claims. The more vital that technology is to the product and the more valuable that product is, the higher the potential damages. With that being said, it is better to demonstrate that multiple products read on your claims, as that increases the value of the market to your competitor and, thus, the damages that you suffered as a result of the infringement.

¶ The rule of thumb is that you should try to assert at least five patents, as it is possible to have one or two declared invalid, but it would be difficult to have five declared invalid and that could still result in substantial damages being awarded to you.

You now need to compare every phrase in your claims, remembering that, in order to be infringed, every component of the claim must be practiced by the product(s) in question. As such, you should first demonstrate that the product reads on at least one of the independent claims. Once that is demonstrated, it is valuable to add the dependent claims that are being infringed. This should be done for each and every product marketed by your competitor that is infringing your claims.

Let us look at what is involved in proving infringement using the following hypothetical patent claim:

1. *An electrophotographic device comprising:*
   A. *A photoreceptive member with a process speed V;*
   B. *A means for charging the photoreceptive member;*
   C. *A means for creating an electrostatic latent image on the photoreceptive member;*
   D. *A means for image-wise depositing toner onto the photoreceptive member, thereby converting the electrostatic latent image into a toner image on the photoreceptive member;*
   E. *A means for transferring the toner image to a receiver;*
   F. *A means of removing toner that failed to transfer from the photoreceptive member to the receiver;*
   G. *Whereby said means of removing toner that failed to transfer from the photoreceptive member comprises a fur brush that rotates in the opposite direction to the process direction of the photoreceptive member and at a surface speed between ¼ and ½ that of the process speed of the photoreceptor.*

It is important to first note that the introductory phrase "*An electrophotographic printer comprising*" would, in general, not be considered by the examiner when prosecuting a patent application. To an examiner, the intended use is inconsequential. What is important is the description of the invention, so that any phraseology up to and including the word "comprising" in the introductory clause is inconsequential to an examiner. However, it is very important when establishing infringement.

Now let us suppose that the Fancy Equipment Company makes and sells a device that can download satellite images and can print those images should an operator choose to do so. You are suspicious that their product may read on your claim, as stated above. What do you have to do to establish infringement?

Although much useful information can be obtained from sources such as owners' or service manuals, in general you will have to obtain the equipment suspected of infringing.

Upon inspecting their product, you find that the Fancy Equipment Company is, in fact, using an electrophotographic process to allow the downloaded data to be printed. Their device contains what appears to be a rigid photoreceptive drum, a corona-charger, a laser-scanner that appears to be able to expose the charged photoreceptor and possibly create an electrostatic latent image, a hopper that holds sheets of paper, a subassembly that can feed paper into what appears to be a nip created by a roller and the photoreceptive drum, a blade that scrapes the photoreceptor, and a fur brush that is located after the scraper blade. Now, let us examine precisely how your claim reads and whether or not the Fancy Equipment Company's product reads on it. It should be remembered that, for someone to be infringing on a claim, the product must read on every component of that claim. Accordingly, let us dissect the claim and see how that compares to the actual product, starting with the phrase:

"*An electrophotographic device comprising…*" The product is an electrophotographic device.

Phrase A. "*A photoreceptive member…*". You will have to show that the component is a photoreceptive member. In other words, you will have so show that, in its normal state, it is a dielectric. However, in the presence of an applied electric field and appropriate illumination, it becomes electrically conducting. The claim does not specify the frequency of the electromagnetic radiation of the illumination, so as long as a member within their device becomes photoconductive, it is reading on this aspect of the claim.

"*…with a process speed V*". You will have to show that the component operates at a process speed V. As long as the process speed is not restricted within the disclosure itself, any process speed will suffice.

Phrase B. "*A means for charging the photoreceptive member*". Earlier in this book, you were warned about writing claims that included so-called "form plus function". Here is where it starts to raise complications. Had the claim merely stated that the device contained a charger, then just the presence of the charger in their product would be sufficient to show that their device was reading on this portion of the claim. However, because the form (i.e. the charger) and its function (i.e., to charge the photoreceptive member) are both included in the phrase, you must show that there is a charger and that the charger is used to charge the photoreceptor. It probably does, but because of the way the claim is written, you must show both. Remember that the burden of proof is on the plaintiff (i.e., you).

Phrase C. "*A means for creating an electrostatic latent image on the photoreceptive member*". Again, proving infringement has become more complicated because of form plus function constraints. Had the claim simply stated something like "an actinic source" or "a source of illumination", the presence of the laser scanner would suffice to show that the product reads upon this phrase. However, because of the form plus function language of the claim, you have to show that the laser scanner creates an electrostatic latent image on the photoreceptor.

Phrase D. "*A means for image-wise depositing toner onto the photoreceptive member*". Perhaps the claim could have just stated "a toner deposition device", but it does not. You have to show that their product contains a subsystem that image-wise deposits the toner. In contrast, for example, their device might be electrically biased in such a fashion so that a uniform layer of toner is deposited on the photoreceptor. If this were the case, their product would not read upon this claim and there would be no infringement.

"*...thereby converting the electrostatic latent image into a toner image on the photoreceptive member...*". You have to show that the toner being deposited converts the electrostatic latent image on the photoreceptor into a toner image corresponding to the electrostatic latent image. It does not have to have high charge regions of the electrostatic latent image corresponding to dark regions on the toner image and vice versa, but there must be some correspondence between the latent and toner images.

Phrase E. "*A means for transferring the toner image to a receiver*". You have to show that their device contains some way of transferring the toner image from the photoreceptor to a receiver. You might be able to argue that the toner could transfer to the aforementioned roller and the roller would thus serve as a receiver. However, unless you defined a receiver as such in the disclosure, its common use would be assumed, which means something that a user can hold and walk away with, such as paper bearing the toner image. To demonstrate this, you will need to show that the paper is fed into the nip with such a timing and manner that the toner is transferred to the paper. It does not matter how transfer was effected, as long as it occurred. If, however, you can show how transfer occurred, such as by electrically biasing the roller to attract the toner towards the paper, you would build a stronger case. Please remember that your intended audience consists of the lay jurors and if they understand how a process works, it becomes much more credible.

The next clause, Phrase F, states "*A means of removing toner that failed to transfer from the photoreceptive member to the receiver*". The Fancy Equipment Company product contains such a means – a cleaning blade.

And now comes the final and most problematic phrase of the claim. Phrase G reads: *"Whereby said means of removing toner that failed to transfer from the photoreceptive comprises a fur brush...".* This is problematic because you have to show that the brush that you describe and that appears to be present in their marketed product removes toner that failed to transfer. However, in advance of the photoreceptor contacting that brush, it first encounters a blade whose function is to remove residual toner. The brush could be there for any number of other purposes, including removing ions from the surface of the photoreceptor or buffing the photoreceptor. Because you linked the form plus function, you need to demonstrate both. At this point, it would be very difficult for you to show that the Fancy Equipment Company's product is infringing your patent. They are simply not practicing every component of your claim.

Now, let us assume that you did not combine the form plus function of the fur brush and rewrite parts F and G to read:

F. *A fur brush that contacts the photoreceptive member;*
G. *Whereby said fur brush rotates in the opposite direction to the process direction of the photoreceptive member and at a surface speed between ¼ and ½ that of the process speed of the photoreceptor.*

This rewriting eliminates the form plus function criterion of this part of the claim. Now, it does not matter that the product has a blade cleaner located between the transfer subsystem and the fur brush. That extra elements are included in the product does not negate the fact that it contains those elements that are specified in your patent. However, there are still some difficulties that, hopefully, you addressed when writing your Detailed Description of the Invention section.

What is meant by the revised phrase F requiring the fur brush to contact the photoreceptive member should be described in the Detailed Description of the Invention section. Does this mean that the fibers should barely contact the photoreceptor or should the fibers be completely compressed in the contact zone or should the contact be somewhere between those extremes? And, if this is specified, how would you determine the amount of contact? Remember that the fibers will have varying heights, which must be factored into your definition of contact and how you would determine the contact. If this detail is left indeterminate, the vagueness may result in the patent being found invalid or, at least, a jury may find that it is impossible to determine whether or not the product infringes your patent. You should also note that the fur brush does not have to be constantly in contact with the photoreceptor. For example, it can articulate as long as at some time during the process it comes into contact with the photoreceptor.

Revised phrase G of the claim now reads: "*Whereby said fur brush rotates in the opposite direction to the process direction of the photoreceptive member...*". Does the fur brush in the product in question rotate opposite to the direction of the photoreceptor? That should be relatively straight forward to determine and, as in the case of the fur brush only having to be in contact during some time during the process, the brush need rotate in the opposite direction only upon occasion. Thus, if the brush articulates into and out of position, it does not have to rotate when out of position.

The final portion of revised phrase G of the claim now reads "...*and at a surface speed between ¼ and ½ that of the process speed of the photoreceptor*". This first requires that the surface of the brush be defined in a manner that it can be determined. Is the surface the outer or inner surface of the presumably hard core or is it somewhere within the fiber knap? Is the surface at the outer extent of the knap (whatever that means) or is it somewhere else such as the height of the knap in the region where the knap contacts the photoreceptor? If the latter, then what is the height of the knap where it contacts, for example, a cylindrical photoreceptor? It can be whatever you want it to be, as long as you defined it in the Detailed Description of the Invention section and you unambiguously described how you would determine that height. Remember, you are describing the invention to the jury members and trying to show how the product in question is reading on your claim. If you have not defined your terms and cannot state how you would measure the specified parameters, it would be very difficult to convince jurors that someone was infringing on your patent.

In summary, for a product to infringe upon your patent, it must practice each and every aspect or component of at least one, presumably the independent, claim. The product can also read on the dependent claims, which would strengthen your case for damages. A competitor's product having additional components does not negate infringement as long as the product is practicing each and every claimed feature. However, if a claim is written so as to incorporate a means plus function, and if the product in question does not practice the claimed function, even if it has the means, it does not infringe the patent. Finally, it is vital that you be able to unambiguously show how the product in question is practicing your technology. This requires that the all aspects of the claimed features be clearly defined and, moreover, it is often desirable to describe the method of establishing infringement in your patent.

Once you have shown that that this product marketed by the Fancy Equipment Company reads on your first claim, it is time to determine whether or not the product is also infringing on other claims. Moreover, does the Fancy Equipment Company have other products that infringe on your patent? Also, does this company's products infringe on other patents in your portfolio? Now that you have completed this exercise for one product and one patent, it is time to repeat it for the company's other products and your other patents. The more infringement that you can demonstrate, the higher your likely damages award or settlement will be.

Filing Patent Applications Internationally

You have put together a patent strategy and filed the appropriate applications with the United States Patent and Trademark Office (USPTO). You did a thorough prior art search and carefully described why the prior art does not predict your inventions. Having done a thorough job working with your legal counsel, you are anticipating that between 70% and 90% of your applications will eventually lead to issued patents that will protect both your intellectual property and your marketplace. Does this course of action provide adequate protection for you? Perhaps. Then again, perhaps not. Specifically, if your patents have been granted in a single country, the United States for example, your intellectual property and your ability to assert your rights are limited to that country. If your business extends beyond that country, you may desire to file patent applications in additional nations.

Whether or not to file applications internationally is a business decision and the factors involved in making that decision and formulating a patent strategy are discussed in *Patent Engineering* [1]. However, as you would likely be involved in the process of filing internationally, we will discuss what is involved here.

In years past, in order to file patent applications in multiple countries, the applicant would have to prepare and file distinct applications for each country in which patent protection was desired. This would involve writing applications that conform to the requirements of each country, including having the application translated into the appropriate language. This changed, in large part, due to the Patent Cooperation Treaty (PCT) [7]. This treaty allows a common application to be used for each of the 152 signatory nations.

When deciding whether or not to file internationally and, if so, in which countries to file those applications depends on whether or not products that use the inventive technology are marketed, produced, or traverse through a particular country. Absent an affirmative answer to at least one of those questions, there would seem to be little reason to build the file history or incur the additional expenses involved in prosecuting patent applications in those countries.

If you decide that it would be beneficial to enhance your patent portfolio by filing internationally, you first need to select the inventions for which you wish to obtain patent protection. Then, assuming that your initial applications were filed in the United States, you must file your PCT applications within 12 months of your priority date. Once submitted to either an issuing country or to WIPO** directly, your PCT application will be forwarded to an International Searching Authority (ISA) that will evaluate your patent applications for novelty and inventiveness (non-obviousness). They will conduct a prior art search and issue a written report on their findings, accompanied by an analysis that classifies the related art as either "A", "B" or "X". "A" means that the art, itself, anticipates your invention. "B" means that the specifically cited art, when combined with other cited art, anticipates your invention. "X" relates to prior art of general interest.

You will be afforded the opportunity to revise your claims as per the findings of the ISA. The report will be published. A favorable report enhances your chances of obtaining patents, but does not guarantee that. Conversely, an unfavorable report pretty much dooms your chances.

Once the ISA report has issued its report and you have been afforded the opportunity to address the perceived shortcomings of your claims, you will select the countries in which you wish to apply for patent coverage. Each country will independently decide on whether or not your application meets their patentability requirements. They may, in addition, conduct their own prior art searches and analyses.

There are advantages to obtaining international patents if the underlying strategy is sound. These advantages include strengthening and increasing the value of your portfolio, and further limiting access by your competitors to your market sites. Having foreign patents also impedes your competition from manufacturing its competing product and transporting it to where it will be marketed. These can be valuable tools for you. However, they also come with liabilities.

First and perhaps the most obvious liability is the increased costs associated with filing PCT applications. PCT itself charges certain fees, as does each country to which you ultimately apply. Once the patents are issued,

---

** World Intellectual Property Organization

there are, unfortunately, maintenance fees that must be paid if you are to retain a proprietary interest in the technology. Much like the United States collects renewal fees, so, too do other countries, which have their own payment requirements.

Then, there is the increased file history. The ISA report is thorough and its arguments and your responses become part of the record, in addition to those between you and the US examiner that are subject to discovery and can be used against you during an assertion. Of course, there will also be discourse between you and the examiners in the specific countries to which you applied. And, do not expect that, just because one country allowed your patent that the same would hold for another country. Each country is independent, with distinct requirements. Moreover, an argument that an examiner accepted in one country does not mean that it will be accepted in another.

The worst case scenario is when either the ISA or a country's examiner finds close prior art that you and the US examiner both missed. This finding, like all other correspondence, becomes part of the discoverable record and can undermine the validity of your patents in an assertion.

Indeed, having an international patent portfolio can be of great value and importance, but it comes with risks. Careful analysis should be undertaken before deciding whether or not to pursue these. The reader is referred to *Patent Engineering* [1] for a more detailed discussion of establishing a strategy that incorporates international patents.

Further Patenting Opportunities

Technology advances over time and your patent portfolio should, in general, advance with it. Moreover, as patents age and expire, it is frequently important to update your portfolio to protect the advances in your intellectual property. Yes, there are occasions when a single patent adequately protects your intellectual property for as long as a product remains commercially viable. Popeil's Veg-O-Matic [8] and Pocket Fisherman [9] appear to be examples of this. However, more often than not, as new problems arise, solutions to those problems are found and give rise to the opportunity and necessity to update your patent portfolio. As an example, consider the wrench, which is a device that has been around for centuries. Originally forged by blacksmiths, today's wrenches are designed to meet today's challenges. Snap-On Tools is the assignee for 92 US patents issued between 1971 and 2016 that specify "wrench" in the claims. Similarly, Stanley owns 35 US patents. Indeed, even wrenches are evolving.

A more high-tech illustrative device is the oxygen or O_2 sensor used in automobiles to control emissions and improve fuel economy. Originally invented and patented in the 1970s, this device continues to be the subject of technological advancements, with ongoing patents being issued. For example, Bosch was assigned its first patent on this device in 1976 [10] and its 110th patent [11] in 2016–40 years later! As discussed in *Patent Engineering* [1], other automotive companies also have extensive and evolving patent portfolios around this technology. Obviously, the original patents have long expired. Yet, this technology remains vital to automobile manufacturers today.

During this period of time, carburetors gave way to fuel injection. The O_2 sensor, located in the exhaust system, originally did not participate in emissions control until it warmed up from the heated exhaust. Today, heated O_2 sensors respond more quickly, thereby limiting the noxious emissions produced by cold engines. The integration of the O_2 sensors with today's central electronic modules has led to both software and hardware developments. The original sensors had a life expectancy of about 15,000 miles. This was rapidly improved, with today's sensors often lasting the life of the car.

Connectors, software, materials, and structures and operations of these sensors have evolved with increasing CAFE[††] standards. As the technology evolved, new technical problems arose and their solutions provided ample patenting opportunities. Are these patents important or valuable? If you were an automotive manufacturer and did not have access to this technology, you would not be able to sell your vehicles. You would either have to buy the technology from other companies, paying whatever price they demanded, or you would need to have a sufficiently broad patent portfolio to force those companies to negotiate cross-licensing agreements with you.

Will your technology be viable in the market in 40+ years? One would have to be an exceptional prognosticator to accurately predict that. However, as discussed by Burke [12], technology rarely blooms forth on its own. Rather, technological advances are built on prior developments, often in seemingly unrelated areas. Perhaps your specific products that you are presently envisioning will become obsolete and will no longer be viable. However, it is likely that new technology and the resulting products will spring forth from the older technology and your patent portfolio, if properly designed and implemented, will continue to bear revenue for you.

---

†† Federally mandated Corporate Average Fuel Economy requirements.

References

1. D. S. Rimai, *Patent Engineering*, Scrivener Publishing, Beverly, MA (2016).
2. https://www.uspto.gov/web/offices/pac/mpep/s1895.html.
3. https://en.wikipedia.org/wiki/Continuing_patent_application.
4. https://patentlyo.com/patent/2012/09/continuations-in-part-and-priority-claims.html.
5. http://www.bitlaw.com/source/mpep/201_08.html.
6. http://www.cambia.org/daisy/patentlens/2645.html.
7. http://www.wipo.int/pct/en/faqs/faqs.html.
8. S. J. Popeil, U. S. Patent #3,933,315 (1976).
9. S. J. Popeil, U. S. Patent #4,027,419 (1977).
10. H. Eisele and G. Stumpp, U. S. Patent #3,942,496 (1976).
11. E. M. Doran, D. J. Cook, J. Oudart, and N. Ravi, U. S. Patent #9,528,426 (2016).
12. J. Burke, *Connections*, Little, Brown, Boston, MA (1978).

15

Final Thoughts

In Case of a Tight Deadline: Provisional Patent Applications

You have seen by this time that building a valuable patent portfolio that creates substantial fences around your intellectual property and impedes others from encroaching into your market space can be, unfortunately, a long and expensive process.

Long is often the operative word. You have to identify the inventions for which you wish to file patent applications, draft proposed claims and do a prior art search on those claims before you start writing your applications. You will obviously have to identify the distinct and separate inventions, as each invention will need its own application. That means a lot of time has to go into proposing those claims and conducting the appropriate prior art searches. You may have to revise your claims, based on your analysis of the search results. Once this is done, you can start writing the applications.

But, how do you proceed should you not have sufficient time for all the steps necessary to implement your patent strategy? Such short time periods often occur under various scenarios. Consider the following cases:

1. You have been feverishly developing technology that will probably be used in your product slated for introduction at the big trade show next week. It is now Thursday and, by Saturday, you will be shipping your product out so that you can set it up at the trade show on Sunday for the start on Monday.

2. You are about to begin jointly developing necessary technology with another company. Whereas you or your company possess the expertise to develop, for example, the mechanical subsystems and the electronics within your product, you need to contract with another company to develop the software. In that capacity, the software company will gain knowledge of the proprietary technology within your product and may invent or think they are innovating solutions to your problems. They will own the patents that result from their applications. Yes, you could contract with them to only supply your company with that technology, but that would preclude your being able to shop around for other suppliers. By the way, technical representatives from that company will be showing up at your door within the next two days to begin work.

3. You are planning to invite your preferred customers to your plant to give them an advanced look at your forthcoming product featuring all the new innovations on which you have been working. This product should blow the socks off of your competitors and garner a major portion of the marketplace for you. You are, of course, cautious and thorough and have carefully vetted all the invitees. Moreover, you had each one sign a nondisclosure agreement (NDA) stating that they will not divulge any of the information to which they were made privy for a period of two years from the date of their visit. Each visitor fully understands the seriousness of divulging the information that they are about to receive and, being ethical, have no intention of disclosing anything. Yet, by accident, while comparing product features with your competitor, one of your customers inadvertently lets slip some of that proprietary information. That constitutes a disclosure and the one year clock to file

your applications begins to tick. Worse, your competitor rushes to figure out how you would solve the problems necessary to offer comparable features, or perhaps was already working on them and speeds up their application process. Remember, the patent is awarded to the first to file. Sure, you can sue your customer for damages, but the loss that you suffered from that disclosure can easily dwarf the ability of your customer to pay. Moreover, do you really want to gain a reputation of suing your customers?

4. We live in a competitive world and you find out that another company is working on the technology that appears to be similar to that which you have been developing. You do not know what their time line for filing applications is, but you are concerned that they may get to the patent office before you. Again, you are reminded that the patents are awarded to the first to file their applications.

There are, undoubtedly, additional reasons why you can be faced with uncomfortably tight deadlines that require the rapid filing of patent applications in order to obtain your priority date before someone else does. How does one go about doing this? The answer is the filing of a provisional patent application.

For all practical purposes, a provisional patent application contains much of the same information that would be present in a patent application except it is missing the claims. You want to include your Detailed Description of the Invention, including the necessary figures, a description the problem and a discussion of why the prior art fails to solve that problem. Once you file a provisional application, you have one year to finalize it, i.e., convert the provisional application into one or more actual patent applications.

During the discussions presented in this book, we emphasized the importance of preparing a thorough patent strategy and writing multiple applications based on that strategy. We also emphasized that, although common disclosures covering multiple inventions could be written, the information contained in those disclosures should be presented primarily to support the claims. Also discussed was the importance of first writing the claims, conducting a prior art search, and possibly revising the claims as a result of the findings of that search. The problem or problems solved would be presented in such a manner so that either single pieces of the prior art or a combination thereof could not predict your invention. You have also reviewed your potential patent applications before filing to ensure that you covered the desired technology and that you did not claim the same invention in more than one application.

When writing a provisional patent application, the picture is greatly changed. You presumably have not written the claims. You need to focus on how you solved perhaps multiple problems because you will likely be filing a single provisional application that you will subsequently convert into several patent applications. In other words, you do not explicitly know what claims your disclosure will have to support and, to make matters more complicated, will have to support to protect multiple inventions. You will likely have to disclose more information than would be necessary if you were to be filing actual patent applications instead of a provisional one. You will also likely not have as clear a definition of the problems that your inventions solved as you would for final applications. Obviously, you would incorporate your knowledge of the prior art, as best you can, when writing a provisional application.

Provisional applications will not be searched and there is no prosecution of them. They do have to either be converted into final applications within the one-year time frame or they will be considered abandoned. The latter situation, of course, relegates them to the prior art and can affect your ability to file actual patent applications on the subject material. This can be especially problematic as, presumably, you have disclosed all your inventions in the provisional application. Writing provisional patent applications is a fine art, as it does require that you anticipate what your claims will ultimately be and what a more thorough search of the prior art might reveal. However, it is a good way of establishing a priority date that would prevent others from filing. In the worst case scenario, you could abandon the provisional application and submit actual applications. However, that would cause you to lose your priority date. With all this, the filing of provisional applications can establish your being the inventor prior to your having to disclose the technology under circumstances such as those described at the beginning of this section.

The Cost of Building and Maintaining a Patent Portfolio Is More Than I Can Afford

The costs associated with building and maintaining a patent portfolio that adequately protects your intellectual property are, unfortunately, quite high. However, it would be improper to consider solely the price of protecting your intellectual property without taking into account the value of your products in the market. How much revenue do you expect to receive from your products? How much did you spend on R&D? How much did it cost you to tool up to produce your products? And how expensive are the costs associated with sales, distribution, and advertising?

It would also be a mistake to just consider your patent portfolio as an expense. Rather, you should consider it as part of your product stream, complete with its own value that reflects how well it establishes your proprietary position in the market, how much access you gain to other's technology through cross-licensing agreements, and how much revenue you could realize from it if you chose to sell or lease rights to use your patents.

And now, after due consideration of the above, you have decided that you cannot afford as extensive a patent portfolio as would be required to totally protect your intellectual property. What can you do?

To answer this question, let us first review why a patent portfolio that allows you to totally own the problem is desirable rather than just having a portfolio consisting of separate patents that protect distinct inventions, with little thought to building a protective wall around your intellectual property.

The reader is reminded that a patent does not give its owner the right to practice the claimed technology. Rather, a patent gives the owner the ability to exclude others from practicing that technology. In an ideal world, your goal would be to build a patent portfolio that allows you to totally own the problem. This includes, not only owning patents that cover the fundamental technology, but also all the alternative approaches that would allow someone to market a competitive product. Owning the problem would also include owning the necessary enabling technology, i.e., the solutions to those problems that are encountered when implementing the fundamental technology. These are generally fairly simple but extremely vital solutions that enable your product to actually function as intended in the hands of the user.

The reader is also reminded that patents have value only when someone else needs access to the claimed technology. Moreover, it is generally impossible to a priori determine which patents are valuable. Sometimes fundamental patents have immense value. However, if a competitor comes up with an alternative fundamental approach that enables the production of a competitive product, it may fall upon the patents covering the enabling technology to prevent intrusion into your market space. As discussed in previous chapters of this book, the Kodak-Polaroid instant photography lawsuit is the quintessential example of this.

Even potentially worse are situations where a company patents certain core or fundamental technology and then fails to follow up with patenting the enabling technology. This leaves an opening for the competition to do so. In a worst case scenario, the competition can totally encompass your fundamental patents and continue to do so as your patents age. There are occasions that the competition succeeds at blocking the originator of the technology from marketing innovative products and does not even have to pay royalties to market its own products as the fundamental patents expire. As previously discussed, patents teach in exchange for the protection given, but if the patent portfolio does not properly protect the intellectual property, you may have just given away a lot of information without obtaining much benefit. And remember, patents do not give you the right to practice your inventions. Rather, they confer on you the right to exclude others from practicing your inventions. A competitor that owns patents that cover necessary enabling technology can readily prevent you from marketing your products using technology that you developed.

In the real world, it is often not feasible to totally own the problem. Rather, it is probable that some of the technology that you will need is protected by patents owned by others. In that case, you want to build a portfolio that will allow you to gain access to that technology through cross-licensing agreements, whereby each company allows the other to use their respective claimed technology in the patents covered by the agreement.

Another, and probably more beneficial way, to avoid being blocked from practicing your own technology by patents owned by others, is to prevent others from obtaining those patents in the first place. This can be accomplished in a less costly manner by selectively choosing material to disclose via some sort of publication.

You should be certain that you do not want to patent the material that you have selected to publish. Once you have determined this, you have several options from which to choose.

One option is to publish your findings in a peer-reviewed journal. This not only enhances your reputation, but also allows you to benefit from making your research a topic of discussion among experts in your field with whom you normally would not have interactions. This is one of the most beneficial ways to broaden your thought processes and enhance your own critical analysis skills.

Publishing in trade journals and conference proceedings are suitable alternatives to submitting your work to peer-reviewed journals. Such publication is generally easier because of the absence of the reviewing process. However, for the same reason, the prestige you gain and the feedback you obtain are also decreased for the same reason. Also, the distribution of conference materials tends to be more limited than that of the peer-reviewed journals. This can be either beneficial or detrimental. It is beneficial because, although the publication of your work does constitute a legal disclosure, it may not be seen by competitors, thereby keeping your advances somewhat under wraps. It is detrimental because the limited circulation impedes your benefitting from the feedback you get from other professionals.

Another alternative for publishing your invention is Research Disclosure [1]. This publication is sent to every major patent office and, under PCT (Patent Cooperation Treaty, discussed in Chapter 14), has to be searched.

Of course, you can publish your invention via a paid advertisement or documented disclosure at a trade show. However, there is yet another route for publishing a disclosure that documents your invention. Consider describing the invention in a related patent application. After all, there is no legal reason why such material cannot be included in a patent application, even if it is not directly relevant to the application under consideration.

Yes, it is acknowledged that you, the reader, have been discouraged in this book from including material that is not supportive of the claims. That policy, in general, is correct because premature or inadvertent disclosures can compromise the patentability of future inventions. However, that is not the case here. You have formulated a patent strategy and have concluded that, despite the fact that the material that you are presently considering likely constitutes an invention, you just are not in a position, financially or otherwise, to include it in your portfolio. However, its being patented by another entity can adversely affect your ability to market your own technology. And, after all, you are planning to publish that invention to block anyone else from patenting it.

The disclosure of the material in question within a patent application should be treated as any material for which you intend to write claims. That is, you define the problem in the Background of the Invention section, include your prior art search results, and discuss how this particular invention solved the problem in the Detailed Description of the Invention section. Naturally, appropriate figures should also be included. In essence, you are including everything in the patent application except for claims around the invention.

This approach has several advantages over the previously discussed methods of publishing. If, for some reason, your proposed patent application is rejected, it allows you to rewrite, perhaps restricting, the claims to include the additional material that is also being included within a new set of proposed claims. Moreover, should conditions change in the near future or, upon reflection, it appears that this additional invention is more valuable than originally supposed, you can now file an additional application as a continuation. Including this material puts you in a strong position to address your patent needs within the time allowed.

There is yet another approach to protecting your technology. Consider not divulging the material and keeping it as a trade secret. The quintessential example of a trade secret is the formula for Coca Cola syrup.

Keeping material a trade secret is most suitable for those areas of technology that cannot be reverse-engineered or analyzed and which would also likely be of value long after the life of a patent has expired. However, there are other instances whereby companies erroneously try to handle intellectual property as trade secrets. These include intellectual property in which the inventive features can readily be discerned. How do you keep something a secret if anyone can see it? Yet, it is not uncommon for a company to unwisely do exactly this.

The other area that is often erroneously treated as a trade secret involves either manufacturing processes or the development of proprietary tools that are used in service industries in which a service, and not the devices, are sold. In both instances, it is mistakenly assumed that an outsider would not be able to ascertain the manufacturing techniques or the design of the instruments being used.

Trade secrets may have, at one time, been an appropriate approach to safeguarding your intellectual property. However, that is no longer the case. The days when employees worked for a single company all their lives and became part of a company's "family" are long gone. Today, the average tenure of an employee with a single employer is approximately five years. The former employees will then either seek employment elsewhere or start their own businesses. In either event, their value in the market is based on what they know, which generally comprises the intellectual property they gleaned while working at your company. And, their having signed nondisclosure or do-not-compete agreements are of limited value to you. Your proprietary information has walked out the door with your former employee, especially if that employee had been laid off or otherwise terminated. The lesson here is that trade secrets should only be used to protect that information that could really be kept as a secret and that you will have to take extreme measures to make sure that, even within your company, access to that information is very limited.

Concluding Remarks

Building and implementing a patent strategy and maintaining the resulting patent portfolio takes a lot of time, effort, and money. However, the costs of not doing so may be that your company is prevented from selling those products for which you have spent so much more in R&D, tooling, and sales, advertising, and distribution. In the worst case scenario, competitors may learn about your technology from your patents and outcompete you, forcing you out of business. Whether you like it or not, patenting is part of doing business.

However, a patent portfolio should not be thought of as just another expense of doing business – something to be minimized. Sure, its costs have to be constrained. However, it is far more beneficial to think of your patent portfolio as part of your product stream – a stream that can produce revenues in the form of licensing fees and allow you to gain access to technology that you need but that is possessed by others through the use of cross-licensing agreements.

There is another advantage to building a patent portfolio. The very process of contemplating your technology in the critical manner necessary to file a complementary set of patent applications forces you to carefully consider both your and your competitors' technologies and what the competing products offer to your customers. You cannot hand wave your way to a patent portfolio. You must carefully consider and describe all aspects of how others have tried to address the problems in the past – the so-called prior art. You must then critically analyze the shortcomings of that art and describe how the technology that you have developed solves those problems, allowing you to offer a product that has significant advantages to your customers. And, the careful analysis that goes into building your portfolio helps you avoid the situation espoused by Lewis Carroll: "'I could have done it in a much more complicated way,' said the Red Queen, immensely proud [2]." Critical analysis at every step is extremely important in today's global, competitive, and rapidly evolving world. The building and implementation of a complete and thorough patent strategy can readily sharpen your technological skills that help drive your company to the next level of success.

References

1. http://www.researchdisclosure.com/
2. http://www.azquotes.com/quote/1304466

Appendix 1

Electrophotography: Building a Patent Portfolio in a Mature but Evolving Field

Background

The electrophotographic process, often referred to as xerography, has been extensively used in this book for exemplary purposes. To facilitate the readers' comprehension of this technology, it is worthwhile to give a brief introduction. For more detailed descriptions of the equipment, materials, and electrophotographic process, the reader is referred to several texts on the subject [1–3].

The use of electrophotography as an exemplary technology for discussing patents was not simply chosen because of the author's background in this area. Rather, it was chosen because, despite its existence for approximately 80 years, during which time printers and copiers using this technology were developed and marketed by numerous companies, electrophotography is still the subject of much development. As a result, it remains an area of intense patent activity despite its being a mature field comprising much prior art. This appendix illustrates how it is possible to address problems arising from an evolving technology that address previously unforeseen applications, thereby producing many new patents.

First, unlike most technological advances, electrophotography arose from the inventions of a single individual - Chester Carlson [4, 5]. His patents, awarded in 1940 and 1942, were filed in 1938 and 1939, respectively. His technology was uniquely disruptive in that it eventually led to the elimination of alternatives such as the use of carbon paper, Verifax copiers*, ditto masters, and mimeographic processes. However, at the time of his invention, the future potential of electrophotography was not appreciated.†

Second, in the approximately 80 years since its invention, electrophotography has morphed from the invention that nobody wanted into a multibillion dollar per year international business encompassing many companies, including Xerox, Eastman Kodak, Ricoh, Canon, Minolta, and many others. In and by themselves, such ongoing activities for an extended period such as have occurred in this field would generate a multitude of patents, as competing companies attempt to gain advantages over each other in the marketplace. However, there is yet another reason for all the patent activity. The use of this technology has evolved to meet new and exciting applications and opportunities that were unforeseen just a few years ago.

Originally, electrophotography was used primarily to reproduce documents. The quality of those reproductions was generally poor and the main requirement was that the copy had to be readable. It was often extremely problematic to make a copy of a copy (often referred to as "second generation" copies) because the image degradation was so extreme. Pictorial content was rare and, at the time, not really suitable for electrophotographic reproduction. Moreover, as office documents consisted mainly of black and white text, the desire for processes that reproduced color was minimal. In fact, up until the 1970s, zinc oxide (ZnO) was incorporated into the paper receiver and served as the photoreceptor. There was no separate photoreceptor or transfer subsystem. The use of the zinc oxide coated paper gave rise to the displeasing feel of the copies.

---

* The Verifax process used silver halide technology to copy a document, which was then transferred to an absorbent paper by pressing the developed silver halide print against the receiving paper.
† The attempts made by Carlson to sell his technology to a multitude of established companies such as IBM and Eastman Kodak is well documented. After repeated failures, Carlson attracted the interest of Joseph Wilson, CEO of a failing photographic paper company named Haloid. Wilson bet his company on this new technology and changed its name to Xerox, derived from the Greek and meaning "dry writing".

In 1959 Xerox introduced the Model 914 plain paper copier.[‡] Building on the photoreceptive technology developed by Dessauer and Clark [6], the novel copier introduced the concept of transferring the toner image from a separate photoreceptor to a paper receiver.

As evidenced by a patent issued to Dessauer *et al.* [7], Xerox realized the importance of being able to electrophotographically produce color documents. Xerox introduced its Model 6500 color copier in 1973. When producing a color document, a separation of each color, generally one of the subtractive primary colors (cyan, magenta, yellow, and black), possibly augmented with certain custom colors, is individually produced and sequentially transferred to a receiver such as paper.[§]

The commercial success of the Xerox 6500 was less than spectacular. At that time there were relatively few color documents, limiting the demand for a color copier. Moreover, the range of colors (a.k.a. the color gamut) and the degree of brightness or saturation obtained with the Xerox 6500 was not extensive. As a result, this copier could not adequately reproduce the high quality color pictures such as those published in art or medical books or in high-quality magazines such as *National Geographic*. Rather, this copier was most suitable for the copying of documents containing graphs wherein the information density could be increased by incorporating color marks and lines. However, as publishers were reluctant to include such graphs in their journals because of the large incremental costs of printing, such originals were rare even in the scientific community. In short, the Xerox 6500 was a product ahead of its time without the ability to meet customer demands when the time ripened.

In short the use of electrophotography was limited to office copiers for which the main criterion was to reproduce primarily black and white alphanumeric documents, using the original document as the source, with adequate quality so as to be readable. However, the world was about to change due to the space program.

---

‡ The term "plain paper copier" is a misnomer, as the properties of the paper, including its electrical resistivity, surface topography, sizing, moisture content, etc. are all carefully controlled. A more proper term is electrophotographic or xerographic paper. A piece of randomly selected paper, such as one suitable for use in a Verifax, mimeograph, or ink jet printer is often unsuitable for use in an electrophotographic printer and can, in fact, damage the printer if it is used.

§ In offset press technology, the separations are sequentially transferred, in register, to an intermediate transfer member and then the entire color print is transferred to the receiver. This simplifies paper handling, as the paper has only to be transported through the printer once, rather than having to be wrapped around a roller that allows the separations to be transferred in register.

The need to launch equipment into space and gather needed information required that electronic devices be made lighter and have greater abilities and faster response times than that of the equipment available at that time. Transistorized electronics, while a great improvement over the earlier vacuum tubes, were still too heavy and slow, and consumed too much power. While computers such as the IBM 360/370 had lots of computing power, they were massive and, as anyone who punched Hollerith cards and waited for their programs to run remembers, they were slow and rather unfriendly to use. Smaller computers such as the IBM 1620 were still massive, consumed too much power, and were too slow for the space age requirements.

The advent of the integrated circuit (IC), in which hundreds or thousands of formerly discrete electronic components were integrated into a single chip, reduced the size, weight, and power consumption of computers. This directly led to several companies such as Tandy Radio Shack and Atari offering to consumers so-called "home computers" in the early 1980s. Within a few years, companies such as Hewlett Packard turned their focus from producing laboratory electronics to manufacturing home computers and printers. Other startup companies such as Microsoft and Apple rapidly grew to become household names.

In addition to electronics, the space program impacted other areas of research, such as materials science. In particular, areas such as polymer and ceramic science showed remarkable advances. Lasers, for example, went from being large and expensive, with limited available light frequencies, to small, inexpensive devices with more available colors. Light emitting diodes (LEDs) became more capable and common. And, controllable electrical properties of polymers added to their utility. These advances directly affected the lives of most people. For example, automobiles are now safer and produce more power and obtain better mileage with fewer emissions due to the confluence of the advances in materials science and electronics. Communications have seen revolutionary changes, with land line telephones giving rise to cellular phones, which, in turn, have given rise to smart phones. It is, today, a rare household that does not have a computer that ties into the internet and has all but eliminated the typewriter of an earlier day. And, the invention of the charge coupled device (CCD) and advances in ceramics that allowed the growing of better silicon crystals that in turn allowed the digital camera, originally invented by Lloyd and Sasson [8], to become household products that all but eliminated conventional silver halide photography. Today, it is unusual for a cell phone to not incorporate the ability to digitally capture images, thereby converting a device originally restricted to oral communications into a device that can capture and send pictures.

In fact, these advances have also enabled modern medical imaging and testing including the use of ultrasonic imaging, CT scans, and MRI.

The increase in both the number and capabilities of electronic devices has led to a world-wide increase in the number of pages being printed each year, especially with electrophotographic printers. According to research conducted by the International Data Corporation in 2011 [9], the number of digitally produced pages increased to 3.1 trillion in 2010, led by an increase of 7.3% over 2009 in developing countries. Most of the increase is in the area of color printing.

The increased ability to produce high quality color electronic originals has resulted in a demand to be able to make high quality color prints of those originals. The printers must have high reliability and, in order to compete with conventional printing technology such as lithography [10, 11], must be able to produce prints at a high rate of speed. These requirements have changed the perceived output of electrophotographic printers from just an office copier for black and white alphanumeric documents to full-color, high quality digital printers. Thus, this field still is ripe for innovation despite its having been first commercialized approximately 80 years ago. It is for these reasons that examples have been chosen throughout this book to illustrate various points. And, although some discussion of the technology was presented in the appropriate sections, a more comprehensive summary is included here to facilitate comprehension by the reader.

The Electrophotographic Process

In an electrophotographic engine (often referred to as a xerographic engine from the Greek meaning "dry writing"), as depicted in Figure A1, a photoreceptor (100) is initially uniformly charged by a charging device (150). An electrostatic latent image is then created on the photoreceptor by image-wise exposing the photoreceptor to electromagnetic radiation (175), generally in the infrared or visible portions of the spectrum. As the photoreceptor rotates into effective contact with a development station (400), toner is deposited onto the photoreceptor, thereby converting the electrostatic latent image into a visible image.

The toner image is then transferred to a receiver (600) by sandwiching the receiver between the image-bearing photoreceptor and a transfer-inducing member (500). Most commonly, transfer is induced by subjecting the receiver to pressure that presses it against the toner image-bearing photoreceptor while urging the electrostatically charged toner particles towards the receiver using an applied electrostatic field.

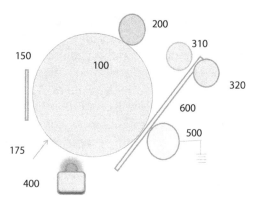

Figure A1 A typical electrophotographic printer.

At this point the image is not fixed to the receiver and can be readily brushed off. To permanently fix the image, the image-bearing receiver is then separated from contact with the photoreceptor and transported through a fusing subsystem. This generally comprises two rollers (310 and 320), of which at least one is heated to a temperature sufficiently high to soften the toner while subjecting the toner to sufficient pressure as to allow it to flow and bond to the receiver.

The photoreceptor is then rotated into contact with a cleaning subsystem (200) that removes any untransferred toner, as well as other contaminants including ions from the charging process, paper dust, etc., thereby preparing the photoreceptor for the next image to be printed.

In some instances it is necessary to produce multiple toner images on a photoreceptor and to transfer those toner images in register to a receiver. For example, this is commonly done when making full-color prints. In this instance, a color separation corresponding to each of the subtractive primary colors¶ (cyan, magenta, and yellow) containing the specific color information to be produced must be transferred while maintaining a color-to-color registration of a few microns. In addition, black toner is commonly added to the primaries, resulting in a print comprising at least four colorants, all of which must be transferred in register.

There are two options for making prints that require a plurality of toner colors. The first is to sequentially produce each color on the same

---

¶ The subtractive primary colors are those colors that, when subtracted from white light, will result in black. These are commonly used in printing and photography to produce color prints. In contrast, the additive primary colors (red, green, and blue) when combined will produce white light. These are used to generate images on televisions.

photoreceptor. In this case the first toner images must be transferred to the receiver prior to producing the second. To accomplish this, if transfer is done to a final receiver, such as a sheet of paper, the paper must be picked up in such a manner, such as wrapping it around the transfer roller, so that the individual toner images can be sequentially transferred in register to the paper. An alternative to this requires that the toner images be first transferred, in register, to another roller known as a transfer intermediate member. The completed print is then transferred to the final receiver in one pass of that receiver.

Although the above configuration works reasonably well for producing color prints, the required multiple transfers cuts productivity significantly. To produce a print requiring four colors, for example, would require four cycles of the printer, compared to one for a simple black and white print.

In order to maintain productivity, high volume/high speed electrophotographic engines frequently gang individual modules together, each capable of producing a print having a single color, in a manner similar to that used in offset lithographic printers.

Finally, before discussing the specific subsystems, let us delve into several aspects that affect perceived image quality that had to evolve with the changing use for this technology. These include, but are not necessarily limited to, granularity, resolution, color gamut, and contrast.

Granularity is the quantitative metric of perceived graininess of a print. Graininess refers to variations in density on a small size scale, often referred to as noise. Mathematically, granularity is essentially the standard deviation of the mean image density within a relatively small area. Factors that affect graininess include toner size, agglomeration of toner particles, and so-called "dot explosion" wherein the highly charged particles repel each other, resulting in the toner particles that were supposed to be deposited into a dark or high density region flying apart or separating and being deposited in areas of the print other than in those desired. Years ago, toner particles as large as 20 μm in diameter were commonly used. Today, it is typical for an electrophotographic engine to use toner particles having diameters in the 6 μm to 8 μm range. To match the granularity of a silver halide photograph, one would need to use toners having a diameter less than 3.5 μm. As will be discussed later in this appendix, reducing the diameter of usable toner has presented many technical challenges that had to be overcome.

Resolution and the closely related issue of mottle, is similar to granularity but on a larger scale. Whereas grain is perceivable as noise occurring with a wavelength of perhaps 0.1 mm or less, resolution involves being able to distinguish features in the range of between about 0.1 mm and 1.0 mm. Mottle refers to random irregularities in the print density with a wavelength greater than 1.0 mm.

Although these noise factors were not terribly important when electrophotography was used principally as an office copier that was used to reproduce alphanumeric documents, they are vitally important when printing images with significant pictorial content.

Color gamut refers to the range of colors that can be produced by a set of colorants. In an ideal world, subtracting each of the subtractive primaries (cyan, magenta, and yellow) from white light would result in black. Moreover, by reducing the amount of a selected primary, one should be able to obtain all colors in the spectrum. However, we live in the real world where toners having ideal subtractive primary colors do not exist. More often than not, just printing with the subtractive primaries would result in a rather muddy, rather than a saturated, black and would require the use of a lot of toner to achieve even that. Accordingly, black is commonly incorporated as an additional subtractive primary and image analysis is performed prior to the actual printing so that colors that would just contribute to the formation of black are eliminated and black toner is substituted for that combination of colors, resulting in a purer black that uses less of expensive toner.

Even with this, there are colors that cannot be accurately produced. Logos such as IBM blue, Coca Cola red, and Kodak yellow are examples of such colors. In these cases it is often necessary to add custom spot colors to accurately print the desired color. This is often done in offset lithography, in which presses with eight or more printing stations, each containing a distinct color, are commonly used.

Finally, let us consider contrast. In every print there are dark regions where a maximum of incident light is absorbed, often referred to as D_{max}. There are other regions where little or no incident light is absorbed. This is referred to as D_{min}. The number of discernable gray levels that a process can generate between D_{max} and D_{min} is referred to as the contrast. Systems that generate many levels of gray are referred to as "low contrast", whereas those that produce only a few are referred to as "high contrast". Depending on the application, it may be preferable to use either a low or high contrast process.

As an example of the benefit obtained with a high contrast system, consider an office copier where the documents to be reproduced consist overwhelmingly of alphanumeric content. Here, it is desirable to sharply reproduce lines without generating a lot of background that may be present on the original document – perhaps smudges from fingerprints or background from the original paper used. Perhaps some of us remember the days when graph paper was sold that had a light ruling that would not reproduce. This was done so that graphs could be accurately drawn and still allow clear copies to be made.

Low contrast is important when pictorial content is to be printed. In this instance, it is important to be able to produce, not only the high density portions, but the mid-tone density regions so as not to lose information and to allow the resulting prints to have a pleasing appearance. Consider, for example, printing a picture of a person standing next to a tree on a sunny day. A high contrast system would capture the predominant high density regions – perhaps an outline of the head and body, and the tree. Lower density regions, such as where the sun is shining on the person, would be lost. Shadow regions, such as the shade cast by the tree on the person and ground, would either be lost or be printed as D_{max}, thereby losing much of the information that is vital when producing a document with pictorial content. Let us now look at how gray scale is obtained with various printing methods.

In lithography, where ink is either deposited as D_{max} in a particular area or no ink is deposited, gray scale is obtained using halftones. This is explained as follows. Consider that the paper onto which the image is to be printed consists of an imaginary grid similar to that of graph paper. For high quality printing, such as in premium journals, there may be 200 lines per inch or more. Lower quality printing, such as that employed in newspapers, may use a grid with as few as 80 lines per inch.

A small drop of ink is deposited onto the intersection of each pair of grid lines. The size of the drop determines the perceived density, which is an average of the D_{max} of the drop and the remaining area of the paper within the cell defined by the grid lines. This method of producing a gray scale is called "halftoning".

It is important that the drops of ink printed on the paper be uniform in shape and in size, as irregularities will give rise to noise perceived as either grain or mottle. It is also vital that, when producing color prints, each color be precisely imprinted on the paper in exactly the same location as the previous colors, as a failure to accurately register the drops will result in a perceived shift in the colors of the print, as well as a blurriness of the image. It is apparent that being able to accurately control the motion of the paper as it traverses from one inking station to the next is crucial if you want to produce high quality prints.

In contrast to using halftone printing, some technologies such as conventional silver halide (AgX) photographic printing generate gray scale using a continuous tone process. In AgX photography, dyes are produced during the development process from so-called "dye couplers" that are incorporated in the light sensitive materials. The more exposure to light, the more dye that is produced and the darker the color. In contrast to lithography, there is no grid pattern onto which D_{max} densities of inks or dyes are deposited. Rather, the amount of dye produced varies continuously over the area of the print, hence the term "continuous tone".

Gray scale in electrophotography can be produced as a halftone, a continuous tone, or a combination thereof, depending on the way the electrostatic latent image is produced. This gives electrophotographic technology the means to control gray level more precisely than either of the other technologies could do. However, benefitting from this capability depends on a number of components. These include the way the electrostatic latent image is produced by a device referred to as a "writer", the properties of the photoreceptor and the charging subsystem, the way the toner is deposited by the development subsystem, the toner properties themselves, and the transfer and fusing subsystems. These technologies are all evolving to meet current and future demands.

To more fully appreciate how the capabilities of electrophotographic technology have evolved to meet the demands of consumers, let us now discuss some of the subsystems employed.

Photoreceptor

The photoreceptor can be considered the central member of an electrophotographic printer, as most of the other subsystems come into contact with it.

The photoreceptor is either a flexible web or a rigid drum. A photoreceptor is a material that acts as an insulator or dielectric in the absence of illumination in the frequency absorbed by the photoreceptor and an applied electric field. However, when appropriately illuminated and with a sufficiently large applied electric field, the photoreceptor becomes electrically conductive.

Why are both illumination and an applied electric field necessary for a photoreceptor to become electrically conductive? The illumination is required to excite an electron from within the photoreceptive molecule. Upon excitation, a free electron is produced, leaving behind a positively charged hole. However, the negatively charged electron is, by Coulomb's law, attracted to the hole and will immediately recombine in a process called "geminate recombination" unless the two are physically separated. The separation requires the presence of the applied electric field.

In the early days of plain paper copiers, amorphous selenium (designated as α-Se), an inorganic material**, was often the photoreceptor of choice. However, organic photoreceptors are generally preferred today.

An electrophotographic engine will contain at least one photoreceptor. However, depending on its configuration and intended applications, there may be multiple photoreceptors. For example, when producing color documents that require the use of the subtractive primary colors, or in instances that incorporate custom colors or clear toner, additional photoreceptors may be present. Whether one or more photoreceptors are required depends on the specific configuration of the engine, as will be discussed in the section of this appendix that covers the transfer process.

Organic photoreceptors have advantages over α-Se. For one, they are nontoxic. However, perhaps more important to their actual performance is that they have a lower dielectric constant. This allows them to experience a stronger applied electric field for a given amount of deposited charge. They may also be flexible, thereby allowing them to be used in a web or belt configuration in addition to the traditional photoreceptive drum. However, organic photoreceptors are generally much more complex than are inorganic photoreceptors. To illustrate this, let us consider the structure of a typical organic photoreceptor.

First, an organic photoreceptor needs some sort of support. This can be an aluminum cylinder when the photoreceptor will take the form of a rigid drum. Alternatively, it can be a strong but flexible polymer belt when the particular engine calls for a photoreceptor in the form of a web. Suitable polymers for belts include Mylar, Estar, and Kaptan-H.

In order to electrically charge and image-wise discharge the photoreceptor, it is necessary to have an electrically conducting ground plane. If the photoreceptor is in the form of a rigid roller, the support can be metallic, as would be the case of the aforementioned aluminum cylinder. Thus, the support can serve two functions. However, if a polymer support or an insulating roller is used, an electrical conductor must be coated onto the support so that it lies between the support and the photoreceptive materials. Obviously, in order to be used as a ground plane, there also has to be some method of grounding the conductive layer as the photoreceptor is moving.

** In chemistry, organic molecules are generally classified as those containing carbon, whereas inorganic molecules do not. The definition of organic molecules has exceptions, as molecules such as carbon dioxide (CO_2) and calcium carbonate ($CaCO_3$) are considered inorganic even though they contain carbon. However, the converse, that molecules that do not contain carbon are classified as inorganic is always true.

The conducting layer generally consists of materials such as a thin film of nickel that had been evaporated onto the polymer support.

Overcoating the conductive layer is the actual photoconductive material or photoconductor. This is the actual component of the photoreceptor that generates the electron-hole pairs when exposed to light.

The photoconductor is generally in aggregate form and is contained within a matrix. It is this composite that is coated onto the electrical conductor and is commonly referred to as the "charge generating layer".

The photoreceptor just described performed adequately for the office copiers of 30 years ago, but does not meet the demands imposed on today's printers. Specifically, the electrostatic latent image can degrade due to a process known as "dark decay". In this process, electron-hole pairs can be created, not just from exposure to light, but from heat. The charges can then migrate to the charge on the surface of the photoreceptor, thereupon combining and neutralizing that charge. This would obviously degrade the electrostatic latent image and the visible print formed by toning the latent image. Whereas that might be tolerable when the process is applied strictly to reproducing alphanumeric office documents (especially in the past when image quality was of lesser importance), it would not be acceptable in today's environment in which high quality pictorial documents are created from electronic files on computers.

To reduce dark decay, the charge generating layer is overcoated with a "charge transport layer" that is designed to conduct either electrons or holes, but not both. Let us consider an example of how such a layer would mitigate dark decay.

Let us assume that the electrophotographic engine is to be configured so that the charged areas of the photoreceptor are developed by the toner. This is commonly done in a copier, where it is desired that the dark regions on the original are reproduced as D_{max} regions on the copy. Let us further assume that the toner particles will be negatively charged and the photoreceptor will be positively charged so that the charged areas of the photoconductor will attract the charged toner particles. Upon an image-wise exposure, the light areas of the original, corresponding to the unprinted areas, will reflect the light that discharges the photoreceptor in the light areas. Conversely, the dark regions of the original document will reflect little light, leaving the photoreceptor charged in those regions.

However, the thermally-induced generation of electron-hole pairs can reduce the charge on the photoreceptor in the non-illuminated portions, resulting in the dark decay of the electrostatic latent image. Obviously, this would inhibit the application of toner in the desired areas and would result in a degraded print.

To reduce the effects of dark decay, the aforementioned charge generating layer is overcoated with a charge transport layer (CTL). In this particular example, the CTL is designed to preferentially conduct holes. The positive charge deposited onto the surface of the photoreceptor consists of electrically-charged molecules from air that are large and tend not to migrate through solid materials. However, the charge generated in the charge-generating layer consists of electrons and holes. The holes are repelled by the positive charge deposited on the photoreceptor. The electrons, which are attracted to those charges, are prevented from migrating to the surface by the CTL, which will not transport them. Thus, the effects of dark decay are reduced.

The saga of advancing requirements on the photoreceptor do not end here. Rather, additional coatings are required to prevent damage and wear to the photoreceptor, facilitate release of the toner during transfer and cleaning, and resist the corrosive effects of the deposited ions, to name just a few of the issues for which continued improvement and innovation are required as the demands on this technology continue to increase.

Development, Developer, and Toner

As previously discussed, it is necessary to deposit electrically charged toner particles onto the photoreceptor in order to convert the electrostatic latent image into a visible one. It is the role of this subsystem to repeatedly deposit the correct amount of the correct color toner onto the correct, often microscopic, regions of the photoreceptor at a rate consistent with the speed of the electrophotographic engine.

The electromechanical device responsible for the image-wise deposition of toner onto the electrostatic latent image-bearing photoreceptor is known as a "development station" or subsystem. To understand the requirements placed on the development station, it is necessary to first discuss toners in order to appreciate the often contradictory factors that are required for their proper functioning.

In past years, all that was required was toner to be deposited in a manner that would create a readable document. Image quality was not of great importance. As the final receiver (the ZnO-coated papers) also contained the photoreceptive material, there was no need to transfer the toner from the photoreceptor to paper. The image had to be permanently fused to the paper, of course. At this time, toner particles had a diameter of about 20 μm, as neither granularity nor resolution were overly important. A typical copied document would consist of perhaps 10% of the paper surface covered by the toner, with the rest remaining bare paper.

With the advent of the plain paper copier, the ability to transfer toner became vital. This change occurred about the same time that customers were beginning to print documents containing pictorial content. While high contrast printing was desirable to obtain sharp, clear alphanumeric characters, gray scale became necessary to produce pleasing pictures. The ability to print solid areas, as opposed to just lines, became important, as did resolution and granularity. The diameter of the toner decreased to about 12 μm. Although it would have been desirable to print with smaller toner particles, the physics controlling the toner-to-photoreceptor adhesion changes, as electrostatic forces governing the adhesion of the toner to the photoreceptor decrease in importance and the relative importance of van der Waals forces increases [12].

The problem of transfer was addressed by applying nanometer-size clusters of silica particles to the surface of the toner particles. As the range of van der Waals forces is extremely short, the silica particles would break contact between the actual toner and the photoreceptor, thereby reducing the forces of adhesion and allowing transfer to occur with toners having diameters as small as approximately 7 μm. However, because the toner particles are all highly charged, reducing van der Waals forces also reduces cohesion between the particles, thereby increasing their propensity to fly apart rather than to tightly pack. This would increase granularity and decrease resolution and D_{max}. Moreover, silica tends to be hydrophilic and the absorption of water on the surface of the toner particles can affect the very charge stability that is necessary for the toner to function.

Toner must also fuse together in order to be permanently fixed to the paper. This generally requires that the toner particles soften and flow under heat and pressure, as applied during fusing. However, the rheological properties of the toner, which must be controlled to allow fusing, must also be limited to prevent the toner particles from cohering, thereby forming bricks while sitting in bottles being transported or stored in trucks and trains in hot climates. Moreover, it is important that the flow be limited in order to prevent stacks of documents from adhering to each other if left in a hot car. And, while this has to be carefully controlled as printers become faster, the ability of the toner to flow more quickly has to be enhanced to allow for shorter fusing times.

The above issues presuppose that the toner particles can be controllably charged and transported into a development nip formed between the development station and the latent image-bearing photoreceptor. This is the role of the development station.

The general requirements of a development station are simple. Toner must be electrically charged so that it can be attracted to the appropriate areas in the electrostatic latent image. It must be transported into operational proximity to that image in sufficient quantity to allow the proper conversion of the latent image into a visible one. Finally, the any residual counter charge remaining in the development station after the charged toner particles have been deposited onto the photoreceptor must be neutralized so that subsequent development will not be impeded.

Although these aspects may appear to be simple, and they may be so for low productivity machines producing marginal image quality, today's demands have required sophisticated technological development in order to deliver the print quality and productivity rates demanded by the consumers.

Development stations today generally consist of cylindrical magnetic cores within a surrounding, nonmagnetic but electrically conducting cylindrical shell. Below these two elements is a sump that holds the developer, which comprises a mixture of magnetic carrier particles mixed with the toner particles.

The carrier particles serve two main purposes: 1) to precisely triboelectrically charge the toner particles (both magnitude and sign of the charge) and 2) to transport the toner particles so as to bring them into operative proximity to the latent image-bearing photoreceptor. It should be noted that only the toner leaves the development station on the photoreceptor. The carrier remains behind.

For small desk-top or low volume printers, the toner and developer are mixed at the factory and, upon depletion of the toner, the entire cartridge comprising the developer, development station, the photoreceptor, and the fuser are replaced. For higher productivity machines, such as those used for commercial applications, the toner is replenished upon depletion. This requires a means for adding and rapidly mixing prescribed quantities of toner with the depleted developer. Both the high and low productivity machines require some means to measure the toner concentration *in situ*.

Charging

As discussed, it is necessary to initially charge the photoreceptor to a uniform and specified initial potential, from which it is image-wise decreased by exposure to light. Traditionally, charging was accomplished using a corona charger that generates ions from air that are attracted to the conductive ground plane incorporated into the photoreceptor. More recently, electrically biased rollers that are in contact with the photorecep- tor have been used to generate the ions. The advantage of biased roller charging is that in generates fewer pernicious ions per level of charge than does a corona charger. The disadvantage of a roller charger is that it con- tacts the photoreceptor and can, therefore, subject the photoreceptor to contamination, wear, and physical damage. To illustrate the challenges associated with charging the photoreceptor, let us consider how a corona charger functions.

A corona charger comprises a wire that is biased with a DC potential (typically over 8,000 V) that is sufficiently high so as to ionize the sur- rounding air[††] without actually causing the air to electrically break down or arc. The ions are attracted to the electrically conducting plane contained in the photoreceptor and are deposited and become trapped on its upper- most layer. This is typically the charge transport or a protective layer, but it could be a different component, depending on the specific structure of the photoreceptor.

The simple corona charger just described would not result in a uniform charge deposition. Moreover, it would continue to charge the photorecep- tor in an uncontrolled manner until its surface potential became so high so that a breakdown of the photoreceptor materials would occur, thereby damaging this member.

To limit the amount of charge that is deposited, an electrically conduct- ing biased grid is placed between the corona wire or wires and the photo- receptor. Ideally, the grid is biased at the desired voltage V_{photo} so that when the potential on the photoreceptor reaches V_{photo} there is no difference of potential between the grid and the photoreceptor, thereby shutting down the current and limiting the voltage to V_{photo}.

Unfortunately, we do not live in an ideal world. Rather, there are many factors that limit this simple corona charger's ability to uniformly charge a photoreceptor to a uniform and selected V_{photo}. These include factors such as contamination on the corona wire that limit the uniformity of the emis- sions, the charging rate that asymptotically approaches V_{photo} instead of instantly reaching that potential, and the effect of the spacing between the grid wires. Each of these factors has been the subject of much research, particularly required as the demands for better image quality and higher process speeds have increased over time.

[††] The ionized air surrounding the wire emits a soft glow analogous to that seen with the Aurora Borealis.

Producing the Electrostatic Latent Image

In the days when electrophotography was used primarily as a copier to reproduce alphanumeric documents, producing an electrostatic latent image was a relatively simple process. The original document was exposed to light for a limited time, generally via a flash exposure. The lines on the original absorbed the light and the rest of the incident light was reflected from the original and focused onto the charged photoreceptor. This allowed the discharge of the photoreceptor in regions corresponding to those portions without text in the original document.

The requirements and uses for electrophotographic printers are different today than in earlier years. Electrophotography is generally used in printers – devices in which electronic files housed in a computer are fed into devices that convert those files into printed documents. Even the technology incorporated into a copier has changed. Now, documents to be copied are first fed into a scanner in which the information contained therein is converted into an electronic file that is then fed into the printer. The documents to be printed often contain multiple colors and, instead of having less than 10% of the printed page covered by toner, as was the case of the office copier, today's documents comprise areas that are totally toner covered, often with multiple layers necessary to achieve the desired color or density.

To understand how an electrostatic latent image is produced on a photoreceptor today, let us consider the halftone grid pattern discussed earlier in this appendix. Although any grid frequency can be used, let us focus, for exemplary reasons, on the 150-line rule. As previously discussed, this can be considered a layout of imaginary perpendicular lines spaced so that, in a one-inch separation, there are 150 such lines. The intersecting lines define square cells, each of which is 1/150 inch by 1/150 inch. Now, let us assume that we can selectively discharge portions of that cell using a writer such as a laser-scanner or an LED array. Specifically, let us assume that the writer has the ability to produce exposed dots at a separation distance of 600 dots per inch.‡‡ In other words, along each line there can be as many as 4 distinct dots, for a total of 16 per cell. These individually addressable regions are called "pixels".

---

‡‡ 600 dots per inch and 150-line rules were the standards of high quality in past years. Presently, higher line rules and dot frequencies are commonly used. The numbers used in the above discussion are for exemplary purposes only.

It may seem that pixels are analogous to the halftone dots used to produce a gray scale in lithography, with 16 pixels allowing for a total of 16 levels of gray as each pixel fills in a distinct region of a cell. This, however, is not the case. In lithography, only the size of the inked dot can be varied. An amount of ink producing a dot of density D_{max} is either deposited on the paper or it is not. The shape of the dot and the amount of ink within the dot cannot be varied. Gray scale is obtained, as previously discussed, by varying the ratio of the inked and uninked portions of the paper.

Today, it is not adequate for an electrophotographic printer to merely be able to produce barely legible copies of typed documents. Rather, such printers must be able to produce high quality prints that comprise both alpha-numeric and pictorial content, generally in full color. This is the result of combining the printer with a computer-driven electrophotographic writer. Yes, the exposure level could be adjusted to give a D_{max}. However, unlike lithography, the exposure level of each pixel can be set so as to only partially discharge the photoreceptor, resulting in a continuous tone gray level. And again, unlike lithography in which the location of each halftone dot is fixed, the exposure of each pixel can be adjusted so that the shape of the resulting toned area within a cell varies. And, of course, each print can differ from the previous or subsequent ones, unlike lithography, where each print is identical to all the others.

The ability to adjust the pixels lies in the mathematical algorithms that drive the writer. These, in turn, get input from the electronic files that are fed into the printer. And, of course, when printing color separations that will have to be superimposed to yield the final print, the timing of each writer must be adjusted so that the color separations are printed in register.

There are yet other adjustments that have to be made to compensate from the skew of a laser writer as it scans the length of the photoreceptor. LED arrays have to correct for individual intensity variations with each LED. It should be apparent that sophisticated mathematical algorithms and sensitive process control methods are necessary for today's electrophotographic printers to produce the desired level of quality for current applications.

Transfer

The transfer of a toner image from a photoreceptor to paper is generally accomplished by pressing the paper against the photoreceptor while applying an electrostatic field to urge the toner particles from the photoreceptor to the paper. However, the constraints placed by nature on toner transfer become more pronounced with the demand for higher quality and through-put and the need to use smaller toner particles. To understand the issues it is first necessary to consider the forces that are acting on the toner par-ticles during the transfer process [13]. Let us first consider the forces that adhere the toner particles to the photoreceptor. These are the electrostatic forces that attract the electrically charged toner particles to the grounded conducting layer within the photoreceptor. These are often referred to as "image forces" because they result from the charged toner particle induc-ing an image charge within that layer [14] and are considered long range forces as they decay slowly with distance.§§

The next type of interaction that comes into play is the adhesion forces such as those arising from van der Waals interactions [10, 15, 16]. These forces, having a range of a few nanometers, are considered to be short range or even "contact" forces, as they essentially require the materials to be in contact to be significant. These forces exist even for particles that are not electrostatically charged and become dominant over electrostatic forces as the particle size decreases. In addition to the surface forces that adhere the toner particles to the photoreceptor, there are also surface forces that hold the toner particles to the receiver, providing those toner particles actually contact the receiver.

Next, there are the electrostatic forces that are applied to the toner to urge the toner from the photoreceptor to the receiver. These are the prod-uct of the electric charge on each toner particle times the net applied elec-tric field. The term "net" is used here because of the presence of a layer of charged toner particles, as in the case of multiple layers of toner being sequentially transferred as would be required to produce a color print from the individual separations. This would generate an electric field due to the toner charge that subtracts from the applied field, thereby decreasing the transfer force being applied to the toner.

And, of course, there are the electrostatic and surface forces that exist between neighboring toner particles. The former, being repulsive as all the toner particles have the same sign charge, would tend to make the toner particles fly apart, thereby increasing granularity and decreasing resolu-tion and sharpness. These are countered by the surface forces that adhere contacting toner particles.

At first, it might be thought that transferring the toner particles should be straight-forward. One may think all one has to do is to increase the

§§ Forces that decay with separation distance r at a rate of $1/r^2$ or slower are generally clas-sified as long range forces. Forces that decay more rapidly are considered short range forces.

applied electrostatic field until transfer occurs. However, that is not the case. Rather, as Friedrich Paschen discovered [17, 18], the dielectric strength of air is limited, resulting in sparking when this limit is reached.

Also problematic is increasing the toner charge, as this would decrease the amount of toner that would be deposited when converting the electrostatic latent image to a visible one. In addition it would increase the electrostatic attraction of the toner to the photoreceptor, as well as the Coulombic repulsion between the toner particles. Moreover, it would also increase the screening of the applied transfer field by an already transferred toner layer, thereby impeding the transfer of subsequent layers.

A discussion of the technology involved in controlling toner charge and van der Waals forces would be well beyond the scope of this appendix. Suffice-it to say, both require sophisticated technology and innovation and remain the subject of future investigation.

Fusing

The final subsystem to be discussed in this appendix, although not by any means the only other subsystem benefitting from innovations, is the permanent fixing of the toner image to the receiver (e.g., paper).

The concept behind fusing is straight-forward: subject the toner image to a combination of heat and pressure to force the flow of the particles and establish intimate interparticle and particle-to-paper contact. In essence, upon raising the toner temperature to above its glass transition temperature or T_g, the normally glassy toner is temporarily converted into a hot-melt adhesive and flows into a coherent mass that bonds to the receiver.

There are several issues that affect fusing. The first is that the softened toner is still highly viscous. It will not flow in the absence of significant applied pressure. Second, is the heat must be applied within a short period of time (typically milliseconds). Third, it is often desirable to control the gloss of the fused print, with required gloss levels ranging from matte for alphanumeric documents to highly specular or glossy for photographic prints. Radiative heat transfer simply has not been effective at addressing any of these issues. Rather, it is necessary to contact the toner-bearing print by pressing it through a nip formed by a pair of rollers or similar device. However, even here, issues abound. Among these are the tendency of the softened toner to adhere to the fusing roller, thereby bonding the paper to that roller. To alleviate this, a carefully monitored release oil is coated onto the contacting roller. When used for fusing alphanumeric documents in which most of the paper does not contain toner, the paper is quite effective at absorbing the trace amounts of oil that is transferred to the print. However, when most of the paper is coated with toner, as would be the case with a full-color pictorial image, the oil is not absorbed. Rather, it creates a blotchy film on the print.

Another issue is that it takes time for the toner to flow, as, even in a softened state, it is still highly viscous. To allow for a sufficiently long time in the fusing nip, at least one roller must be compliant, which requires that it be coated with a relatively thick elastomeric blanket. The problem encountered by doing so is that elastomers are not especially good thermal conductors. As heat is drained from the surface of the roller by fusing one print, it becomes too cool to fuse a second one under the high process speeds required, especially for commercial printers. And, heating the roller to a higher temperature is problematic as it merely aggravates the tendency of the viscous toner to further adhere to the roller.

Opportunities for Building a Patent Portfolio in a Mature but Technologically Evolving Field

There is no attempt made in this appendix to describe all the challenges faced in electrophotography, especially as advances allow this process to be used for diverse applications ranging from high quality color printing to medical imaging to functional printing, whereby operating devices are actually produced. Rather, this appendix was written to allow the reader to have a greater appreciation for the patent examples cited throughout this book, as well as an understanding of how an aging technology can still afford a plethora of patenting opportunities. Indeed, one can speculate that, had Chester Carlson fully appreciated a fraction of the technical challenges encountered in this field, he may have become discouraged and have never invented electrophotography.

And, such opportunities are not limited to electrophotography. Rather, advances occur in many areas. These occur in part because of new demands and evolutionary changes. The automobile of today bears little resemblance to that invented by Karl Benz in 1885. The fuel cells that power exploratory cars today bear even less similarity to the hydrogen-powered internal combustion engine invented by de Rivas in 1808. The rockets that power exploratory space vehicles or allow modern precision-guided ordnance bear little resemblance to the rockets immortalized by Francis Scott Key in his poem "The Star Spangled Banner" and even less to those developed by unknown Chinese inventors in the 13th century.

In other instances, technological advances occur because someone has the insight to recognize how several distinct and separate items, often in totally unrelated fields, can be combined to create novel products. The space program, announced by President Kennedy in his inaugural address, created the demand for smaller electronics to control the rockets that were to launch people to the moon. The development of compact electronics containing integrated circuits was a giant step towards developing the microprocessors that are used in automobiles and eliminated the need for carburetors and distributors, yet still allowed the production of more reliable automobiles that perform better while using less gasoline and polluting less than those of previous decades. And, of course, this same technology has displaced the typewriter, slide rule, and graph paper, as small but powerful computers have changed the way the average person lives today, from the methods of paying bills and buying merchandise to the medical tests and treatments that have lengthened our lives to the ways in which we communicate, perform our work, and obtain our entertainment.

Inventions do not necessarily arise from someone combining technological advances in a nonobvious fashion to solve a problem. In some instances an inventor sees a better way of doing something or a shortcoming in the present solutions to a problem. An example of this is in the area of building fine wooden furniture. To make tops for tables, desks, and other cabinets generally requires that narrow boards be glued on edge to each other to produce a board of sufficient width. To facilitate the alignment of the boards, it was common to drill holes into which dowels were inserted. This required very precise positioning of the holes both along the board and across its thickness if the multiple round dowels used were going to allow the boards to come together. Along comes an inventor with the idea of using flat wooden biscuits that provided a stronger bonding of the boards than that achievable with dowels, but shaped in a manner that allowed for the alignment to be self-correcting. Accompanying the invention of the biscuits was a power tool that cut slots into the edge of each mating board in a precise location quickly and easily. The biscuits were even designed to swell slightly upon application of glue, thereby making a strong, tight, permanent bond.

The bottom line throughout this discussion is that it does not matter if the field is old or new or if the device is an improvement on existing technology or an innovative stand-alone advancement. If you are solving technical problems and your solutions are not obvious to someone of ordinary skill in the art and are novel, you probably have patentable inventions. Your inventions could be worth a lot of money. In order to derive benefit from them, you need to protect your intellectual property. Implementing a well-designed patent strategy will allow you to achieve this.

References

1. R. M. Schaffert, Electrophotography, Focal/Hastings House, New York (1975).
2. E. M. Williams, *The Physics & Technology of the Xerographic Process*, John Wiley and Sons, New York (1984).
3. L. B. Schein, *Electrophotography and Development Physics*, Laplacian Press, Morgan Hill (1996).
4. C. F. Carlson, U. S, Patent #2,221,776 (1940).
5. C. F. Carlson, U. S. Patent #2,297,691 (1942).
6. J. H. Dessauer and H. E. Clark, U. S. Patent #2,901,348 (1959).
7. J. H. Dessauer, U. S. Patent #2,962,374 (1960).
8. G. A. Lloyd and S. J. Sasson, U.S. Patent 4,131,919 (1978).
9. http://idc-cema.com/eng/about-idc/press-center/48450-three-billion-pages-printed-every-day-in-emea-according-to-idc.
10. M. H. Bruno (Ed.) *Pocket Pal: A Graphic Arts Production Handbook*, 16th Edition, International Paper, Memphis, TN (1995).
11. F. Cost, *Pocket Guide to Digital Printing*, Delmar Publications, Albany, NY (1997).
12. D. S. Rimai and D. J. Quesnel, *Fundamentals of Particle Adhesion*, Global Press, Moorhead, MN (2001).
13. G. Wright, T. N. Tombs, A. Chowdry, D. S. Weiss, and D. S. Rimai, "Toner Transfer: Effects of Size Polydispersity", J. Imag. Sci. Technol., 49, 531 (2005).
14. P. Lorrain and D. Corson, *Electromagnetic Fields and Waves*, 2nd Ed., W. H. Freeman and Co., San Francisco, CA (1970).
15. J. Israelachvili, *Intermolecular and Surface Forces*, 2nd Ed., Academic Press, New York, NY (1992).
16. K. Kendall, *Molecular Adhesion and Its Applications*, Kluwer Academic/Plenum Publishers, New York, NY (2001).
17. F. Paschen, *Annalen der Physic* 273 (5), pp. 69–75 (1889).
18. J. D. Cobine, Gaseous Conductors: *Theory and Engineering Applications*, Dover, New York City, NY (1958).

Index

Also of Interest

Patent Engineering
Guide to Building a Valuable Patent Portfolio

By Donald S. Rimai
2016 ISBN: 9781118946091

Description
Patents are a vital asset in the modern business world. They allow patent holders to introduce new products in to a market while deterring other market players from simply copying innovative features without making comparable investments in research and development. In years past, a few patents may have provided adequate protection. That is no longer the case. In today's world, it is critical that innovative companies protect the features of their products that give them a competitive advantage with a family or portfolio of patents that are strategically generated to protect the market position of the patent holder. A patent portfolio that deters competitors from introducing competitive products in a timely manner can be worth billions of dollars. Anything less than this is an expensive and possibly fatal distraction.

Patent Engineering provides a strategic framework for cost efficient engineering of patent portfolios that protect your investments in research and development and extend the market advantages that these investments provide. In addition, the book:

- Demonstrates the value by organizing patent engineering efforts around the problems that you solve for your customers rather than the technologies developed to solve these problems
- Illustrates the use of the problem centric framework to enable the efficient creation of individual patents and patent portfolios that have significant value in and by themselves and allow your company to control its product market
- Teaches how to use the problem centric framework to help address the challenge of designing international patent portfolios

- Introduces the concept of a patent engineer whose role it is to organize input from legal, business and technical communities and organize portfolios and patents using the problem centric framework
- Provides a non-expert with a solid working knowledge of patents that will enable him to work effectively with legal counsel to produce solid patents